PRISON SLAVERY

by
Barbara Esposito & Lee Wood
Editor: Kathryn Bardsley

Committee to Abolish Prison Slavery

Cover photo from *Conversations with the Dead* by Danny Lyons—Magnum Photo

PRINTED BY
JOEL LITHOGRAPHIC, INC.
SILVER SPRING, MARYLAND

First Edition
Library of Congress Card Number: 82-072547
ISBN 0-91007-00-4

*As in the original prison slavery paper by
Lee Wood, this book is dedicated to the memory of
Sergio Adgigo.*

Address orders to
Committee to Abolish Prison Slavery
P.O. Box 3207, Dept. B.
Washington, D.C. 20010

Contents

Sergio died yesterday, October 26, 1973, in the California Medical Facility at Vacaville...

For the past week, Sergio had been complaining of severe abdominal pains and urinating blood. Several times he went to the Doctor's Line for treatment, but they said nothing was wrong with him.

Then, as he got off his job as a first floor porter Thursday night and started up to the second floor, he fell backwards down the stairs. The previous day Sergio was given a 115 disciplinary write-up for "Disrespect Toward a Doctor." This same Doctor declared that nothing was wrong with Sergio. His doubled-up body was not sufficient to warrant admission into G-2 Hospital. His roommates had to help him into the bed and they also state that he complained of unbearable pain. The next morning a roommate tried to awaken Sergio... but he was dead.

This one is for you Sergio. As we always agreed, "A threat to one is a threat to all." And as you would have wanted it, it is for all the Sergios of the past, and the present, and for all the Sergios of the future.

Acknowledgements

Credit for the research and writing of this book belongs to the Committee to Abolish Prison Slavery and all those who have worked with C.A.P.S. over the past six years. *Prison Slavery's* final editing, production and distribution has been the responsibility of the Inalienable Rights Institute.

Because development of this book has been part of the Committee's program to build a new abolitionist movement to end "slavery...as a punishment for crime," the research and writing of its many drafts cannot be separated from C.A.P.S.'s ongoing education and organizing program with hundreds of prisoners who contributed to this book. C.A.P.S.'s national circulation of the Petition to Abolish Prison Slavery has elicited the questions from concerned supporters and non-supporters which this book seeks to answer. Many hundreds of hours have been spent researching answers to those questions within the abolitionist perspective developed through the Committee's grass-roots education, organizing, lobbying and legislative-action programs. This book's development has been one part of a meagerly-funded organization's many-faceted struggle for slavery abolition, and reflects that struggle's collective process of development. We are grateful to prisoners who have patiently endured delays in correspondence, and to members who have waited three years for this book's completion, especially those members who sent contributions towards its completion. It is designed to explain our mutual quest for slavery abolition.

Research and writing of the first manuscript was financed by donations from community supporters in Berkeley and Oakland, California. The Poverello Fund in San Francisco gave C.A.P.S. its first grant for book production in 1978. After consulting with several activist supporters across the country who had reviewed that first draft, we learned that we needed to answer new questions and do more research and analysis to augment our thesis. We then relocated our national operations in Washington, D.C., were given shelter by several Quakers and prisoner supporters, borrowed office space from the National Moratorium on Prison Construction, and dug into research and writing again.

With the assistance of the American Friends Service Committee, we published *Prison Slavery in the Thirteenth Amendment* in 1978, a booklet adapted from one chapter of that year's book draft. The next year, we asked prisoners to contribute work for an anthology of prison slave writings. Lack of funds made that project impossible, but a small grant from the P.B.P. Foundation of New York enabled us to reprint the booklet and combine prison slave writings with data already gathered for this book. Just as much work remains in the struggle to restore citizenship, labor and human rights to prisoners and the communities from which they come, much research remains in the immense task of prison slavery abolition which lies before us. It is our hope that this work will encourage others to join that struggle.

Several foundations have provided funding which has enabled us to complete the arduous research and writing to substantiate our case. Among them are the American Friends Service Committee, the P.B.P. Foundation of New York, the Poverello Fund of San Francisco, the United Methodist Church Board of Global Ministries Office of Urban Ministries, the Department of Political and Human Rights of the Board of Church and Society of the United Methodist Church, the Women's Division of the United Methodist Church General Board of Global Ministries, and the Program Agency of the United Presbyterian Church in the United States of America.

Periodic consultation with Dr. Thorsten Sellin and recourse to his book *Slavery and the Penal System* have made the task easier. While most of those who given assistance, support, encouragement and counsel know who they are, we would like to give special acknowledgement to Marcy, to Ruth Cohn, Scott Christiansen, Congressman Ronald V. Dellums, Dr. Dorothy Donnelly, C.S.J., Christopher Dunne, Jackie Foster, Bob Heaney, Barbara Moffit, Pete Ortiz, Sandra Turner, and Brad Zigler.

Mrs. Abby Hadley shared her home with us for a year, R.W. McCoy and the Reverend Guillermo Chavez have given understanding and inspiration in difficult moments, Dr. H.B. Franklin has given invaluable encouragement and Christopher Fisher made important personal sacrifice. Special thanks go to Kathryn Bardsley, who stuck with us through several months of editing by the interruptions meager resources create, and to John Morris, who proofread the final copy.

The greatest acknowledgement belongs to prisoners and their family members. Because this book belongs to all of them, choosing from among their testimony was a painful process. We have included the identities of those now released from prison, omitting or giving pseudonyms to those still inside or on parole. To give them their rightful recognition would make them vulnerable to punishment and harrassment by corrections officials. It is because of prison slavery that they must remain unnamed; it is because of the courage of these men and women, and their commitment to generations after them, that this book can begin to expose "slavery...as a punishment for crime."

Credit for this book must be extended to two more: Richard Myers and Abre Lee Wood. Throughout the course of its writing, Richard Myers, once full-time volunteer organizer with the Committee, kept its production going by long hours of dedicated labor at tasks upon which the survival of our struggle depends. And Abre Lee Wood, born and stolen from her father's love because of the slavery which still tears children from their parents' breasts - she has been an inspiration for this work. It is for her, and millions of children like her, that this book has been written. So that, someday, she and they will understand.

Introduction

Slaves are in the tribe, but not of it. Without citizenship, slaves are outside the realm of jural personality, and their debased status does not contradict the slaveholders' notions of social equality · for themselves, exclusive of the slaves.

· E. Adamson Hoebel[1]

America responds to lawbreakers by making slaves of them: a shocking statement but true. This book has been written to document the historic and class-based roots of slavery as a punishment for crime. It seeks to explain how our prisons are the last vestige of constitutional slavery.

In 1970, defendants awaiting trial in the New York City Tombs were beaten when they protested against the conditions forced upon them. The next year California prison activist George Jackson was murdered in San Quentin and prisoners at Attica were gunned down in the State of New York's response to their demands.

Like many other caged brothers and sisters throughout the country, those of us imprisoned in California were strongly moved by the struggles of our fallen brothers. Our lives were constantly pressed by poor diet, inadequate and irresponsible medical care, isolation from our loved ones, meaningless labor forced upon us for pennies or no pay at all, and the continual servility that was demanded to "earn" parole. A few of us had been singled out for exceptionally harsh punishment or transferred from prison to prison in an attempt to neutralize our efforts to organize for better conditions. Several had been through prison work strikes at Susanville, Folsom, San Quentin and Tombs which had been squashed by our keepers. We had been pitted against each other by the divisive tactics of our masters; we had been beaten and had watched others being beaten for refusal to bend to whimsical demands. Divided and conquered, we were rendered powerless to create change.

A few days after the Attica massacre we began quietly discussing the oppressive conditions that faced all of us locked inside. Our discussions led to the formation of a small study group which we were careful to keep hidden from the prison administration, since visible prisoner organizing was - and is - rapidly crushed. Through study and discussion, we were trying to find out *who* and *what* we were as prisoners. At one meeting a prisoner declared he was a "slave". Although this made gut sense, we "knew" slavery had been abolished after the Civil War. Another participant brought his paperback copy of the U.S. Constitution to the next meeting and read the Thirteenth Amendment:

> Neither slavery nor involuntary servitude, EXCEPT AS A PUN-
> ISHMENT FOR CRIME WHEREOF THE PARTY SHALL HAVE
> BEEN DULY CONVICTED, shall exist within the United
> States, or any place subject to their jurisdiction.*

The book was passed around so everyone could see the EXCEPTION. This - the constitutional denial of our basic human, citizenship, and labor rights - was the common denominator of our mutual oppression.

A few of the original study group members were paroled during 1975 and 1976, and proceeded to contact those community people to whom we had previously smuggled our analysis. Together we organized the Committee to Abolish Prison Slavery. When we reached the point where we could mimeograph leaflets to inform the community about the reality of "slavery...as a punishment for crime" and the need for its abolition, we went to the people with our struggle. The nickels and dimes dropped in our campaign buckets were not enough, so we took full- or part-time jobs and put our earnings toward building a new slavery Abolitionist Movement. Since our beginning, we have obtained several thousand signatures on the nationally distributed Petition to Abolish Prison Slavery and, through grassroots methods of organizing, we grow closer to the abolition of prison slavery and the return of inalienable citizenship, labor, and human rights to our incarcerated brothers and sisters.

Slavery is a harsh word, having different associations for different people. Among historic accounts of slavery are bondage in the ancient civilizations of Egypt, Greece and Rome, convict slavery of those who rowed the massive ships of European kings during the fourteenth through seventeenth centuries, American antebellum chattel slavery, the industrial servitude of wage slavery, and the concentration camps of Nazi Germany. Slavery has three attributes: ownership, possession or control of a person; denial of citizenship rights; and denial of labor rights (the rights to sell one's own labor). American imprisonment meets all three criteria: convicts are completely controlled by the State, are denied the practices of their citizenship - virtually all expression of "guaranteed" freedoms are squashed - and they are either forced to work without just compensation and worker protections or are not allowed to work at all.

Prison is the last stop on the line for the poor, the minorities, the disenfranchised of our nation. Our large and ever-increasing prison and jail populations are among the highest in the world. Each year, a half million Americans are denied participation in the democratic process while over $5 billion of our yearly tax bill is spent to maintain human bondage. With over 500,000 people in federal and state prisons and jails, we spend an average of nearly $10,000 to confine one person in prison for one year. Thus, we invest more money in denying

---

*Capitalization of the slavery proviso is ours, and we use it throughout to emphasize the importance of this exception...then and now.

citizenship, labor and human rights to each prisoner than it would cost to send that same person to a public university and financially support his or her family.[2]

As with many contemporary injustices, prison slavery is more deceptive and sophisticated than its historical counterparts. Its most visible cruelties are hidden from general public awareness behind closed doors and high prison walls. Because prisoners are denied the right to vote, no elected representative is politically obliged to listen to prisoner needs. Denied the practices of their citizenship, prisoners lose their freedoms of speech, press, association, due process, freedom from undue search and seizure, and other democratic protections. Like chattel slaves in the antebellum South, today's prison slaves are separated from, and often lose, their families. They are forced into submission and subjected daily to the cruel and unusual punishments of an environment devoid of democratic process. Prison slavery teaches failure, disempowering the convicted and diminishing their capacity to reenter society. Our nation's high rate of recidivism can be easily understood by watching people released from prison finding themselves lonely, bitter, impoverished, and unskilled in the practices of a society reluctant to give them any opportunity to succeed.

As the fear, force and degradation emitted from this nation's prisons colors and corrupts the fabric of our society, efforts to reform our prison systems fail. They fail because they seek to change the superficial methods and forms of treating offenders and do not confront the issue of our prisons being historically, legally, and intrinsically based in the institution of slavery. Slavery cannot be reformed, it can only be abolished.

More than half of American prisoners are black or other minority and practically all are poor. They have had few educational opportunities, and have suffered unemployment, underemployment, negligent medical care, toxic and hazardous physical environments, high rates of illness and death, and all forms of institutional discrimination. Those who suffer under prison slavery are not new to exploitation and victimization. As the late Soledad Brother Fleeta Drumgo wrote from prison:

> It seems at times that the oppression and violence inflicted upon us here in the maximum security is more intense than that inflicted upon us in the minimum security, but really it's utterly impossible for me or any of us here to distinguish the oppression and violence we are all victimized by. I am constantly thinking about unemployment, under-employment, poverty and malnutrition that are the basic facts of our existence; it's this which sends persons to these concentration camps; it's this which causes so-called crime in general.[3]

In contrast, the crimes of the wealthy go largely unpunished and are instead rewarded with decontrols and tax breaks. The crimes of cor-

porate industries rip off millions, yet such crimes are practically ignored by the State; unsafe working conditions and over-exposure to
toxic industrial substances cause untold numbers of illnesses and
deaths each year. American University Professor Jeffrey H. Reiman
has shown that life can be far more dangerous in the workplace than
the streets: 390,000 people were reported injured at work while 218,383
were injured in acts of crime, and 114,000 died from occupational-
related diseases and accidents while only 9,285 died from "crime."[4]
The richer the culprit, the more lenient the hand of justice. In a study
of seventy of the largest U.S. corporations over forty years, Edwin
Sutherland showed that

> generally, the official records reveal that these corporations
> violated the trade regulations with great frequency. The
> "habitual criminal" laws of some states impose severe pen-
> alties on criminals convicted the third or fourth time. If this
> criterion were used here, about 90 percent of the large cor-
> porations studied would be considered habitual white-collar
> criminals.[5]

But our prisons do not house the well-to-do:

> Of the 7724 inmates of *federal* prisons and reformatories in
> 1970 who had an income in 1969, 4491 (nearly 60 percent)
> reported an annual income of under $2000. Of 141,600 per-
> sons confined in *local* jails throughout the nation in mid-1972,
> 61,800 (44 percent) had a prearrest annual income of less than
> $2000 - only 11 percent reported a prearrest income of $7500
> or more. "The 1972 U.S. median income of $9255 was exceed-
> ed by roughly 10 percent of the inmates. Only 6 percent had
> prearrest incomes of more than $10,000."[6]

While such statistics indicate that more dangerous corporate
crimes are largely untouched by prosecution and public outrage, the
processing of street crimes is permeated with class and racial
discrimination, given hourly "cops and robbers" media coverage and
subjected to manipulation by political candidates.

Government failure to weigh the consequences of economic inequalities among its citizens enables it to cloak injustice by asserting
that "equal opportunity" and "equal protection before the law" are
upheld by government when in reality they are not. When the law does
not consider the economic inequalities among its people in judging
them, there can be no equal opportunity and equal protection before
the law:

> ...legal equality in the face of the existence of economic in-
> equality is repressive...to treat unequals equally is scarcely
> just...If the law is indifferent to the distinctions between
> rich and poor, it follows that the law will necessarily support
> and maintain this distinction.[7]

As eighteenth century slavery abolitionist John Woolman warned, "while oppression in the extreme appears terrible," oppression in its most refined forms "remains to be oppression, and when the smallest degree of it is cherished it grows stronger and more extensive."[8] Slavery consumes lives and constantly expands in its pursuit of power; that is the nature of slavery: increasing power of the few by subjugation of many.

Punishment in the form of slavery is the centuries-old method of maintaining class-based rule. As this book is readied for press, economic class lines are becoming sharper in America. Unemployment is increasing, government is slashing aid to the poor and the needy, and crime in our communities continues to increase. A new "war on crime" has begun, harsher laws are being passed, legal aid for the poor is being withdrawn and new protections have been given to the wealthy. Meanwhile, prison populations are increasing and record numbers of poor people wait on Death Row.

Most Americans do not know that our Constitution still authorizes slavery or that prisoners are slaves. For many who have never been imprisoned, the reality of this enslavement may be difficult to absorb. For most who have been imprisoned, it epitomizes the many oppressions suffered inside. Regardless of our experience, the exception within the Thirteenth Amendment represents a painful and offensive reality which victimizes all of us.

As defined in *Instead of Prison* by the Prison Research Education Action Project, victims are "all those who have suffered either by collective or individual acts of violence. Victims usually feel powerless to alter their situations since few avenues for relief are available."[9] The cycle of violence begins with poverty, unemployment, underemployment, substandard housing and medical care, poor education, unequal opportunity and protection before the law, and unequal political representation for the needy by a government more favorable to the well-financed representation of the rich and the privileged. Increasingly fewer avenues for relief are available, and "without relief for constructive action, feelings of powerlessness can easily turn into rage and violence."[10]

Victims of gross misrepresentation, we have unwittingly participated in the destruction of prisoners, their families, the communities from which they come and the communities in which we live. As victims of crime and the inequities that encourage crime, we have become unknowing self-oppressors in our function as taxpaying slaveholders. In any form, slavery dehumanizes, cripples and destroys anyone who willingly or unwillingly partakes in its practice. Until the abolition of all slavery is obtained, we all remain victims.

Slavery's poisons pass in undetected ways through literary resources, cultural imperatives and human limitations to all of us, and slavery's continuance cannot be separated from the inequities most of us consciously and unconsciously live with. This book touches upon the long history and profound victimization of prison slavery. It also contains limitations resulting from the urgent need for its publication. Its completion has taken a number of years with very limited finances. Hence, we ask that particularly those who read from non-Western perspectives recognize its shortcomings as contrary to our intent and dictated by the limitations of time, resources and the urgent need to bring the cause of slavery abolition to the American public. This book is only a beginning, one part of a many-faceted struggle to abolish "slavery. . . as a punishment for crime."

Thirteenth Amendment:

> Neither slavery nor involuntary servitude, EXCEPT AS A PUN-ISHMENT FOR CRIME WHEREOF THE PARTY SHALL HAVE BEEN DULY CONVICTED, shall exist within the United States, or any place subject to their jurisdiction.

C.A.P.S.' Proposed Amendment Change:

> Neither slavery nor involuntary servitude shall exist within the United States or any place subject to their jurisdiction.

Notes

1. E. Adamson Hoebel, *Anthropology: The Study of Man,* (New York: McGraw Hill), p. 410.

2. The estimated U.S. detention population in Fall 1981 was 579,772.[2a] ("Cage Count," *Jericho* [National Moratorium on Prison Construction, 324 C Street, S.E., Washington, D.C. 20003], no. 26, Fall 1981, p. 12).

Based on prison maintenance costs reported to the U.S. Department of Justice Statistics on 1978, the National Moratorium on Prison Construction estimates the average cost per state prisoner in the United States to be $9,143 per year. Limited to "direct" institutional costs, this amount does not include legal, medical and educational costs, additional welfare benefits paid to families with incarcerated breadwinners, prison construction[2b] and other bills payed by the taxpayer. (More detailed explanation of costs of imprisonment is found in Note 9, Chapter 7.)

> 2a. The actual number of Americans subjected to imprison-ment is much larger - there are 6.2 million commitments to jail each year. ("Fact Sheet on American Jails," National Coali-tion for Jail Reform, 1333 New Hampshire Avenue, N.W., Suite 1220, Washington, D.C. 20036.)

> 2b. Prison construction is expensive. As reported by the Na-tional Moratorium on Prison Construction (*Jericho,* no. 26, p. 12), a general cost analysis for "New [Prison] Facilities Pro-posed or Under Construction" in Fall 1981 follows:

No.	Type	Average Capacity	Average per facility cost	Average per bed cost
8	Federal	176	$ 6.9 million	$39,204
182	State	450	$23.22 million	$51,600
459	Local	159	$ 6.68 million	$42,013

Total facilities: 649
Total estimated capacity: 156,288
Total estimated cost: $7.35 billion

3. Fleeta Drumgo, "Letter from Fleeta," Angela Y. Davis, Ruchell Magee, Soledad Brothers and other political prisoners, *If They Come in the Morning: Voices of Resistance,* forward by Julian Bond (New York: The Third Press, Joseph Okpaku Publishing Company, Inc., 1971), p. 115.

4. Jeffery H. Reiman, *The Rich Get Richer and the Poor Get Prison: Ideology, Class and Criminal Justice* (New York: John Wiley and Sons, 1979), pp. 65-69.

5. Edwin Sutherland and Donald R. Cressey, *Criminology,* 9th edition (Philadelphia: Lippincott, 1974), p. 41; quoted in Reiman, p. 108.

6. Reiman, pp. 126-127, and cites U.S. Department of Justice, U.S. Law Enforcement Assistance Administration, National Criminal Justice Information and Statistics Service, *Survey of Inmates of Local Jails: Advance Report* (Washington, D.C.: U.S. Government Printing Office, 1974), pp. 3, 4, 16.

7. Isaac D. Balbus, *The Dialectics of Legal Repression: Black Rebels before the American Criminal Courts* (New York: Russell Sage Foundation, 1973), p. 5.

8. John Woolman, *The Journal of John Woolman and A Plea for the Poor,* introduction by Frederick B. Tolles (Secaucus, N.J.: Citadel Press, Inc.), p. 249.

9. Prison Research Education and Action Project, *Instead of Prisons: A Handbook for Abolitionists* (Syracuse, N.Y.: Prison Research Education Action Project, 1976), p. 21.

10. Ibid.

Chapter 1:
Roots

One should always address a slave in the language of command. One should not sport or jest with slaves, whether male or female; for though this is often done, it is a senseless practice and its result is to spoil the slave, making his life of servitude more difficult to bear and the authority of the master harder to maintain.

- The Athenian Stranger, *The Laws*, Plato[1]

It's really cold in the East Wing this day in April. But my cell was colder in January, so I shouldn't complain. It gets my mind off the depression of solitary (or segregation, isolation, lock-up or whatever they're calling it today). But it would help if they started giving me the iron pills the doctor cut off last week, and if I started getting the diet for hypoglycemia I might stop blacking out each time I get up from the bed. This will probably take awhile; the doctors here wouldn't even give me a high-protein diet when I was pregnant - told me to eat crackers - told me pregnant women don't need extra protein. And when I asked why there was such a high percentage of poor women with inadequate diets who had retarded children, he said I don't want to be confused with facts and walked out. This was the competent doctor. He had promised me the month before he would set up a "pregnant diet" for the 30 pregnant women here. He had promised. . . .

I remember the last time, the police put me in a cell with a grill over the window. I could only see shadows passing in front of the sunshine. This cell is a lot better. It has a view of the prison grounds in the distance and a five by ten inch opening through the bars so I can feed the cats most of my food. Sometimes, even they won't touch it. Then the birds get it or the possums come around at night. Maybe we should start naming our animals - this is working out to a long-term relationship.

I'm not having my nightmares lately. The last one was about my mother. I dream about her a lot in prison. It's always dark. This time I was a little girl and sleeping next to her. A whole wall of our house was missing and when I opened my eyes, I could feel the evil of the wind blowing over my clothes - they were sheets - and watched the ripples, terrified of the evil. . . The rippling quieted, then returned, and I turned to my mother and cried, "Why, Mama, why?" She kept on sleeping.

Solitary is a long hall with cells on both sides. The cells don't have bars, but heavy steel doors - just like on the main unit of PTU [Psychiatric Treatment Unit] - and bars on the windows. But in solitary there is no closet, desk or commode cover - just a sink, a commode without a seat, and a single bed. Someone hypothesized last night that we were living in a bathroom; as I looked around and realized they were right, I had a surreal feeling of sleeping in a Greyhound bus station ladies room - in Tijuana.

I've been thinking about my friends here and on "campus." They're mostly 189's - that's murder. And I'm just small time - welfare fraud; even smaller - I didn't do it. It's hard to explain to the people "outside," I wouldn't have been able to understand what I am about to say when I was "outside" *either. People in prison, I thought, who take lives must be incredibly evil, and there is no way of rationalizing what they did so that they don't deserve it all; it's payback time. I couldn't possibly like these people. I thought. Yes, intellectual and wise as I was, as just and fair, and self-righteous; I thought. I know.*

The people here are like those from any neighborhood. One could be the girl smiling back at the cashier's check-out stand, another might be the secretary in your accountant's office, or at your attorney's or dentist's office or the life-guard at the beach, or the president of the P.T.A. The difference between you and them is that just one time they did just one thing that society says can't be done.

You can separate the people from their "crimes." Most people here don't talk about their cases, unless they're professional thieves and are proud of their skills, or are hypes who need the momentary self esteem rip-off stories get them. But then hypes have been looking for things all their lives which always seem to come real close, to surround them and then disappear. . . .

Nearly every morning of the last ten months I've awakened and promised myself I'd try to get through the day without thinking or feeling. It's too painful to think. It hurts too much to feel. My ex-husband kidnapped my four- and five-year-old children; they're 3,000 miles away, maybe happy and healthy. I can talk about my children, but I can't just sit and think about them. It hurts too much to feel. . . .

They won't allow me to go to school here because I won't work anywhere except the law library. (In the law library, I can file writs and appeals and get women out of here.) Even when I was pregnant, the adminstrators said I was too pregnant to work in the law library, but wanted me to work in "industry." Only a few credits away from an A.A. and they won't let me "program" my way - everything is punitive here.

The police walk by and lock through my door-window. I'm sitting on the toilet. But then, I should be used to this by now. There are room searches, skin searches. There is no privacy.

It must take a special kind of person to believe in prisons.

Tonight, I'm being released, going back to PTU "Proper." But I have another 10 days coming for another refusal to work - whenever they feel like giving it to me, then another, and another for contesting my baby's transfer to my home county. . .

It's my right to go to court. I feel helpless and hold the anger inside. It's my right!

Two people escaped a few nights ago. My heart is overflowing with good will for them - I dance inside.

Legend has it I'm a problem here; I'm a "troublemaker," the chief medical officer said. Even when I was pregnant, I was a "threat to the institution" because I asked to see a good gynecologist at the nearest county hospital. They locked me down even tighter, then sent me to a mental institution so I wouldn't screw up the prison budget. My baby was born there. The mental institution sent me back.

Why is nothing being done, I wonder as I gaze at the faces, the expressions, see the cries in people's eyes, hear the screams. Who would do this to another creation of God? Civilization. Yes, that is the answer. Tearing children from their mothers - tearing away at colors of life, blindly; the whirlwind. A Kafka story I'm trying to understand.

The perimeter car circles, our bodies are counted again, and as the nurse's tray squeaks down the hall, I see the girl who swallowed gasoline and stabbed herself with a pin - a long one near her heart. What good is it doing her to be locked back here in solitary, I wonder.
But then, I ask "why" too often. I ask: WHY?

- Marianne Hricko Stewart, #W13238
"A Day in the Life of a Prison Slave," 1979

How Did It All Begin?

Slavery denies human rights, treats people as property and exploits their labor. For centuries, slavery has existed as a spoil of war, as a class status and as a punishment for crime. Contemporary prison slavery is only one sophisticated version of that slavery triad. Slavery as a spoil of war may be as ancient as migrating tribes fighting over use of water holes. Captives may have been released, killed, adopted as tribal members, or enslaved. According to anthropologist E. Adamson Hoebel, however, the two forms of slavery internal to a tribe - slavery as a class status and slavery as a punishment for crime - occur only in "advanced primitive societies with quasi-capitalistic practices of borrowing and lending."[2] We find all three forms of this "peculiar institution" occuring throughout civilization, a stage in social development characterized by nation-states, ownership of private property, and division of the population into economic classes.

Civilization, however, is only three thousand years old and we know little of how people lived before that time. Since precivilization remains a matter for theoretical controversy, we turn to anthropologist Evelyn Reed's *Woman in Evolution,* which has empowered the women's movement while causing debate among her colleagues. Anthropologists generally divide precivilization into two stages: "savagery," a hunting and gathering economy lasting about a million years, and "barbarism," which coincided with the development of agriculture and lasted for five thousand years. As Reed explains it, more than 99 percent of human history falls within the stage of development called savagery during which people knew no private property, no state and no patriarchal family. They hunted and gathered food and owned all property communally within the tribe. There was complete independence in division of labor - men hunted while woman tilled the soil. The nuclear family did not exist and the role of the father was social rather than biological or sexual. Family relations were reckoned through the mother's line and people lived in self-governing communities where all members shared equally in economic functions, enjoying social and sexual equality.[3]

During the period known as barbarism, agriculture developed as men learned the skills of husbandry - husbandsman means tiller of soil. Due to their division of labor, men were responsible for the cattle, and as farming developed, they came to own the herds. As greater value accrued to labor because the cattle multiplied faster than the family members who tended them, captives of war were increasingly used as slaves, instruments of labor; and human labor power came to be used like the cattle themselves. Hence, the word for property in people - "chattel" - derives its meaning from "cattle," the first form of private property.[4]

Women were not always oppressed; it was the inception of private property during barbarism and, finally, slavery which sealed their fate. As ownership of property increasingly fell to the men in the tribe, inheritance evolved from being matrilineal to patrilineal, eventually resulting in the "child price," exchange of a gift of cattle for a man's right to a woman's children. Patriarchy gradually replaced matriarchy and today we see remnants of the "child price" in the tradition of dowry payments in marriage.[5]

Gradual enslavement of those without property by property owners developed into civilization with its wealth-based class distinctions. A wealthy few ruled the early civilization of Egypt, Greece and Rome:

> Forced labor had existed in Egypt since time immemorial. It had built the tombs, pyramids, and monuments, impressed by rulers who owned all the natural resources and whose subjects were in reality their bondsmen. It is not impossible that such forced labor was used as a punishment for crime at quite an early date. In fact, Sabbacus, an Ethiopian king of Egypt in the eighth century B.C., abolished the death penalty during his reign and substituted penal labor in chains on public works.[6]

Ancient Greece

We find the influence of ancient Greece tnroughout American institutions, in philosophy, education, law, government and in the controversy over slavery which has persisted throughout history. Some Greeks, like Aristotle, held that foreigners were natural slaves; others, like Antiphon, believed that all men were born free and equal - that fate, not nature, made some men free and other men slaves. Regardless of philosophical or moral argument, slavery remained as intrinsic to the Greek socioeconomic structure as it later became to the American antebellum South. Those Greeks who held the most property were those with the greatest political power.[7]

After Solon (640-558 B.C.) divided Athens into social classes according to the amounts of property owned, only 20 percent of the total Athenian population had the right to vote. This ancient practice of restricting the vote to those who held the most property continued through to 1787 when less than 15 percent of the population in the young republic of the United States were allowed to vote.[8] The top fifth of the Greek population included four classes ranked according to property, wealth, and accompanying privileges. Remaining Athenians who otherwise retained full civil rights could not vote. Called metics, this large, immigrant class consisted of craftsmen, artists, bankers and businessmen - occupations held in low regard by the voting classes. At the bottom of the social ladder were slaves. Owned by the state for use on public works or by citizens for domestic service, they were chattel who had no rights. Since most slaves were non-Greeks, considered naturally inferior, it was deemed appropriate to enslave and rule them.[9]

There existed two systems of punishment in Greece: one for citizens and one for non-citizens. With the exception of treason, all citizen crimes were punishable by payment of fines. The greatest dishonor faced by a citizen was exile or death; in contrast, those without property paid for their crimes in their bodies. Floggings and penal slavery were the lot of many throughout the Greek city-states.[10]

Rome and the Birth of Criminal Law

We also inherit much from the Roman Republic; our language reflects its roots in Roman tradition. *Webster's New World Dictionary of the American Language* cites the root word for "slave" as being of Latin origin: "sclavus" in Middle Latin, or "Sklabos" in Late Greek. The word initially referred to captives of Slavic origin in southeast Europe enslaved by the Romans.[11] Even the word for the cornerstone institution of modern civilization, "family," has Latin origins. "Familia" signified the totality of slaves belonging to one person and came from the word "famulus," meaning household slave. The Romans invented the expression to signify the paternal power of life and death over all.[12]

As in the Greek city-states, native-born and wealthy Romans possessed the greatest power and could outvote other citizens. The lowliest citizens were proletarians, propertyless laborers. Below these came the coloni, or sharecropper peasants, bound by heredity to the land no matter what changes occurred in its ownership. Beneath the coloni were the slaves.[13]

Before the birth of criminal law, civil law was the only system of justice. Under civil law, Rome did not claim itself as victim in crimes. Unlike today, few offenses were considered crimes against the State, but the State did lend its services as arbitrator in criminal disputes, receiving payment for its services in court fees.[14] Excepting the crimes of treason and patricide, Roman citizens rarely suffered the punishment of death and could not be flogged or executed without opportunity to appeal to the Centuriate. Noncitizens and slaves, on the other hand, had no access to the assembly to appeal convictions and were often victims of the arbitary justice of the magistrate, who could sentence them to death, floggings, fines, confiscation of property, and crucifixion in the case of slaves.[15]

As Roman courts evolved, officials were appointed to particular kinds of cases such as treason, patricide, and murder. The Roman judicial system grew more intricate and became a lucrative source of revenue for the State. Soon there were citizens charged not only to discover and try offenses that had been committed but also to anticipate potential crimes. The State began to classify crimes and, in 149 B.C., a mandate enabling provincials to recover funds a Governor-General had taken improperly marked the beginning of Roman criminal law.[16] The criminal justice system became more intricate as Rome forced other nations to surrender to its rule. In addition to increasing judicial revenues to the State from court fees, fines, and convict labor, Rome's new criminal code increased control over its expanding empire. Property rights determined wealth, wealth determine nobility and class, and class determined punishment. Criminal law displaced civil law, punishment for crime took on forms formerly reserved for slaves and, by the third century A.D., torture was being used to extract information from lower-class criminal suspects. The Romans laid the ground-work for what would follow: class-based criminal law and "slavery...as a punishment for crime."

The Germanic State in the Middle Ages

The most severe punishment in the Germanic states was death. Fines were imposed for most crimes, the amount dictated by the seriousness of the crime. If an offender could not pay for his crime, he and his family could be enslaved by the victim. Traditionally, retribution was a private matter, an issue to be resolved between victim and offender; however, as the State increased in power, vengeance became government-administered and punishment again emerged as a major source of revenue for the State.[17]

Around the tenth century A.D., serfdom and servitude were quite prevalent.[18] Big landowners and a military aristocracy ruled the common people who, though greatest in numbers, had no political power. The maturing feudal system began to eliminate the need for chattel slaves as serfs came to serve the primary economic needs of the ruling class. Criminal justice remained in the hands of the aristocracy and slavery and its particularly brutal punishments were reserved for disobedient commoners.[19]

By the end of the twelfth century, slave punishments were enshrined in law and applicable to free and unfree alike.[20] Lower class freed-people, like those of Greece and Rome, were without the resources of their wealthier countrypersons and subject to the judicial punishments of civil death and enslavement. As historian Gustav Radbruch wrote:

> To this day, the criminal law bears the traits of its origin in
> slave punishments.... To be punished means to be treated
> like a slave. That was symbolically underscored in olden
> times when...flogging was joined with the shearing of the
> head, because the shorn head was a mark of the slave....
> Slavish treatment meant...not just a social but a moral deg-
> radation. "Baseness" is thus simultaneously and inseparably
> a social, moral and even an aesthetic value judgement. The
> lowly born is also a "mean fellow." ...In both French and
> English the unfree peasant and the scoundrel are called vil-
> lains.... In the illustrations in the *Sachsenspiegel* the faces
> of the common people are pictured as ugly and coarse. The
> diminution of honor, which ineradicably inheres in punish-
> ment to this day, derives from slave punishments.[21]

Vagrancy Laws

The fourteenth through sixteenth centuries witnessed the fall of
feudalism and the rise of commerce and industry. As urban centers
flourished, wages for free workers rose and the plight of feudal landlords worsened. Pressed to pay higher wages for free labor, landowners could not provide even the standard of living they had formerly
supplied their serfs. Serfs had no alternative but flight from the land
should they choose to better their position. Such flight might mean
both freedom and better conditions, since the possibility of work in
the new weaving industry was great and the chance of being caught
small.[22]

Loss of lives during the Black Death of 1348 and the crusades hastened the demise of feudalism. Exorbitant costs of war pressed some
feudal landlords into selling freedom to their serfs. Refugees from
serfdom migrated to cities that "offered bright but illusory hopes of
success and prosperity," most of them sinking even further into poverty as increasing city populations resulted in business-designed barriers to keep newcomers out.[23]

Migration to the cities also threatened the state with vast, indigest-
ible socioeconomic changes. Between 1349 and 1351, in an effort to
avert the inevitable, England issued the Statutes of Labourers which
forced every able-bodied person lacking means of support to accept
the low wages prevailing before the Black Death. The statutes forbade
migration from one county to another where a worker might find higher
wages and forbade poor people to spend money in any manner that
might represent them as other "than a poor and dependent person."[24]

An abundant labor supply meant owners could afford to place little
value on workers and less on the jobless. Given the limited and oppressive alternatives defined by the vagrancy laws, the poor could do
little to improve their situation. Some worked for power-hungry lords,
while most sank into bitter poverty.

The Statutes of Labourers not only victimized the poor, they reinforced the attitude that immorality rather than oppressive inequality caused crime. Harsh criminal codes directed at the poor were among the first fruits of free enterprise. Crimes against property were common during the latter part of the fifteenth century, but poor people were not the only thieves. Increase in the size of aristocratic families over the course of generations produced large numbers of younger sons with no prospect of inheritance. Many of these landless knights took to highway robbery, just as their subjects did on a smaller scale. While destitute peasants had to rob openly, however, these knights could camouflage their activities under the pretexts of legitimate warfare or of avenging the pauperized masses on rich city merchants who "ruined the populace bodily, economically, and morally."[25]

As feudalism gave way to the need for a mobile free labor force, the vagrancy laws fell into disuse until 1530, when England directed its attention to criminal offenders. As demonstrated by a 1547 statute, new vagrancy laws not only prosecuted offenders, but also those deemed capable of crime - the poor and the jobless:

> Whoever man or woman, being not lame, impotent or so aged or diseased that he or she cannot work, not having whereon to live, shall be lurking in any house, or loitering or idle or wandering by the highway side, or in streets, cities, towns, or villages, not applying themselves to some honest labour, and so continuing for three days; or running away from their work; every such person shall be taken for a vagabond. And...upon conviction of two witnesses...the same loiterer (shall) be marked with a hot iron in the breast with the letter V, and adjudged him to the person bringing him, to be his slave for two years...[26]

New law also "provided that all vagrants who refused to work or ran away could be adjudged slaves of their masters for two years; second offenders could be sentenced to slavery for life, and third offenders to death."[27]

While vagrancy laws were initially aimed at inhibiting the political and economic changes ushered in by capitalism and industrial development, they came to serve new functions dictated by economic changes in the fourteenth through sixteenth centuries.[28] Labor acquired new value and vagrancy laws helped control the common labor pool in the best interests of the powerful few. While lawful distinctions between lord and serf became outmoded under capitalism, vagrancy statutes which criminalized even "honest" efforts of the poor to advance themselves crushed all hopes for social mobility. Threatened punishments kept workers in servant roles and those who tried to improve their condition found few lawful means to do so. If people left their jobs in search of better pay or working conditions, they were guilty of vagrancy; if they crossed county lines or were caught begging or stealing, they were criminals. While property holders enjoyed the protection of the State, those without property were forced to devote their labor to maintaining the status quo.

As in times before, the wealthy were not only free of the need to commit crimes to survive but, should they be found guilty of crime, their punishments were limited to fines or banishment, in which case they took their riches with them. Owning property not only enabled the upper classes to pay fines but automatically conferred personal honor, while the term "villain," orginally designating a person of low economic status, also came to mean a person of immoral character.[29]

The Punishment of Slavery Benefited the State

> Methods of punishment began to undergo a gradual but profound change toward the end of the sixteenth century. The possibility of exploiting the labor of prisoners now received increasing attention. Galley slavery, deportation, and penal servitude at hard labor were introduced, the first two only for a time, the third as the hesitant precursor of an institution which has lasted into the present.... These changes were not the result of humanitarian considerations, but of certain economic developments which revealed the potential value of a mass of human material completely at the disposal of the administration.[30]

Galley slavery, which existed in ancient Greece and Rome, appeared in France and Spain during the fourteenth and fifteenth centuries. Since wage laborers refused to work rowing the massive ships of the kings, government turned to the convenient labor source of convict slaves. Prisoners, proclaimed civilly dead upon conviction, were chained in ship galleys. Galley slavery, "tantamount to a slow and painful death,"[31] inspired many convicts to save themselves through disabling injuries. Self-mutilation became so prevalent among galley slaves that, in 1677, French law ordered the death penalty for it.[32] As more sophisticated sailing methods replaced teams of oarsmen, use of galley slaves declined in the eighteenth century. However, the following royal mandate indicates that convict slaves served the reigning monarchs well:

> Since His Majesty urgently needs more men to strengthen His rowing crews...to be delivered at the end of the following month, His Majesty commands me to tell you that He wishes you to take the necessary steps in His name in order to have the criminals judged quickly.[33]

A fundamental development in the exploitation of prisoner labor was provided by the Houses of Correction of sixteenth century England. Run by wealthy, state-appointed citizens for government profit, these houses were thought to humanize punishment by providing job training for convicted vagrants. Custom dictated use of "shackles of iron for the taming of wild and lewd persons"[34] and, as in all forms of penal slavery, corporal punishment disciplined the laborers. Workhouses in sixteenth and seventeenth century Amsterdam followed the same tradition and, spreading throughout the continent, "they became state factories serving the mercantilistic policies of rulers more concerned with the balance of trade than with the reformation of criminals."[35] Like contemporary prison manufacture of license plates, many workhouses secured trade monopolies. Those monopolies meant that freed prisoners would find their workhouse experience of no use in securing employment. And, as if a mirror were held up to reflect today's prejudices against hiring ex-convicts, people released from workhouses were excluded from guilds and rejected by potential employers.

European governments discovered the flexibility of penal servitude and, by the seventeenth century, were using slave labor to fill production gaps left by work too expensive or too harsh to be done by paid laborers. The Thirty Year War (1618-1648) resulted in a diminished labor force throughout Europe and, just as today's convicts erect prisons and state buildings and maintain highways, seventeenth century convicts were put to work in the fortresses of the State and, over the next three centuries, on public works.

> In France, the revolutionary penal code of 1791 introduced a punishment "in irons" as a substitute for sentences to the galleys. The convicts were to be "employed at forced labor to the profit of the state, either in a *maison de force* [maximum security prison] or in ports and arsenals, or in the extraction of ores, or in draining of marshes, or, finally, in any other painful labor which upon demand of a department [administrative district] might be determined by the legislative assembly."[36]

Brutal Punishments

Corporal punishment accompanied penal slavery and the poorer the offender, the harsher the punishment. Before the nineteenth century, the death penalty punished many minor offenses and torture extracted "the truth" from the accused. Without riches to protect them, punishment of poor people became grotesque spectacles comparable to the Roman practice of sentencing errant slaves and lower class citizens to die in the arena:

> Publicity was officially believed to enhance the deterrent value of punishment. Thieves were more often left hanging in the air than buried in order that everyone might see them and fear a similar fate. But the whole system was primarily the ex-

pression of sadism, and the deterrent effect of publicity was negligible. That is why the most morbid imagination today can hardly picture the variety of tortures inflicted. We read about executions by knife, ax, and sword, heads being knocked off with a plank or cut through with a plough, people being buried alive, left to starve in a dungeon, or having nails hammered through their heads, eyes, shoulders, and knees, strangulation and throttling, drowning and bleeding to death, evisceration, drawing and quartering, torture on the wheel, torture with red-hot tongs, strips being cut from the skin, the body being torn to pieces or sawed through with iron or wooden instruments, burning at the stake, and many other forms of cruelty.[37]

Since punishments inflicted by a society at any given time reflect prevailing social relationships, the forms of cruelty have changed.[38] Much has been done with little effect, however, to remedy the inequities of punishment inflicted on the poor or to alter the justification for capital punishment voiced in the following eighteenth century statement:

No man of common humanity or common sense can think the Life of a Man and a few shillings to be of equal Consideration, . . .[but] the Terror of Example is the thing proposed, and one man is sacrificed for the Preservation of Thousands.[39]

In the twentieth century, the Nazis also rationalized use of the death penalty as a deterrent, although statistics show no conclusive evidence that increased punishment deters crimes.[40] A more accurate expression of the import of the death penalty may have come from the German theoretician who stated that "the necessity of retaining it in the National Socialist state requires no defense. The death penalty is the expression of the domination of the whole over the individual . . ."[41] Historians George Rusche and Otto Kirchheimer explain Nazi repressive punishment in this way:

A significant feature . . . is the avowed necessity to keep down the living standard of the lower strata. In order to facilitate the acceptance of this program by the masses, considerable effort is spent in cultivating a moral distinction between those who are poor but honest and the strata which have become criminal.[42]

We can apply this understanding to American justice today, especially in light of recent invocations of the death penalty. John Spinkelink, a Florida prisoner who claimed he murdered in self-defense, was executed on May 23, 1979. Only four days before, San Francisco conservative council member Dan White, who admitted shooting defenseless Mayor George Moscone and gay council member Harvey Milk in their separate city offices, was found guilty of voluntary manslaughter, which carriers a sentence of no more than eight years' imprisonment.

The startling contrast between these two convictions and sentences reflects biases that still determine criminal punishments.

In the current period of deepening recession and high unemployment, government reinstatement of the death penalty exhibits a vindictiveness characteristic of historic responses to an over-abundant labor force. Death is always the slavemaster's ultimate weapon but when the supply of slaves runs short, he looks to other methods of punishment. While sixteenth through eighteenth century justice promoted the death penalty as the best deterrent to crime, increased need for labor in the colonies of the new world prompted European governments to offer slavery as a reprieve from death. Convict transportation to America in indentured servitude became a popular way to escape execution.

Notes

1. Plato, *The Laws,* Book VI, line 778a.

2. Hoebel, p. 410.

3. Evelyn Reed, *Woman's Evolution: From Matriarchal Clan to Patriarchal Family,* (New York: Pathfinder Press, Inc., 1975), pp. xiv-xx, 69-72, chaps. 4-7, 11 (for social organization). The terms "savagery" and "barbarism" are used for scientific description. As Evelyn Reed explains:

> The terms "savage" and "primitive," often used in a derogatory, colonialist or racist sense, are here used exclusively in a scientific way. "Savage" is simply a designation for our earliest ancestors. Without their collosal achievements over a span of a million years, humanity could not have walked the last mile to civilization. (Ibid., p. xviii)

4. Ibid., pp. 312-313, chap. 14 (especially pp. 412-415, 429-430); Hoebel, p. 422.

5. Reed, chap. 14, especially pp. 412-413, 429-430.

6. J. Thorsten Sellin, *Slavery and the Penal System* (New York: Elsevier Scientific Publishing Co., Inc., 1976), p. 18.

7. Ibid., p. 5.

8. Ibid., pp. 5-6 for Solon's division of Greek social classes; Linda Grant De Pauw, "Land of the Unfree: Legal Limitations on Liberty in Pre-Revolutionary America," *Maryland Historical Magazine,* 68 (1973): 363-365 for percentage of voting Americans. De Pauw's article is reprinted in *The American Revolution: Whose Revolution?,* James Kirby Martin and Karen R. Stubaus, eds. (Huntington, New York: Robert E. Krieger Publishing Co., 1977).

9. Sellin, pp. 3, 5-10.

10. Ibid., pp. 12-18.

11. *Webster's New World Dictionary of the American Language,* 2nd college ed. (1970), s.v. "slave."

12. Frederick Engels, *The Origin of the Family, Private Property and the State,* intro. and notes by Eleanor Burke Leacock (New York: International Publishers, 1972), p. 121; Reed, p. 430.

13. Sellin, pp. 23-25.

14. Gilbert M. Cantor, "An End to Crime and Punishment," *The Shingle,* 39 (1976): 99-100.

15. Sellin, pp. 25-26.

16. Cantor, p. 100.

17. See Sellin, pp. 30-33.

18. Ibid., p. 39.

19. Ibid., p. 41.

20. Ibid.

21. Ibid., p. viii, Sellin quotes from "Der Ursprung des Strafrechts aus dem Stande der Unfreien," reprinted in Gustav Radbruch, *Elegantiae juris criminalis* (Basel: Verlag für Recht und Gesellschaft, 1950), pp. 11-12.

22. William J. Chambliss, "A Sociological Analysis of the Law of Vagrancy," *Social Problems,* 12 (1964): 69.

23. Ibid. for black death and the crusades; The President's Commission on Law Enforcement and Administration of Justice, Task Force Report: Corrections 88 (1967), "The Collateral Consequences of a Criminal Conviction," *Vanderbilt Law Review,* 23 (1970): 946.

24. Chambliss, pp. 69-70; quotation is from Beatrice Webb, *The English Poor Law* (London: Oxford University Press, 1928), p. 1.

25. Georg Rusche and Otto Kirchheimer, *Punishment and Social Structure* (New York: Russell and Russell, 1968; reprint ed. Columbia University Press, 1939), pp. 12-13. (Complaint against city merchants is on p. 13. The citation given for this quotation is W. Andreas, *Deutschland vor der Reformation* [Stuttgart, 1932], p. 289.)

26. Chambliss, p. 73.

27. Rusche and Kirchheimer, p. 39.

28. See Rusche and Kirchheimer, pp. 14-18; Chambliss, pp. 69-74.

29. Rusche and Kirchheimer, p. 15.

30. Ibid., p. 24.

31. Sellin, pp. 46-48; Rusche and Kirchheimer, p. 57 for description of galley slavery as a slow and painful death.

32. Rusche and Kirchheimer, p. 57.

33. Ibid., p. 55, quotes a February 21, 1676, letter to the public prosecutor in Paris.

34. Sellin, p. 72.

35. Ibid., p. 81.

36. Ibid., p. 60.

37. Rusche and Kirchheimer, pp. 21-22.

38. Ibid., p. 23, as follows:
> Brutal punishment cannot be ascribed simply to the primitive cruelty of an epoch now vanished. Cruelty itself is a social phenomenon which can be understood only in terms of the social relationships prevailing in any given period.

39. Alan George Lewers Shaw, *Convicts and the Colonies* (London: Melbourne University Press, 1977; reprint ed. Faber & Faber, Ltd., 1966), p. 28, quoting Henry Fielding.

40. Rusche and Kirchheimer, p. 183.

41. Ibid, quoting E. Wolf, "Das künftige Strafsystem und die Zummessungsgründe," *Zeitschrift für die gasamte Strafrechswissenschaft,* 54 (1935), 546-547.

42. Ibid., p. 182.

Chapter 2:
A New Nation

> What, to the American slave, is your Fourth of July? I answer;
> a day that reveals to him, more than all other days of the year,
> the gross injustice and cruelty to which he is a constant vic-
> tim. To him, your celebration is a sham; your boasted liberty,
> an unholy license; your national greatness, swelling vanity;
> your sounds of rejoicing are empty and heartless; your de-
> nunciation of tyrants, brass fronted impudence; your shouts
> of liberty and equality, hollow mockery; your prayers and
> hymns, your sermons and thanksgivings, with all your reli-
> gious parade and solemnity, are to him, mere bombast, fraud,
> deception, impiety, and hypocrisy · a thin veil to cover up
> crimes which would disgrace a nation of savages. There is
> not a nation of the earth guilty of practices more shocking
> and bloody than are the people of these United States, at this
> very hour.
>
> · Frederick Douglass
> Independence Day Speech, 1852[1]

Of Class, War, and Punishment

The first slaves in America were its own conquered and exploited people. Even the Puritans who fled England for their own religious freedom made slaves of their neighbors.

> No new community in the midst of virgin soil ever had enough
> labor to satisfy it, and the English settlers at once began to
> enslave their neighbors, soothing their consciences with the
> argument that it was right to make slaves of pagans. Fierce,
> intractable, unaccustomed to continuous labor, the Indians
> fled or died in captivity, leaving few of their descendants in
> bondage. Rather by way of experiment than with any confi-
> dence in their usefulness, in 1619 the Virginians began to im-
> port African negroes, first from the West Indies; later by a
> steady direct trade from Africa.[2]

Not until 1726 to 1788 did African slavery begin to supplant indentured servitude in Virginia. During the earlier period of colonization,
trade in Europeans was found cheaper than African slave trade. It is
possible that the first Africans brought here were treated like indentures. Slavery in all three forms had found its way to new soil: Native
Americans and Africans were spoils of European wars on their villages, impoverished Europeans were slaves of punishment or class
through indentured servitude. As the peculiar institution of chattel
slavery became entrenched in the colonies, Afro-Americans became
slaves of class when, after 1640, they and their unborn children were
sold as life-long chattel.[3]

Native American Resistance

More than a century before the American Revolution, Native Americans were enslaved by colonists. Regarded as useful in the profitable fur trade and in knowledge of the land, business interests guided colonial attempts to enslave them. The Puritans engaged in wars with native tribes, taking as many into bondage as they could while still keeping their friendships with the "more important" tribes. During the war with the Pequots, the Puritans made women and children captives slaves while shipping the men to slave traders abroad.[4] The following 1637 description of the Puritan disposition of women captives indicates the base regard many colonists had for their new neighbors:

> There is a little squaw that Steward Calient desireth, to whom he hath given a coat. Lieutenant Davenport also desireth one, to wit, a small one that hath three strokes upon the stomach.[5]

When the supply of European indentures grew short, colonists bargained with the natives for their labor.

> Their labour was desired by the European settlers. So much so, in fact, that when the Indians for one reason or another wished no employment their labour was acquired by subterfuge. A group of Indians could be persuaded to contract, say, to build a stone fence, for a certain sum and within a certain time. If they became reluctant to go through with their task, if, perhaps they found out that they had contracted for too small a price, they were forced by legal process to go on with their work and in some such cases they were put to the lash and forced to work at the end of a whip![6]

Some Iroquois even apprenticed their children to colonists for the purpose of learning the new language and trades, but the children were treated harshly and many were sold to slavers for the West Indies trade.[7] In spite of their lack of advanced weaponry, the Native Americans were not easily enslaved. Unlike the people stolen from Europe and Africa, they had not been torn from their native systems of support and knew the land and its resources. Although the following statement does not treat Native Americans fairly, it helps clarify the victimization of these people during the period of colonial expansion:

> The North American Indians, inasmuch as they had not emerged from the hunting stage, could not be enslaved; they were too 'wild'. So the English colonist slew them, drove them away, or bought them off, and put his own back to the labours of the fields.[8]

Indentured Servitude

England's Vagrancy Act of 1547, authorizing magistrates to sentence vagrants to work as slaves for their masters, was repealed in 1550. In 1598, a reenactment of the statute declared "that any rogues appearing 'dangerous to the inferior sort of people' or 'such as will not be reformed of their roguish kind of life'" could be transported or sent to the galleys.[9] Transportation became a favorite means of getting rid of "undesirables," particularly political dissidents. Building prisons would be expensive, transportation "was defended as cheap punishment,"[10] and the bonded labor of the criminal element would fill the need for free labor power to colonize the New World.

In 1611, Sir Thomas Dale requested convicts for Virginia so that criminals "might be rather corrected than destroyed and that in their punishmentes some may live and yeald a profitable service to the commonwealthe in partes abroad."[11] In 1656, England ordered the "apprehending of lewd and dangerous persons... who have no way of livelihood... and treating with merchants for transporting them to the English plantations in America."[12]

The Habeas Corpus Act of 1679 forbade transportation without a trial but also legalized the pardoning of prisoners if they agreed to serve a sentence of indenture in the colonies. Between 1679 and 1699, 4,500 convicts agreed to be transported in lieu of impending corporal punishments or death.[13]

Between 1688 and 1819, nearly 187 capital offenses were added to the original 50. Menial crimes such as stealing or injuring gates, deer, fish, and shipwrecked goods became punishable by death and the available free convict labor to the crown also increased as servitude was offered as a reprieve from death. During the Seven Years War (1756-1763), convicts were used more in the war efforts than in transportation.[14] John Lauson, sentenced to fourteen years of indenture, left a rare account of indentured servitude in *The Felon's Account of his Transportation at Virginia:* "...Of honest parents did I come tho' poor/ Who besides me had no children more..."[15] John ran away from his master, taking part in a robbery with seven others, all of whom were apprehended. Three of his friends were hanged, he and the others transported.

> The Captain and the Sailors, us'd us well,
> But kept us under lest we should rebel.
>   We were in number much about Threescore,
> Wicked and cruel lousy Crew as ever went over,
> And after sailing Seven weeks or more,
> We at VIRGINIA all were put ashore,
>   Then, to refresh us, we were all made clean,
> That to our Buyers we might better seem....
> Some ask our Trades and others ask'd our names,
>   Some view'd our Limbs turn'd us around,

> Examining like Horses if we were sound,
> What trade, my lad? said one of them to me,
> A Cooper, Sir, that will not do for me.

Not sold on the first day ashore,

> Down to the harbour I was took again,
> On board a Ship bound with an iron chain,
> Which I was forc'd to wear night & day,
> For fear I from the sloop should run away.

Finally sold,

> At last to my new masters house i came,
> To the town of wicowoco call'd by name,
> Here my Europon cloaths were took away from me,
> Which never after i could see.
>   A canvass shirt and trowers me they gave,
> A hop-sack frock in which i was a slave
> No shoes nor flockings had i for to wear
> Nor hat, nor cap, my hands and feet went bare,
>   Thus dress unto the fields i next did go,
> Among Tobacco plants all day to hoe
> At day break in the morn our work begun,
> And lasted 'till the setting of the sun.
>   My fellow slaves were five transports more
> With eighteen Negroes, which is twenty-four,
> Besides four transports women in the house,
> To wait upon his daughter and his spouse.
>   We and the negroes both alike did fare,
> Of work and food we had an equal share. . . .
>   But if we offer once to run away,
> For every Hour we must serve a Day,
> For every day a Week, they're so severe,
> Every Week a month, every month a Year.
>   But if they Murder, Rob, or Steal when there,
> They're hang'd direct, the Laws are so severe. . . .
>   At last it pleased God I sick did fall,
> Yet I no favour did receive at all,
> For I was forc'd to work while I could stand,
> Or hold the Hoe within my feeble hands.
>   Much hardship then indeed I did endure,
> No Dog was ever nursed so before:
> More pity the poor Negro Slaves bestow'd,
> Than my Inhuman brutal Master show'd.

John's master eventually sold him to another who treated him more kindly. After serving his full fourteen years, John Lauson returned to England.

> And in my heart I often griev'd to see,
> So many transport Felons there to be;

Some who in England had liv'd fine and brave,
Was there like horses forc'd to trudge and slave.

Not Just For Punishment

More than half the European colonists migrating to this nation were indentured servants. Regardless of the laws passed to prevent abuse of the system, people were also transported illegally. The term "kidnapping" originated with the stealing of indentured servants, or "kids." They were lured with sweetmeats or promises of a life of leisure, seduced by ladies of the night or forcibly carried off. The practice became so popular that the ladies of the royal court and the mayor of Bristol were suspected of sharing in its profits.[16]

Besides the involuntary indentured servants convicted of crimes or kidnapped, there were many Europeans who willingly leased themselves for a two to seven year term of indenture in exchange for their voyage to America. For those rendered hopeless by economic conditions at home, indentured servitude in America provided an alternative. The agreement was usually made with a representative of the colonial master in England, who later transferred the contract to the servant's master. Many voluntary servants not yet of age were considered apprentices who would serve a colonial master while learning a trade. Those apprenticed included youngsters who had no family capable of supporting them and were a burden the state was not willing to assume. Other voluntary indentures were redemptioners, usually Germans, many of whom later settled in Pennsylvania. They came to England to sign contracts that included the voyage of entire families to the colonies. The redemptioner signed an agreement to have colonial friends or relatives pay the ship's captain for the voyage upon arrival. If he was not "redeemed," the captain could sell him and his family into indenture to the highest bidder.

The "voluntary" nature of such indentures is questionable since the recruitment process was enmeshed with deceit. Contractors employed agents all over Europe who received commissions on tickets sold to America. Among those who earned a reputation for promoting immigration through lies were the Nuelanders (new landers) who were the subject of warning in a letter from Muhlenburg, Germany, published in 1769:

In order to accomplish their purpose the more readily, they resort to every conceivable trickery. They parade themselves in fine dress, display their watches, and in every way conduct themselves as men of opulence, in order to inspire the people with the desire to live in a country of such wealth and abundance. They would convince one that there are in America, none but Elysian fields abounding in products which require no labor; that the mountains are full of gold and silver, and

> the wells and springs gush forth milk and honey; that he goes
> there as a servant, becomes a lord; as a maid, a gracious lady;
> as a peasant, a nobleman; as a commoner or craftsman, a
> baron. . . . Now, as everybody by nature desires to better his
> condition, who would not wish to go to such a country![17]

The demand for indentured servants was greater than the agents could supply. Their slave labor was preferred to free labor and remained so "until the population increased enough to provide a surplus of men making it possible to hire and fire at will."[18] Those involved in human traffic spent little to assure the health and safety of their victims. For all transports, the long voyage to America was dangerous: ships were overcrowded, ventilation poor and nourishment inadequate. Voluntary and involuntary servants alike suffered terrible conditions.

> During the eight to twelve weeks voyage, there was "on board
> these ships terrible misery, stench, fumes, horror, vomiting,
> many kinds of sea-sickness, fever, dysentery, headache, heat,
> constipation, boils, scurvy, cancer, mouth rot and the like . . .
> and . . . add to this want of provisions, hunger, thirst, frost,
> heat, dampness, anxiety, want, afflictions, lamentations."
> Conditions on board were probably no worse than in many
> contemporary gaols, where the felons lay "worse than dogs
> or swine and are kept much more uncleanly than those an-
> imals are . . . the stench and nastiness are so nauseous that
> no person enters without the risk of his life and health"; yet
> they were overcrowded with prisoners lodged in irons be-
> tween the decks.[19]

The labor of the indentured servant belonged to the master. A servant could own no property other than what the master allowed, could not marry without permission, or frequent taverns. Indentures could be sold away from their families against their will or seized to pay for their master's debts.[20] They were subjected to cruel corporal punishments, even to service in irons. As with chattel slavery, the conditions under which indentured servants lived varied according to the cruelty or kindness of their masters and to laws dictating their treatment within the several colonies.

> "What we unfortunat English People suffer here is beyond
> the probability of you in England to Conceive," lamented one
> girl to her father; "let it suffice that I . . . am toiling almost Day
> and Night, . . . and then tied up and whipp'd to that Degree
> that you'd not serve an Annimal, scarce any thing but Indian
> Corn and Salt to eat and that even begrudged . . . almost naked
> no shoes nor stockings to wear, and . . . slaving during Mas-
> ters pleasures . . ."[21]

Whether stolen, transported as convicts, apprenticed or voluntary, all "indentured servants were temporarily chattel."[22]

They were recognized as property; they sold themselves or were sold for given terms, and had no protection as to the place or nature of their service except such as was extended by quite general legislation. Indentured servants often got scant justice under the laws of the time. Into the nineteenth century this form of labor was often termed slavery.[23]

African Slavery

With the initial shipments of Africans to the colonies and the first regular charter voyage in 1631, the African slave trade became a lucrative and important business, "especially in the south, where the master class of tobacco, rice, sugar, and cotton planters found slavery an invaluable, unequaled source of profit." After 1640, blacks were sold into life-long slavery, their unborn children and grandchildren sold with them. In 1662, Charles II chartered the "Company of Royal Adventures" for the African trade and, in 1713, England secured a monopoly of colonial slave trade by a treaty with Spain knows as the Asiento.[24]

Before the American Revolution, England engaged in a triangular slave trade with Africa, transporting between 40,000 and 100,000 slaves to America each year.[25] Slave ships, loaded with goods to exchange with slavers for kidnapped Africans, completed their trade in Africa and carried their victims to the colonies. Many died from the cramped and diseased conditions aboard ship, some committing suicide rather than face bondage. In the colonies, these men, women and children were traded for rum, cotton, and other goods which were carried back to England.

Europeans and Africans labored side by side under early American servitude. It is possible that the first Africans brought to Virginia in 1619 were treated like indentures, since it was one half-century after the first permanent settlement before chattel slavery of blacks "became an important substitute [for indenture], chiefly because the supply of indentured servants was insufficient." Indentured servitude paved the way for the colonial master's receptivity to chattel slavery and, as chattel slavery became entrenched in the colonies, indentured servitude more and more resembled the condition of African slaves.[26]

Increased plantation production generated the need for craftspeople to build barns, warehouses, and the like. When there were not enough indentured servants, the plantation master had indentures train slaves in their crafts, increasing the monetary value of the slave. The common bondage of Europeans and Africans on plantations created a sense of kinship, mutual struggle, love and resulting marriages. In response, a 1691 Virginia law forbade further marriages between white indentures and black slaves. The new law forbidding "miscegenation" was aimed at dividing the master's slaves and preventing them from uniting against him.[27]

Indentured servitude differed from chattel slavery in three main respects - bondage was temporary rather than lifelong; indentures could sue their masters for violating their rights to a minimal standard of living; and successful escape was much easier for the white servant. Black and white servants often ran away from their masters but runaway Europeans were much more difficult to find since they assimilated easily into the free white population. Parallel to fugitive laws for runaway slaves, penalties were imposed on anyone found harboring a fugitive indenture. Many newspaper ads offered rewards for the capture of runaways. Searching for escaped slaves, however, was more attractive, since the redeemer had to release the unclaimed servant but could keep the unclaimed slave for his own use.[28]

As plantation colonies flourished, southern masters came to prefer black slavery to white indenture and used their white servants as overseers, slave drivers, and superintendents.[29] The lifelong service of chattel slaves and their descendants proved more profitable for plantation owners. Chattel slavery supplanted indentured servitude when, after the American Revolution, transportation of indentures from England ended.

Lacking plantation economies, the northern colonies did not purchase slaves in great numbers but did nevertheless profit from the slave trade. New England colonists purchased slaves and traded them for ship-building materials in South Carolina, molasses in the West Indies and large barrels in other colonies. Traders made West Indies molasses into New England rum which they poured into the barrels to ship to Africa in exchange for more slaves. In the West Indies, Connecticut colonists traded horses for slaves to sell in other colonies. Newport, the hub of the business in the North, became a thriving port because of the pre-Revolution slave trade. No lawful measures against the trade were taken in any part of New England until the first few years of American independence.[30]

Those slaves purchased to live in New York and New England were treated in the same manner as servants generally, while those living in Pennsylvania were treated much like serfs. The aristocratic caste system, and its "peculiar institution" of chattel slavery, flourished in the plantation colonies of the South.[31]

Several authors of the Declaration of Independence did not believe that slavery would be upheld in the new nation. Thomas Jefferson, Virginia plantation and slave owner who professed a loathing for slavery, participated in its writing and was responsible for the following section of the original document, which charged the king with waging a

> ...cruel war against human nature itself, violating its most
> sacred rights of life and liberty in the persons of a distant
> people who never offended him, captivating and carrying them
> into slavery in another hemisphere, or to incur miserable
> death in their transportation thither. This piratical warfare,

the opprobrium of *infidèl* powers, is the warfare of the *Chris-tian* king of Great Britain. Determined to keep open a market where *men* should be bought and sold, he has prostituted his negative for suppressing every legislative attempt to prohibit or to restrain this execrable commerce. And that this assem-blage of horrors might want no fact of distinguished die, he is now exciting those very people to rise in arms among us, and to purchase that liberty which he has deprived them, by mur-dering the people on whom he also obtruded them: thus pay-ing off former crimes committed against the *liberties* of one people with crimes which he urges them to commit against the *lives* of another.[32]

The above portion of the Declaration of Independence was deleted be-cause it did not win approval by all the delegates. Jefferson later ex-plained that it was

"struck out in compliasance to South Carolina and Georgia, who had never attempted to restrain the importation of slaves, and who, on the contrary, still wished to continue it. Our northern brethren also, I believe," said he, "felt a little tender under those censures; for though their people had very few slaves themselves, yet they had been pretty considerable carriers of them to others."[33]

Whose Revolution Was It?

Although Britain could be charged with initiating the African slave trade, many wealthy colonists, including Thomas Jefferson, partici-pated in the loathsome system. Jefferson's words rang true, how-ever, in accusing the king of encouraging rebellion among the slaves. In 1775, royal governor Lord Dunmore of Virginia decreed that all re-belling colonists were traitors, and offered freedom to slaves who would fight for the British:

I do hereby further declare all indented servants, Negroes, or others, (appertaining to Rebels,) free, that are able and willing to bear arms, they joining His Majesty's Troops, as soon as may be, for the more speedily reducing the Colony to a proper sense of their duty, to His Majesty's crown and dignity."[34]

Even before his November proclamation, Dunmore was known to sail "up and down the river, . . . and where he finds a defenceless place, he lands, plunders the plantation and carries off the negroes." Colonial masters tried to discourage their slaves from joining the British, fur-ther accusing Dunmore of innoculating blacks with smallpox and sending them ashore to spread the disease. Thousands of slaves join-ed the British and sailed their war vessels, bore their arms and for-aged plantations at night for food and livestock to earn their promised liberty. Several went to England in freedom after the war.[35]

With the exception of those who supported the British in exchange for their freedom, slaves and indentured servants fought according to the desires of their masters. During the war, feelings against slavery rose and, in recognition of their participation in battle, the North emancipated many of its slaves after the Revolution. The South, however, demanded that the slave trade continue since "slaves, by pillage, flight, and actual fighting, had become so reduced in numbers during the war..."[36]

Although history texts speak little of them, working class women also fought among American troops. An eyewitness account of the battle of Monmouth records that

> A woman whose husband belonged to the artillery and who was then attached to a piece in the engagement, attended with her husband at the piece the whole time. While in the act of reaching a cartridge and having one of her feet as far before the other as she could step, a cannon shot from the enemy passed directly between her legs without doing any other damage then carrying away all the lower part of her petticoat. Looking at it with apparent unconcern, she...continued her occupation.[37]

In "The Truth About Molly Pitcher", John Todd White explained how women who followed their working-class men into battle have been historically misunderstood as having been limited to domestic camp chores because of nineteenth century attempts to romanticize their role and transform them "into an acceptable legend of middle class femininity."[38]

Another social class of women, the wives of the new American lawmakers, are known to have tried to persuade their men to give women the right to vote, as illustrated by the famous but ineffective appeal from Abigail Adams to her husband John:

> - and by the way in the new Code of Law which I suppose it will be necessary for you to make I desire you would Remember the Laidies, and be more generous and favourable to them than your ancestors. Do not put such unlimited power into the hands of the Husbands. Remember all Men would be tyrants if they could. If perticuliar care and attention is not paid to the Laidies we are determined to foment a Rebellion, and will not hold ourselves bound by any Laws in which we have no voice, or Representation.[39]

Despite such appeals, the plight of women worsened under the new government. American widows received only one-third of their husband's estate and were often forced to work by necessity or by the compulsory work requirements of poor laws, unless a male relative took them in. Divorces, much easier to obtain under British rule became "practically impossible for a woman to obtain" after the Revolution.[40]

Instigated and led by wealthy colonists whose political aspirations were frustrated by their lack of recognition by the ruling British, the American Revolution is more properly called the War for Independence.

> Indeed, leadership analysis tends to conclude that the confrontation after 1763 resulted not so much from a class struggle as from a struggle within the ruling class...[41]

Although the Declaration of Independence called for consent of the governed, few Americans were sufficiently "equal" to have their consent measured in ratification of the Constitution of 1787. Those delegates who drew up the proposed Constitution represented the propertied interests of America. They were "practical men" with the interests of their own class at heart. Some actively preferred aristocratic rule to protect government from what they feared as the incompetent and anarchistic sentiments of the lower classes. Seeking to ensure economic advantage for their own interests, the delegates fought over whether to determine government power by city or agrarian property,[42] but the main dispute, said James Madison, was over the issue of slavery:

> "the States were divided into different interests not by their difference of size, but by other circumstances; the most material of which resulted partly from the climate, but principally from the effects of their having or not having slaves...the institution of slavery & its consequences formed the line of discrimination" between the contending states.[43]

Slavery continued under the new government. Oliver Ellsworth, delegate from Connecticut, offered one convincing argument for patience:

> As slaves multiply so fast in Virginia and Maryland that it is cheaper to raise than to import them, whilst in the sickly rice swamps foraging supplies are necessary, if we go no further than is urged, we shall be unjust towards South Carolina and Georgia. Let us not intermeddle. As population increases, poor laborers will be so plenty as to render slaves useless.[44]

There were already many poor laborers in new nation. Most colonists who fought for the right of self-government did not participate in it: more than 85 percent of the American population did not meet the property requirements to vote on the proposed document for new government. Almost one quarter of the disfranchised population were chattel slaves; about 12 percent of the voteless were indentured servants; and another 6 to 13 percent were free white men not owning enough property to qualify them to vote in their respective states. The rest of the voteless population were women and children.[45] These statistics do not include Native Americans, generally regarded as aliens on "American" soil; their fate would be determined by the imperialistic policies of a government which would steal their lands. Three-fourths of the adult male population did not vote on the Constitution of 1787, "either on account of their indifference or disfranchisement by property qualifications," and not more than one-sixth ratified the Constitution.[46]

In fact, the proposed document caused considerable controversy. The Federalists, nicknamed the "aristocracy" by their opponents, represented the propertied classes and favored ratification. They put the great advantage of their wealth into proratification propoganda in privately owned newspapers, printing and distributing leaflets, and other means to defend their cause.[47] As Charles Beard concluded in his *Economic Interpretation of the Constitution of the United States,* the "Constitution was not created by 'the whole people' as the jurists have said; neither was it created by 'the states' as Southern nullifiers long contended; but it was the work of a consolidated group whose interests knew no state boundaries and were truly national in their scope," growing out of their economic base in currency, public securities, manufacturing, trade and shipping. "The Constitution," wrote Beard, "was essentially an economic document based upon the concept that the fundamental private property rights are anterior to government and morally beyond the reach of popular majorities."[48]

Chattel Slavery in the Constitution of 1787

Slavery and the slave trade embarrassed the writers of the American Constitution and they took great pains to avoid discussion of the issue. Nevertheless, the topic required attention and debate ensued between those for and against perpetuating the right of private property in human beings.

Luther Martin of Maryland regarded it [the slave trade] as "inconsistent with the principles of the revolution, and dishonorable to the American character."[49]

[Delegates from South Carolina and Georgia] - Baldwin, the Pinckneys, Rutledge, and others - asserted flatly, not less than a half-dozen times during the debate, that these States "can never receive the plan if it prohibits the slave-trade"; that "if the Convention thought" that these States would consent to a stoppage of the slave-trade, "the expectation is in vain."[50]

"Every principle of honor and safety," declared John Dickinson of Delaware, "demands the exclusion of slaves."[51]

Rutledge...[of South Carolina] declared: "If the Northern States consult their interest, they will not oppose the increase of slaves which will increase the commodities of which they will become the carriers." This sentiment found a more or less conscious echo in the words of Ellsworth of Connecticut, "What enriches a part enriches the whole."[52]

Pressure successfully applied by delegates from states like Georgia and South Carolina resulted in a compromise favoring Southern slaveholding interests. While anti-slavery factions consoled themselves with the belief that slavery and its trade would die by degrees, slave-trade continued under a policy of *laissez-faire.* Article I, Section 9 of the Constitution of 1787 resolved the slave-trade question by permitting it to continue without interference until 1808, and by imposing an import duty of no more than ten dollars per slave. The assembly further decided that delegates to the House of Representatives would be determined by the population of each state, each slave to be counted as three-fifths of one person.[53] Article IV, Section 2 of the Constitution contained the following fugitive slave clause:

> No Person held to Service or Labour in one State, under the Laws thereof, escaping into another, shall, in Consequence of any Law or Regulation therein, be discharged from such Service or Labour, but shall be delivered up on Claim of the Party to whom such Service or Labour may be due.[54]

W.E.B. DuBois said of the Continental Congress that

> To be sure, the South apologized for slavery, the Middle States denounced it, and the East could only tolerate it from afar; and yet all three sections united in considering it a temporary institution, the corner-stone of which was the slave-trade. . . . Instead of calling the whole moral energy of the people into action, so as gradually to crush this portentous evil, the Federal Convention lulled the nation to sleep by a "bargain," and left to the vacillating and unripe judgement of the States one of the most threatening of the social and political ills which they were so courageously seeking to remedy.[55]

The Constitutional article pertaining to slave-trade did not go unrebuked by concerned Americans. In a letter from "Centinel," published in tne *Independent Gazatteer,* the following Quaker statement demonstrates the presence of abolitionist sentiment in the United States in 1787:

> We are told that the objects of this article are slaves, and that it is inserted to secure to the southern states the right of introducing negroes for twenty-one years to come, against the declared sense of the other states to put an end to an odious traffic in the human species, which is especially scandalous and inconsistent in a people, who have asserted their own liberty by the sword, and which dangerously enfeebles the dis-

tricts wherein the laborers are bondsmen. The words, dark and ambiguous, such as no plain man of common sense would have used, are evidently chosen to conceal from Europe, that in this enlightened country, the practice of slavery has its advocates among men in the highest stations.[56]

Prison Slavery in the Northwest Territory Ordinance

Land speculators from the Ohio Company of Associates and the Society of Cincinnati who wanted to establish colonies provided the impulse for the Northwest Territory Ordinance.[57] In 1784, the first Northwest Territory Ordinance was adopted. Thomas Jefferson, chairman of the committee in charge of its writing, is largely credited for Article 5, which read:

> That after the year 1800* of the Christian era there shall be neither slavery nor involuntary servitude in any of the said States, OTHERWISE THAN IN THE PUNISHMENT OF CRIMES WHEREOF THE PARTY SHALL HAVE BEEN DULY CONVICTED TO HAVE BEEN PERSONALLY GUILTY.[58]

Defeated by a narrow majority, Article 5 was dropped from the final document. Several attempts were made to readmit the article, including one by Rufus King in 1785, but nothing came of such efforts until 1787, when a new ordinance was drafted to provide more efficient territorial government.

As Jefferson was in France at the time of its writing, Nathan Dane and Rufus King of Massachusetts, Richard Henry Lee of Virginia, and Revolutionary soldier and statesman Timothy Pickering are held responsible for Article 6 of the Northwest Territory Ordinance of 1787, modeled after the old Article 5.[60] Article 6 of the Ordinance of 1787 stated:

> There shall be neither slavery nor involuntary servitude in the said territory, OTHERWISE THAN IN THE PUNISHMENT OF CRIMES WHEREOF THE PARTY SHALL HAVE BEEN DULY CONVICTED. *Provided, always,* That any person escaping into the same, from whom labor or service is lawfully claimed in any one of the original States, such fugitive may be lawfully reclaimed and conveyed to the person claiming his or her labor or service as aforesaid.[61]

Many of the delegates participating in the writing of the Ordinance of 1787 had also been delegates to the Constitutional Convention in

---

*The reason for "after 1800" seems to be that slavery had already been introduced into the territory due to slaveholding settlers from Virginia and France's Louisiana.[59]

Philadelphia. Since the Constitution's fugitive slave clause already ensured legal protection of the master's right to claim runaway slaves and plantation owners desired to maintain their monopoly of cheap labor south of the Ohio River, the southern delegates agreed to the inclusion of Article 6 in the Ordinance.[62]

In 1775, twelve years before the passage of Article 6, Timothy Pickering wrote to Rufus King, stressing the need to prevent slavery from spreading to the Northwest:

> For God's sake, then, let one more effort be made to prevent
> so terrible a calamity. It will be infinitely easier to prevent the
> evil at first than to eradicate it, or check it at any future time.[63]

Pickering's words proved a sad warning, for although chattel slavery was prohibited by the 1787 law, slavery and involuntary servitude for "the punishment of crimes" endures today. That exception to prohibition of slavery in Article 6 served as the model for the Thirteenth Amendment to the United States Constitution 77 years later, and we, nearly two centuries later, inherit the enormous task of its abolition.

Since Thomas Jefferson is credited with the original 1784 article, we looked to his ideas on punishment to explain it. Like many political thinkers in the "Age of Enlightenment," Jefferson believed that laws should result from and uphold the social contract and he valued Cesare Beccaria's ideas on law and punishment as being humane and conducive to strong government.

Cesare Beccaria, Father of Prison Slavery

Cesare Beccaria (1738-1794) was an Italian nobleman of Jesuit schooling whose theories were embraced by many leaders of the "Age of Enlightenment" besides Thomas Jefferson. Beccaria's 1764 *On Crimes and Punishments (Dei delitti e delle pene)* was revolutionary in its time, so much so that he originally published it anonymously. At the time of his writing, punishments had become grotesque spectacles. Torture was used to elicit "truth" from the accused and justice was so arbitrary that a person could be found guilty of committing an act not previously declared unlawful. Beccaria knew little of penology and relied on his friend Allessandro Verri, the Protector of Prisons in Milan, Italy, to advise him. Based on the social contract theory, which supposes that citizens agree to give up certain liberties to ensure peaceful government, Beccaria's treatise insisted that laws, not town magistrates, should instill fear and respect in the people. He criticized the popular practice of using torture to elicit confessions from the accused, calling for due process by trial before one's peers and insisting that punishment should be only as severe as the crime. It was certainty, he said, rather than cruelty or severity of punishment that would deter crime, and speediness of trial that would link punishment with the crime and therefore serve as an effective example for others.[64]

Beccaria argued that laws must treat all equally and that the example of punishment should deter others from committing crime. He therefore warned against use of pardons since they weaken the effectiveness of example. He spoke against banishment as being more hurtful to society than suicide: the suicide leaves his property behind while the migrator takes his property with him, causing society a double loss. Keep people happy at home, he said, so they will not leave.[65]

While he criticized frequent use of the death penalty as too cruel, Beccaria also challenged its effectiveness as a deterrent to crime. Instead, he said, lifelong slavery would serve as the most influential example of punishment:

> The strongest deterrent to crime...[would be] the long and painful example of a man deprived of his freedom and become a beast of burden, repaying with his toil the society he has offended.... No one today, in contemplating it, would choose total and perpetual loss of his own freedom, no matter how profitable a crime might be. Therefore that intensity of the punishment of lifelong slavery as a substitute for the death penalty possesses that which suffices to deter any determined soul. I say that it has more. Many look on death with a firm and calm regard - some from fanaticism, some from vanity, which accompanies a man beyond the tomb, some in a last desperate attempt to cease to live or to escape misery - but neither fanaticism or vanity dwells among fetters and chains, under the rod, under the yoke or in an iron cage, when the evildoer begins his sufferings instead of terminating them .... Were one to say that perpetual slavery is as painful as death and therefore equally cruel I would reply that...the former would be even worse.[66]

Sir Thomas More had written two centuries earlier "that it is unwise to execute offenders since their labor is more profitable than their death,"[67] but Beccaria warned rulers that frequent use of the death penalty would also encourage revolution. Instead of protecting propertied interests, frequent executions encouraged direct attacks against the rich. Beccaria's analysis emphasized the practicality of diluting punishment to prevent social revolution and preserve existing power relations.[68]

Although Beccaria can be credited with voicing some humanitarian concerns, he wrote for a privileged audience who wished to protect their own wealth and whose best interest lay in preserving the status quo. Attributing equal value to property and liberty, he considered that invasion of property deserved enslavement. In defending the privileges of his own class, Beccaria wrote that, "leisure attending riches [is] acquired by industry."[69] He tolerated the "industrious" pauper but encouraged punishment of vagrants - an attitude which prevails today towards persons on welfare. Beccaria believed that the rich as well as the poor should be bound by justice and based his ideas on the supremacy of laws derived from the social contract, the theoretical agreement of all members of a society to live by certain rules in order to ensure peace and harmony.

Like Beccaria and his contemporaries, Thomas Jefferson failed to consider the implications of laws which secure the privileged by prosecuting anyone, rich or poor, for villain-like crimes. The inherent injustice was best captured by Anatole France when he described "the majestic egalitarianism of the law, which forbids rich and poor alike to sleep under bridges, to beg in the streets, and to steal bread."[70]

Beccaria's theories became American law, to a considerable degree through Thomas Jefferson's influence on American criminal justice. "The principle of Beccaria is sound," said Jefferson. "Let the legislators be merciful, but the executors of the law inexorable."[71]

In a proposed "Bill for Proportioning Crimes and Punishments" for Virginia, Jefferson held that punishment should be "proportioned to the injury so that men would feel it their inclination as well as their duty, to see the laws observed." This 1779 bill called for transportation of offending slaves to another land to continue there in slavery, the identical maiming of a person who had maimed another as well as forfeiture of half of the offender's estate to the victim, castration for sex crimes and hard labor at public works for most property crimes. Like Beccaria, Jefferson would have limited the scope of the death penalty and hastened executions: death would be punishment for the crimes of treason and murder and offenders would be executed the day after conviction.[72]

In his *Commonplace Book,* primarily notes for his own study, Jefferson quoted Beccaria at length. His advocacy of Beccaria's "punishment worse than death" found reflection in his plan to have convicts work at "hard labor on roads, canals, and other public works," reforming the criminals while making them "long continued spectacles to deter others from committing like offenses."[73]

Many of Jefferson's Virginia colleagues thought his proposals too permissive, favoring instead a policy of *lex talionis,* "an eye for an eye, a tooth for a tooth." As an acceptable daily condition for African slaves and European indentures, slavery probably did not seem a punishment severe enough for convicted "villains." Although he had trouble gaining support for the 1779 bill, Virginia adopted most of his bills concerning crime and punishment by 1796. After recidivism increased in other states which displayed convicts at hard labor on public works, Jefferson turned his attention to the European model of confined convict slavery and designed a prison for Virginia which received its first prisoner in 1800.[74]

Convict slavery, which had victimized the homeless poor in Europe and helped colonize the New World, became law in the Northwest Territory Ordinance of 1787. The precedent-shaping exception for prison slavery in Article 6 was written by men adhering to social contract theory and to Cesare Beccaria's ideas on punishment, and it found its way into the Thirteenth Constitutional Amendment of 1865 and the jails and prisons of America.

Notes

1. Philip S. Foner, *Frederick Douglass* (New York: Citadel Press, 1969; International Publishers, Co., Inc., 1964), p. 127.

2. Albert Bushnell Hart, *Slavery and Abolition, 1831-1841* (New York: Negro University Press, 1968; reprint ed. Harper & Brothers, 1906), p. 50.

3. James Curtis Ballagh, *White Servitude in the Colony of Virginia* (New York: Burt Franklin, 1969; reprint ed. 1895), p. 65; Sellin, pp. 133-134.

4. William Christie MacLeod, *The American Indian Frontier* (New York: Alfred A. Knopf, 1928), pp. 295-296.

5. Ibid.

6. Ibid., p. 308.

7. Ibid., p. 303.

8. Ibid., p. 313, quoting Lauber in Ross, *South of Panama* (n.p., n.d.). While MacLeod criticizes Lauber's "naive" generalization of history, we also disagree with MacLeod's interpretation of history, especially the following example found on page 311:

> The facts observable [in the history of Native Americans] on the Pacific Coast make it plain that a forced-labour system, not free labour, is the thing needed for backward peoples. Forced-labour systems make possible the protection of the natives under some paternal scheme during the period when they are learning to accommodate themselves to a new economic and social environment.

9. Shaw, p. 23.

10. Ibid., p. 18.

11. Ibid., pp. 23-24.

12. Ibid., p. 24.

13. Ibid.

14. Ibid., pp. 24-25. On page 34 Shaw explains:

> During the Seven Years War, 1756-1763, fewer were transported, for many convicts were sent to the army, the navy and the dockyards. For example, out of 154 who were sentenced to death or transportation at the Old Bailey between November 1760 and January 1762, while twelve were pardoned unconditionally and thirty-four on the condition of transportation, five were pardoned on the condition of serving in the navy, and sixty-three in the army. Other somewhat curious reasons for reprieve were that a criminal submit to have a limb amputated 'to test the styptic medicines discovered by

Mr. Thomas Price', and because it would help a member's electioneering in the boroughs of Launceston and Newport.

15. John Lauson, *The Felon's Account of His Transportation at Virginia in America*, reprinted and edited from original by J. Stevens Cox (Mount Durant, St. Peter Port, Guernsey, C.I. via Britain: Toucan Press, 1969), p. 6. The passages quoted from Lauson's *Account* are from pp. 9-12 of this 12-page booklet.

While the original date of Lauson's *Account* is unknown, the original work was sold by an English press which did business during the mid-eighteenth century (Cox, p. 4). Cox also reports that Lauson was shipped to Essex County, Virginia. "Wicowoco" was a hundred miles up the Essex River (p. 2).

16. Philip S. Foner, *Labor and the American Revolution* (Westport, Ct.: Greenwood Press, 1976), p. 7; Ballagh, pp. 38-39. Foner states: "An estimated 80 percent of all immigrants who came to the colonies, whether voluntary or in chains, were either white indentured servants or black slaves.... Not less than 50 percent, and probably closer to 65 percent, of all white immigrants in America before 1776 were indentured servants."

17. Karl Frederick Geiser, *Redemptioners and Indentured Servants in the Colony and Commonwealth of Pennsylvania* (New Haven: Tuttle, Morehouse & Taylor Co., supplement to *Yale Review*, 10, 1901), pp. 18-19. The letter was published in the German newspaper *Hallischen Nachrichten*.

18. Abbot Emerson Smith, *Colonists In Bondage: White Servitude and Convict Labor in America 1607-1776* (New York: W.W. Norton & Company, Inc., 1971; reprint ed. University of North Carolina Press, 1947), p. 28.

19. Shaw, p. 35.

20. DePauw, p. 50.

21. Shaw, p. 32 quotes from "Letter from Elizabeth Sprigs to her Father from Maryland" dated September 22, 1756.

22. Cheesman A. Herrick, *White Servitude in Pennsylvania: Indentured and Redemption Labor in the Colony and Commonweath* (Freeport, N.Y.: Books for Libraries Press, 1970; reprint ed. 1926), p. 3.

23. Ibid.

24. W.E.B. DuBois, *The Suppression of the African Slave-Trade to the United States of America, 1638-1870,* intro. by Philip S. Foner (New York: Dover Publications, Inc., 1970; reprint ed., Harvard University Press, 1896), pp. 2-3; Sellin, p. 134 for quotation on slavery in the South.

25. DuBois, p. 5.

26. Sellin, p. 133, says that the first Africans brought to Virginia may have been treated like indentures; Herrick, p. 11, for quotation on slaves becoming an important substitute for short supply of indentured servants; Ballagh, p. 68, says that indentured servitude prepared "the way both legally and practically for the institution of slavery as it existed in Virginia."

27. Marcus Jernegan, *Laboring and the Dependent Classes in Colonial America, 1607-1783,* (New York: Frederick Ungar Publishing Co., American Classic Series; reprint ed. 1931) pp. 7-11, 55; Herrick, p. 22. Jernegan also reports that slaves occupied many skilled trades. "In the files of the *South Carolina Gazettes,* 1732-76, we find evidence of slaves trained in and practicing at least twenty-eight different trades specifically so named." (p. 13) Wood,

leather and craftspeople, ship builders, silver and blacksmiths, navigators, pilots, and house builders are among the broad range of occupations occupied by slaves. (See Jernegan, pp. 13-23.)

28. Samuel McKee, Jr., *Labor in Colonial New York, 1644-1776* (Port Washington, New York: Ira J. Friedman, Inc., 1963; reprint ed. Columbia University Press, 1935), pp. 110-112.

29. See Herrick, pp. 21-22.

30. DuBois, pp. 27-29.

31. Ibid., p. 6.

32. Ibid., pp. 48-49.

33. Ibid., p. 49.

34. Benjamin Quarles, "Lord Dunmore as Liberator," *William and Mary Quarterly*, 5 (1958): 494. This article is reprinted in *The American Revolution: Whose Revolution?*, op. cit.

35. Ibid., p. 497, quoting an October 28, 1775, letter from a Norfolk resident to a friend in England.

36. DuBois, p. 49.

37. John Todd White, "The Truth About Molly Pitcher," *The American Revolution: Whose Revolution?* (This article is a reprint of White's same titled paper presented at the Conference on Women in the Era of the American Revolution, Washington, D.C., 1975), p. 105. White quotes the eyewitness record of Joseph Plum Martin.

38. Ibid., p. 105.

39. Quoted from a letter dated March 31, 1776, L.H. Butterfield, Marc Friedlaender, and Mary-Jo Kline, eds., *The Book of Abigail and John,* (Cambridge: Harvard University Press, 1975), p. 121.

40. DePauw, p. 360.

41. James Kirby Martin, *Men in Rebellion: Higher Governmental Leaders and the Coming of the American Revolution* (New Brunswick: Rutgers University Press, 1973), p. 189. Also in article of same title by Martin in *The American Revolution: Whose Revolution?*, p. 45.

42. See Charles A. Beard, *An Economic Interpretation of the Constitution of the United States* (New York: Macmillan Company, 1929).

43. Staughton Lind, "Beyond Beard," Barton J. Bernstein, ed., *Towards a New Past: Dissenting Essays in American History* (London: Chatto & Windus, 1970), p. 59.

44. Beard, p. 176.

45. DePauw, pp. 358-365, states that black slaves comprised 20 percent of the colonial population, with a very small and unmentioned number of free blacks who enjoyed almost no legal distinction from slaves; the white servant population was about half as large as the black slave population; and disenfranchised white men made up 5-10 percent of the population. The remaining disenfranchised were women (half of the adult population) and children, including males between the ages of 16 and 21 who were taxable and liable for military duty and made up one-quarter of the male population.

46. Beard, pp. 324-325.

47. Ibid., pp. 217-299, especially 250-252. On pp. 294-295 Beard wrote:
> Perhaps the spirit of the battle over ratification is best re-
flected in the creed ironically attributed to each of the con-
tending parties by its opponents. The recipe for an Anti-Fed-
eralist essay which indicates in a very concise way the class-
bias that actuated the opponents of the Constitution, ran in
this manner: "Wellborn, nine times - Aristocracy, eighteen
times - Liberty of the Press, thirteen times repeated - Liberty
of Conscience, once - Negro slavery, once mentioned - Trial
by jury, seven times - Great Men, six times repeated - Mr. Wilson, forty times.... put them all together and dish them up at
pleasure."
>
> To this sarcastic statement of their doctrines, the Anti-Fed-
eralists replied by formulating the "Political Creed of Every
Federalist" as follows: "I believe in the infallibility, all-suf-
ficient wisdom, and infinite goodness of the late convention;
or in other words, I believe that some men are of so perfect a
nature that it is absolutely impossible for them to commit er-
rors or design villainy. I believe that the great body of the people are incapable of judging in their nearest concerns, and
that, therefore, they ought to be guided by the opinions of
their superiors.... I believe that aristocracy is the best form
of government.... I believe that the new constitution will
prove the bulwark of liberty - the balm of misery - the essence
of justice - and the astonishment of all mankind. In short, I believe that it is the best form of government which has ever
been offered to the world. I believe that to speak, write, read,
think, or hear any thing against the proposed government is
damnable heresy, execrable rebellion, and high treason
against the sovereign majesty of the convention - And lastly I
believe that every person who differs from me in belief is an
infernal villain. Amen."

48. Ibid., pp. 324-325.

49. DuBois, p. 54.

50. Ibid., p. 55.

51. Ibid., p. 54.

52. Ibid., p. 56.

53. ibid., p. 61; Richard Kluger, *Simple Justice* (New York: Alfred A. Knopf, 1976), pp. 32-34.

54. Kluger, p. 34.

55. DuBois, pp. 61-62.

56. Ibid., p. 63.

57. "The Northwest Territory Ordinance, July 13, 1787," Henry Steele Commager, ed., *Documents of American History,* 5th ed. (New York: Appleton-Century-Crofts, Inc., 1949), p. 128.

58. C.B. Galbreath, "The Ordinance of 1787, its Origin and Authorship," *Ohio Archaeological and Historical Publications,* 33 (1924): 118.

59. Edward Coles, *History of the Ordinance of 1787* (Philadelphia: Historical Society of Pennsylvannia, 1856), pp. 16-18.

60. Galbreath, pp. 112-113, 116, 176; W.E. Gilmore, "The Ordinance of 1787," *Ohio Archaeological and Historical Publications,* 14 (1905): 157.

The authorship of Article 6 is credited to several men. C.B. Galbreath says that Nathan Dane was primarily responsible for passing Article 6 and that Dane mentioned Melancton Smith of New York and R.H. Lee of Virginia to be committee members who were "in hearty sympathy with him and very materially assisted in the preparation of the Northwest Territory Ordinance." (p. 176) W.E. Gilmore concludes that "the great ordinance, like almost every important and permanent legislative enactment, grew [over its four-year process of finalizing]; gradually accreting the best suggestions of Jefferson, King, Dane; and doubtless also Grayson [Virginia], Carrington [Virginia], R.H. Lee [Virginia], Pickering, and other grand men of the day..." (p. 157)

While Nathan Dane, Rufus King, and Richard Henry Lee are mentioned frequently by both Gilmore and Galbreath, we have also credited Timothy Pickering. Pickering's 1783 "Proposition for Settling a New State..." was apparently the first plan offered to draft a government for a new state in the Ohio Valley (Galbreath, pp. 112-113). Section 11 of his proposal required "total exclusion of slavery from the State to form an essential and irrevocable part of the Constitution." (Galbreath, p. 116)

61. Commager, p. 129.

62. Galbreath, p. 167, quotes Virginia delegate William Grayson's letter to James Monroe:

> The clause respecting slavery was agreed to by the southern members for the purpose of preventing tobacco and indigo being made on the northwest side of the Ohio, as well as for other political reasons.

63. Gilmore, pp. 151-152.

64. Elio Monachesi, "Cesare Beccaria (1738-1794)," *Pioneers in Criminology,* Hermann Manheim, ed. (Montclair, N.J.: Patterson Smith, 1972), pp. 36-47.

65. Cesare Beccaria, *An Essay on Crimes and Punishments,* translation and commentary by de Voltaire (London: E. Hodson, 1801), "Of Suicide," pp. 126-129.

66. Sellin, p. 66, quotes Beccaria.

67. Rusche and Kirchheimer, p. 53.

68. Ibid., p. 76.

69. Beccaria, "Of Idleness," pp. 84-85.

70. *The Oxford Dictionary of Quotations,* 3rd ed. (New York: Oxford University Press, 1979), s.v. "Anatole France," p. 217 as quoted from *Le Lys Rouge* (1894), ch. 7.

71. "Answers to Questions Propounded by M. De Meusnier," Saul K. Padover, ed., *The Complete Jefferson* (Freeport, N.Y.: Books for Library Press, 1969), p. 61.

72. Ibid., "A Bill for Proportioning Crimes and Punishments," pp. 90-102.

73. C. Randolph Benson, *Thomas Jefferson as Social Scientist* (Rutherford, N.J.: Fairleigh Dickenson University Press, 1971), pp. 145-148 for Jefferson quotation on keeping convicts at hard labor; Padover, p. 91 for Jefferson's comment on the spectacle of prisoners at hard labor serving to deter others from crime.

74. Benson, pp. 145-148; Orlando F. Lewis, *The Development of American Prisons and Prison Customs, 1776-1845* (Montclair, N.J.: Patterson Smith, 1967; reprint ed. Prison Association of New York. 1922), p. 210.

Chapter 3:
Setting the Stage for Civil War

Ay, even if slaveholders treated their slaves with the utmost kindness.... Slavery is, not to belong to yourself - to be robbed of yourself. There is nothing that I so much abhor as that single thing - to be robbed of one's self. We are our own legitimate masters. Nature has not created masters and slaves.... I go for emancipation of all kinds - white and black, man and woman...there should be no slaves of any kind among them.

- Ernestine L. Rose[1]
August 4, 1853

Contradictions in the policies of our new government toward servitude would remain for a long time: dispute over chattel slavery developed into battles over gaining new territories; contempt for tribal nations' rights to their native lands resulted in broken treaties and war; racist prejudices justified the servitude of immigrants, stolen peoples, and those from whom land was stolen. The Northwest Territory Ordinance's provision for slavery as a punishment for crime spread to new states and, while northern workers suffered under industrial servitude, prisons were being built to reinforce their bondage.

Early Contradictions within the Movement for Abolition

As colonists were beginning to complain of taxation without representation, Native Americans were being pushed from their ancestral lands, indentured servitude had become the cornerstone of seventeenth century industrialism in the North, and the labor of chattel slaves was building the plantation aristocracy of the South. Few cried out against the injustice of slavery; few had an effective voice in the new government. While wealth determined whose best interests would be protected by government, the most gaping inequality was the blight of chattel slavery, protected by the Constitution of 1787 and reinforced six years later by the Fugitive Slave Act. The 1793 law authorized the capture of runaway slaves and imposed a five hundred dollar penalty on anyone who obstructed a master's "rightful" claim to his human "property."

Chattel slavery violated the teachings of the Gospels but professed Christians would be among the last to break their slavemaster chains.

The first American Christian congregation to be free of slaveholding was the Quaker meeting of Germantown, Pennsylvania, in 1688. During the 120 years that followed, several Quakers who spoke out against slavery were disowned by their congregations. By 1776, however, Philadephia Quakers were clear of slaveholding and, by 1808, every American Quaker meeting had taken steps to rid its membership of slave-owning.[2] Quakers earned unfavorable reputations among slaveholders, but, as a group, turn-of-the-century Quakers began to retreat from abolitionism as they turned inward to church concerns.[3] At a time when slavery was most vulnerable to attack, abolitionists were the weakest. As W.E.B. DuBois would later write:

> That the various abolition societies and anti-slavery movements did heroic work in rousing the national conscience is certainly true; unfortunately, however, these movements were weakest at the most critical times. When, in 1774 and 1804, the material advantages of the slave trade and the institution of slavery were least, it seemed possible that moral suasion might accomplish the abolition of both. A fatal spirit of temporizing, however, seized the nation at these points; and although the slave-trade was, largely for political reasons, forbidden, slavery was left untouched.[4]

While the British had introduced slavery to the colonies, they could not be held responsible for policy toward its continuance. In 1792, the Dutch abolished their slave traffic and, after the "united efforts of Sharpe, Clarkson, and Wilberforce...began to arouse public opinion by means of agitation and pamphlet literature,"[5] Britain began a legislative battle culminating in 1807 with abolition of its slave trade. The United States also passed legislation to prohibit slave trade in 1807, but, as with all measures taken regarding the United States traffic in slaves before the Civil War, no effective prohibition occurred. Throughout the 1820's and 1830's, the government refused to participate in international efforts to end the trade. In 1842, the United States signed the Treaty of Washington with Britain but failed to participate in a joint Right of Search of vessels in order to halt the trade. The slave trade continued under the American flag until 1862, when, under the leadership of President Lincoln, the United States "immediately expressed a willingness to do all in its power to suppress the slave trade."[6]

American Quakers also lagged behind British Quakers in taking a firm stand against slavery. During the years before they emancipated their slaves, American Quakers were severely criticized by their British brethren. Friends played a vital role in purging this land of chattel slavery but their unwillingness to see the roots of oppression represents the failing of many abolitionists of that era. An important exception to this failing was American Quaker John Woolman.

John Woolman: Quaker Vanguard of Abolition

John Woolman (1720-1772) was twenty-three when he gave up his lucrative merchant's career in New Jersey to become an abolitionist. The crisis point in his life came when he wrote a bill of sale for a slave. "Suddenly it flashed upon his conscience that the whole institution of slavery was inconsistent with the religious testimony for equality."[7] Woolman traveled throughout the colonies to convince slaveholders, particularly those of his own faith, to give up their slaves. He brought his testimony to fellow Quakers in religious meetings, and with gentle staunchness, criticized habits of wealth that yielded oppression to others.

> The love of ease and gain are the motives in general of keeping slaves, and men are wont to take hold of weak arguments to support a cause which is unreasonable.[8]

He urged that people boycott businesses profiting from the slave trade:

> To trade freely with oppressors without laboring to dissuade them from such unkind treatment, and to seek for gain by such traffic, tends, I believe, to make them more easy respecting their conduct than they would be if the cause of universal righteousness was humbly and firmly attended to by those in general with whom they have had commerce...[9]

In 1762, John Woolman initiated the tradition of Quaker gray by refusing to purchase colored cloth dyed by slave labor. A man ahead of the times, Woolman endured ostracism from Friends in stylish circles.

> In attending meetings [Quaker Church services] this singularity was a trial to me, and more especially at this time, as white hats were used by some who were fond of following the changeable modes of dress, and as some Friends who knew not from what motives I wore it grew shy of me, I felt my way for a time shut up in the exercise of the ministry.[10]

Unlike many who would later try to emulate his ministry, he did not separate slavery from the sufferings of the poor and exploited elsewhere. In "A Plea for the Poor," he wrote that labor and wealth should be shared and that those who exploit others are slaves "to a selfish spirit." Woolman saw the relation among all forms of slavery and realized that abolition would not occur until the inequalities that breed all suffering end.[11]

Woolman's concern for the plight of all oppressed people provides an important lesson for modern abolitionists. Addressing himself also to crimes against Native Americans and the poor, he knew that one form of oppression gives rise to another and abolition demands a fight on many fronts. John Woolman did not subscribe to contemporary prejudices, and in 1763, traveled among tribal villages to better understand Native Americans. He had for many years, he said,

> felt love in my heart towards the natives of this land who dwell far back in the wilderness, whose ancestors were formerly the owners and possessors of the land where we dwell, and who for a small consideration assigned their inheritance to us. . . [12]

Ignoring warnings from his friends of the potential dangers of such journeys, Woolman traveled without harm among the Native Americans. In Wyoming, he recorded his meeting with an "ancient man" who, though greeting him with mistrust, soon invited him into his home.

> Though taking his hatchet in his hand at the instant I drew near to him had a disagreeable appearance, I believe he had no other intent than to be in readiness in case any violence were offered to him.[13]

As history proved again and again, the old man was wise in his distrust of a stranger's call upon his people. After American independence was secured, the fight for tribal land accelerated with United States government plans of westward expansion.

In June 1772 John Woolman made his final voyage to England, where he died of smallpox four months later. He traveled among Friends to convince them to relinquish participation in the slave trade. On July 12th, he wrote in his journal:

> I have felt great distress of mind since I came on this island, on account of the members of our Society being mixed with the world in various sorts of traffic, carried on in impure channels. Great is the trade to Africa for slaves; and for the loading of these ships a great number of people are employed in their factories, among whom are many of our Society.[14]

He was greatly distressed by the poverty he found in England:

> Great numbers of poor people live chiefly on bread and water in the southern parts of England, as well as in the northern parts; and there are many poor children not even taught to read. May those who have abundance lay these things to heart![15]

And, in closing paragraphs of "A Plea for the Poor," he wrote:

> Thus oppression in the extreme appears terrible; but oppression in more refined appearances remains to be oppression, and when the smallest degree of it is cherished it grows stronger and more extensive.[16]

He placed responsibility for slavery and poverty in the hands of those who reap the fruits of other people's labor without equal sharing. He sought to convince those engaged in the struggle for wealth that riches are always "attended with power...and hence oppression."[17]

John Woolman created an important model for future abolitionists and his teachings remain to remind us of the need to end slavery, that "dark gloominess hanging over the land" which stands "grievous to posterity."[18]

> Many slaves on this continent are oppressed, and their cries have reached the ears of the Most High. Such are the purity and certainty of his judgments, that he cannot be partial in our favor. In infinite love and goodness he hath opened our understanding from one time to another concerning our duty towards this people, and it is not a time for delay.[19]

Although John Woolman's life and writings provided a source for inspiration, few followed his devout path to abolition. "To turn all we possess into the channel of universal love," he said, "becomes the whole business of our lives."[20] For Woolman, abolition of African slavery was but one vital step toward achieving equality. John Woolman marked a difficult path to follow, especially since Quakers not only had a testimony against slaveholding but also a testimony against going bankrupt. This testimony against permitting themselves to fall into poverty prevented many Quakers from understanding the roots of slavery in the relationship between wealth and oppression.

The Ironies of Philanthropy

The atrocities of the African slave trade brought cries of indignation from humanitarians, but plantation slavery also served as an influential model for disciplining poor workers in the growing private industries which required new methods of labor management. As plantation slavery was increasingly exposed as controlled by torture, less obviously cruel forms of discipline were sanctioned. One example of domestic oppression sanctioned by antislavery advocates was that of British Quaker and abolitionist Josiah Wedgewood, whose sugar mill kept men, women and children laboring from dawn until dark under constant watch of his overseers. Conditions suffered by his workers were so severe that they, like chattel slaves, resisted management pressures to increase their work output and finally rioted in 1783, only to be suppressed by the police.[21]

In Britain and in the United States, the abolitionist movement was fraught with many internal contradictions. As David Brion Davis stated in *The Problem of Slavery in the Age of Revolution, 1770-1823,* "Even where slavery is of marginal economic importance, it will be sheltered by a concern for the rights and security of private property."[22] Several abolitionists were people whose wealth afforded them leisure for philanthropy but whose status nevertheless depended on a social order that kept workers subordinated by low wages. For these philanthropists, abolition represented personal and national self-purification rather than true equality for all people. While abolitionists concerned themselves with removing the personally exploitive relationship between master and slave, most of them advocated, however naively, a more "impersonal" exploitation for the future when, as Davis wrote,

> All workers would be citizens, subject to the same laws and the same forces of the market. . . . According to [Britisher] Thomas Clarkson, there was nothing inequitable about slavery when considered merely as a form of labor. Any state, for example, might legitimately use convicts to clear rivers, repair roads, or work in the mines."[23]

While influential citizens championed the cause of slavery abolition, their participation in preserving the existing social order helped pave the way for oppression of the industrial poor. Out of this grew the American prison movement.

The Institutionalization of Prison Slavery

While abolitionists were fighting to throw off slavemasters' chains on the political front, human cages for slave punishments were being built at home. Cesare Beccaria justified slavery as "a punishment worse than death" that would ensure the continued power of society's rulers. Thomas Jefferson, under the guise of preventing slavery from spreading, enshrined it as punishment for crime in the Ordinance of 1787. Yet convict slavery was nothing new to civilization. Even in America, it had enjoyed brief trials. Boston opened its first jail in 1635 and its first house of corrections thirty years later. Shortly after, William Penn, Quaker and colonial protecter of Pennsylvannia, provided for houses of correction where offenders would pay their debts to society in hard labor. Penn's system was discontinued after 1718, the year of his death, and the colony returned to the more traditional practice of corporal punishments and executions.[24]

Misguided but well-intended, Pennsylvania Quakers initiated the prison movement. In response to Pennsylvania's harsh penal code of 1786 forcing convicts to labor on public roads while secured to each other by heavy chains, Quakers and like-minded citizens formed the Philadelphia Society for Alleviating the Miseries of Public Prisons. Abhorring practices of corporal and capital punishment, the Society convinced the legislature to approve the proposed Walnut Street Jail which would be founded on the Society's belief that "solitary confinement to hard labor and total abstinence from spiritous liquors will provide the means of reforming these unhappy creatures."[25]

Influenced by the European principle that "the concept of crime was blended with that of sin,"[26] the Society attempted to speak to the "inner light" of prisoners by keeping them in complete silence and solitary confinement, working at such daytime jobs as "shoe-making, weaving and tailoring; clipping logwood, grinding plaster of Paris, beating hemp, sawing and polishing marble. . . [and] picking oakum."[27] Corporal punishment was forbidden but, like slaves, prisoners had no rights, were forced to labor, and their lives depended upon the kindness of their keepers.

Caleb Lownes, member of the Society, is credited with the publicity that attended the Walnut Street Jail under his directorship. Lownes co-authored the *Account of the Alteration and Present State of the Penal Laws of Pennsylvania* which influenced legislatures of several states to reform their penal codes.[28]

In 1796, Quaker Thomas Eddy and General Philip Schuyler visited the Walnut Street Jail and, upon returning to their native New York, convinced that legislature to pass a bill substituting imprisonment for corporal punishments. Designed by Eddy and built in 1796, the Newgate Prison in Greenwich Village housed felons rather than the vagrants and misdemeanants of the Pennsylvania model. By 1803, Newgate showed a small profit over expenses and corporal punishments were prohibited, but conditions soon deteriorated, largely from severe overcrowding. In 1804, Eddy resigned from Newgate's directorship to build a better designed prison.[29]

While Eddy helped plan the new Auburn Prison, designed for congregate labor during the day and complete solitary confinement at night, Philip Williams was imprisoned in the Washington, D.C., jail for failure to pay his debts. In an 1806 letter to an abolitionist, the jailed debtor described the fate of black prisoners confined with him:

> Was it not that I owe money, of which I have no means or prospect of paying, I could be much better reconciled to my fate - I owe perhaps 1,000 dollars, & am now worth not a cent. However when I look round me and hear the piteous moan of so many fellow Prisoners & fellow creatures, doomed to perpetual servitude, & oppression's bloody scourge, I feel reason to bless GOD for the small portion of hope which yet remains with me; & which these poor creatures cannot enjoy - Since my confinement here, more than *"One Hundred"* of the poor blacks have been taken out of this one prison, manacled, & driven off to Georgia, by those monsters in human shape call'd *"negro Buyers"* or *"Georgia-men."* Several members of congress have been concerned in this traffic, during the late session - They were often at the Jail - I saw them. . . These members pretended they were only buying for their own use, but it is notorious that it was for speculation - It is common to

> see at the starting of these *droves* (I have often seen it with anguish) children parted from their parents, brothers from sisters, & husbands from wives, with all the agonizing tortures, which separations are calculated to produce.[30]

Permanent destruction of families would be forced upon millions victimized by slavery in southern plantations and by the expanding prison movement, which was attracting as much fervor on the part of its followers as the abolitionist movement, but more quietly.

In antebellum America, racial minorities, which make up a disproportionate number of our poor and convicted peoples today, faced other forms of slavery: Native Americans were fighting for the right to live on their ancestral lands, Mexicans and Asians were in some form of indenture or peonage, and most Blacks were chattel slaves or running from slave catchers.

Prison evangelists were devoted to encouraging the errant poor to adjust to their status in society and to develop an attitude of complacent obedience. By 1812, New York, Virginia, Massachusetts, Vermont, Maryland and New Hampshire built their first prisons, but the cruel refinement of prison slavery took shape in the Auburn plan. Auburn Prison was built in 1816. The War of 1812 had ended and crime increased as soldiers returned home to unemployment. Growing population and rising industrialism engendered a new form of class struggle which contributed to the growing unease of those benefiting from the status quo. New York legislators reacted to overcrowded conditions and deteriorating discipline in prisons by imposing repressive punishments upon convicts. In 1819, they passed a law permitting corporal punishments and use of stocks and irons in their prisons.[31]

> Paradoxically, the new law actually made it possible for criminals to be punished more inhumanely than would be the case under the old penal code. Whereas a thief might be given thirty-nine lashes under the old system and then set free, he could now be sentenced to a long prison term and flogged repeatedly if he did not conform to certain rules under confinement.[32]

Under the Auburn plan, prisoners were forbidden to talk, were kept in solitary confinement at night and at harshly supervised congregate labor during the day, were marched to and fro in rigid lock-step and forced to keep their eyes cast down at all times. Developing practices in American punishment treated the convicted as subhuman.

> From the moment a convict entered the prison at Auburn he was subjected to a process of calculated humiliation, in which every attempt was made to strip away whatever pride and self-respect he possessed. At Newgate, prisoners had been obliged to wear different types of uniforms, depending upon how many convictions appeared on their records. Under the Auburn system, all inmates wore black-and-white striped

outfits which made them look grotesque and ridiculous. Although the convicts were forbidden visitors of their own, citizens who paid a fee could come to the prison as if they were animals in a zoo. The word of an inmate was never to be taken. A convict was to use the most polite terminology when speaking or referring to prison officers, but to refrain from any titles or expressions of respect when talking about his fellows.[33]

The prisoner's time was forfeit to the State. His labor was part of that forfeit. He was the slave of the State. He had forfeited his citizenship.[34]

Auburn prison designer Thomas Eddy objected when the contract-labor system was initiated at Newgate but contract labor gained special favor in the eyes of New York prison keepers because of financial gains available from convict slave labor. The state leased the labor of prisoners to private businesses which came into the prison to work the confined population, selling their slave-made products on the open market to the great profit of the state and private contractors. Auburn advocates believed that prisons should pay for themselves and indeed they did, for prisons built on the self-supporting model showed impressive increases in revenue after 1820: Auburn made twenty-five dollars in 1830 but this increased to $1,800 by 1831; Connecticut's Wethersfield Prison showed a profit of $1,000 in 1828, more than $3,200 in 1829 and nearly $8,000 in 1831; and Baltimore made $11,500 in 1828 and nearly $20,000 in 1829.[35]

Advocates of the Pennsylvania solitary system, the main rival of the Auburn plan, built the Cherry Hill Prison in Philadelphia in 1827. Louis Dwight, defender of the Auburn plan and outspoken leader of the Boston Prison Discipline Society, criticized the Pennsylvania system as an "insanity breeder."[36] True, the solitary system was cruel, but it became especially cruel when reformed as an experiment at Auburn Prison. Reacting to outbreaks of prisoner unrest in New York and in Pennsylvania's overcrowded Walnut Street Jail, in 1821 New York legislators ordered more punitive methods of convict treatment. Therefore, on Christmas 1821, 81 prisoners at Auburn were placed in complete solitary confinement without work or recreation for the remainder of their sentences. A state-ordered investigation discovered that most of the men in solitary had gone insane or were suffering from serious illness, and the Governor faced the embarrassing task of ordering their release from prison.[37] Louis Dwight nevertheless continued his mission of converting other states to the Auburn plan and his arguments exploited the economic differences between the two systems: the Pennsylvania plan cost money while the Auburn plan brought in profits. Massachusetts's Charles Sumner, who would later make crucial contributions in the U.S. Senate to the abolition of slavery, also belonged to the Boston Society and criticized Dwight's advocacy of the Auburn plan. The Auburn system, however, remained the victor.[38]

While the Quakers who started the Walnut Street Jail were, like other philanthropic reformers, incorrect in their assessment of what caused crime and how to alleviate injustice, they meant well. Limiting their understanding of crime to that of sin, they fell victim to the myths that insulate the privileged from understanding the causes of crime. With introduction of the Auburn plan, penal philosophy changed from the Quaker design of addressing the "Christ within" to conquering the "innate depravity of man."[39] Both the Pennsylvania and the New York systems were forms of slavery in their denial of human rights and in their exploitation of labor. The victory of the Auburn system proved a victory for a punitive philosophy based on the same motives that guided plantation masters - financial gain. What began as an attempt to reform the law-breaker turned into the cruelty of institutionalized convict slavery.

Prison slavery, like all slavery, became a lucrative business attractive to the greed of many state governments. Auburn-inspired prisons were built in the South and the West, and, in 1802, Ohio became the first state to include prison slavery in its constitution. According to Article 6 of the Northwest Territory Ordinance of 1787, Ohio was to prohibit "slavery or involuntary servitude, OTHERWISE THAN IN THE PUNISHMENT OF CRIMES WHEREOF THE PARTY SHALL HAVE BEEN DULY CONVICTED." Following that precise mandate, Article 8, Section 2 of Ohio's first Constitution read:

> There shall be neither slavery nor involuntary servitude, in this state, OTHERWISE THAN FOR THE PUNISHMENT OF CRIMES WHEREOF THE PARTY SHALL HAVE BEEN DULY CONVICTED.

When, however, that sparsely settled state put its constitution into effect, it had not yet institutionalized prison slavery. The first settlers had arrived only 24 years earlier under the direction of the New England based Ohio Company. Colonial traditions in corporal punishments prevailed in Ohio until 1812: petty larceny was punishable by death, destruction of fruit trees by 50 lashes, robbery by 79, and second-offense theft by 100.[40] Building its first state prison in 1817, Ohio "modernized" its punishments, emulating changes already instituted in the more "civilized" eastern states. In 1820 and 1831, penal advisors to the State of Ohio recommended that it adapt the Auburn plan to its prison system. In 1832, the Ohio penitentiary was built on the Wethersfield, Connecticut model, a prison which shaped itself after the New York plan.[41] Hence, the first *prison slave state,* that is, a state authorizing slavery "for the punishment of crimes" by constitutional mandate, was fully implementing its consititutional proviso. In 1848, the Governor of Ohio stated that "our penitentiary was never before in so flourishing a condition. The earnings and profits of the prison exceed all expenses by $23,000."[42]

Elam Lynds, Sing Sing's first warden, summarized American penal philosophy when he said, "In order to reform a criminal you must first break his spirit."[43] Expansion of this simple statement is found in Rusche and Kirchheimer's critique of European penal practices during the Industrial Revolution:

> In like manner, the 1825 report on the prison of the canton Waad [in Europe], one of the most valuable documents of the whole prison literature of the period, insisted first of all that mere deprivation of liberty is no effective punishment for the lower classes. The conclusion was reached that the necessary condition for the prisoner's reentry into society is unconditional submission to authority, a conclusion which has remained unshaken by reform programs and tendencies up to the present. If the prisoners resign themselves to a quiet, regular, and industrious life, punishment will become more tolerable for them. Once this routine becomes a habit, the first step toward improvement has been taken. As far as possible there must be a guaranty that the improvement will continue after the prisoner has been released. Obedience is demanded not so much for the smooth functioning of the prison but for the sake of the convict himself, who shall learn to submit willingly to the fate of the lower classes.[44]

Expanding Slave Territory

The "free" states that entered the Union under the precedent of the Ordinance of 1787 may have been free of chattel slavery, but they were not free of slavery. In 1816 and 1818, respectively, Indiana and Illinois joined Ohio as *prison slave* states. Another category must be recognized in determining the true nature of the "free" North: those states that practiced prison slavery without specific state constitutional authorization, *without proviso* states. In 1820, the northeastern State of Maine joined the Union without a constitutional stipulation regarding slavery or its use in punishing the convicted. Soon following the prison slave punishments established by its neighbors, Maine joined New York, New Jersey, Connecticut, Pennsylvania and Massachusetts in practicing prison slavery without a specific state constitutional proviso authorizing that punishment.[45]

Slavery in all its forms represented the victory of the interests of private property over human needs. While the Mason-Dixon Line divided two economic systems, it did not insulate the practice of prison slavery to the North or chattel slavery to the South.

> Although in 1830 no person could be born into slavery north of the Mason and Dixon's Line, slavery and the incidents of slavery continued to exist in most of the free states. In Maine, Vermont, New Hampshire, and Massachusetts no permanent

slaves appear; in Rhode Island, Connecticut, New York, New Jersey, and Pennsylvania, the census of 1830 shows a total of about twenty-seven hundred slaves; and in 1850 New Jersey still counted two hundred and thirty-six. All the northwestern states except Michigan contained a few slaves in 1840, in part old slaves held previous to 1787, in part persons who had come in previous to 1820 under what were termed indentures with their masters.[46]

Carved out of the Louisiana Territory purchased from France in 1803, Louisiana entered the Union as a slave state in 1812. Slave states had little need for large penitentiaries since most of their labor force was already in bondage. While the Carolinas adhered to the old colonial practices of corporal and capital punishments, other southern states erected small prisons to house their few ex-slave and white convicts. But the reputation of lucrative prison slave industries in the North traveled southward. By 1835, Louisiana opened its Baton Rouge Prison with a cotton mill and shoe factory to compete with the prices of northern capitalists. Mississippi put its convicts to work at a cotton mill which paid for the prison's maintenance. Auburn-inspired prisons were erected in the states of Kentucky, Tennessee, and Alabama, where contractors seized the opportunity to lease convict slaves for profit.[47] Even in the South, slavery crossed racial lines. For example, an abolitionist imprisoned in a penitentiary in the slave state of Missouri from 1841 to1845

found it an awful place of cruelty and wretchedness, in which the warden came home drunk at midnight to drag white men out of their cells to be whipped before him, and where white women prisoners were sometimes chained to the wall.[48]

Punishment in slavery reinforced class barriers and continued to grow. The South, attracted by the lucrative profits of the prison movement in the North, added that form of slavery to her own cruel traditions.

How Free Was "Free"?

Economic differences between slave and free states were acted out during the Industrial Revolution. While northern participation in the slave trade fed the South, the slavocracy fed northern industries raw materials for production. In New England and the Middle Atlantic States, there were 800 cotton factories in 1831, increasing to 1200 factories by 1840. Fuel for industrialism became big business: mining expanded after 1838, with anthracite coal added to charcoal and coke and, in 1846, bituminous coal was introduced in Ohio.[49] The North developed rapidly into an industrial nation stoked by the labor of propertyless citizens subject to a system of free enterprise that cared nothing about just wages. Government protection of the slavemaster's right to property assured capitalists of continued pursuit of private wealth through exploitation of workers.

The bourgeoisie of the late eighteenth century threw off the chains of British royalty, and their greatly publicized answer to centuries of aristocratic rule was the doctrine of equality among all men. They nevertheless identified the right to pursue happiness as the right to pursue private property, placing few restrictions upon the emerging competitive system of free enterprise.

Many colonists fled to this country seeking religious freedom. Among the values they brought with them was belief in the natural inferiority and immorality of propertyless peoples. The sixteenth century Protestant reformer John Calvin preached that salvation was predestined before birth and his followers came to believe that the identity of those chosen for eternal happiness could be guessed at on earth by their good fortune. A successful and prosperous citizen easily translated into one chosen for eternal reward. The Protestant work ethic was rooted in Calvin's teachings, and even Quakers, intent on recognizing the inherent goodness of each person, were bound to a testimony that prevented them from learning what it was like to be indigent. The stigma of sin reinforced old prejudices against the poor, and punishment for crimes moved toward the cruelties of institutionalized slavery. Successful industrial capitalism became a new means to prove one's salvation.

The freedom to pursue happiness was cherished by those who demonstrated their social "worth" by exploiting the labor of others. Class privilege contradicted equal opportunity and equal protection before the law. Seeds of that inequality could be seen in the proportion of Americans allowed to vote on the American Constitution - less than 15 percent of the population: those safe from slavery, safe from indentured servitude and relatively insulated from economic hardship by the property they owned. The contradiction intensified as, increased by poor Europeans brought here to provide a cheap work force, the ranks of industrial laborers swelled. No laws protected workers from exploitation and the opportunity to pursue happiness was scarcely equal for those without means to pay for education, medical expenses, insurance, clothing, or surplus funds to invest in security. Those who had the capital to invest in factories and raw materials gained control of the free market and its workers; those who worked in the growing industries far outnumbered those who owned and profited from them.

The Industrial Revolution did not bring with it laws protecting the fruits of workers' labor and was not marked by star-spangled banners or heroes' graves. Medals were given in cash and power; those who fell in battle fell quietly from long, hard hours of meagerly rewarded labor, poverty-stricken in new-made ghettos, or as slaves of the state in recently built prisons. Workers, "duly convicted" of straying from the accepted paths of good, became slaves of the State rather than personal slaves of any one master.

For most abolitionists, slavery was synonymous with American chattel slavery and chattel slavery became a scapegoat issue rather than one tragic symbol of the inequalities of an "enlightened age" of liberty and free enterprise. As Davis indicated,

> Most of the philanthropies linked with the abolition cause had two broad aims: to protect an urban population from disease and disorder, thereby ensuring the smooth functioning of the social and economic system; and to inculcate the lower classes with various moral and economic virtues so that workers would want to do what the emerging economy required.[50]

Those whose wealth afforded them the leisure for philanthropy were also those whose status depended on a social order that kept workers subordinated by subsistence wages.

Hidden behind prison walls and inserted between two commas in the Northwest Territory Ordinance, the institution of prison slavery grew naturally from unacknowledged inequalities. The pursuit of happiness and the right to personal property, even human property, were protected by the Constitution with little regard to the victimization of others. The crimes of the rich, while affecting large numbers of people, were rarely subject to prosecution. As today, the wealthy paid for their crimes in fines while poor people paid in slavery. Most of the convicted committed crimes after having endured long periods of inequality and suffering; punishment in slavery was designed to train people to accommodate themselves to being exploited. As the 1820 report on the prison at the canton of Waad stressed, convict submission was "demanded not so much for the smooth functioning of the prison but for the sake of the convict himself, who shall learn to submit willingly to the fate of the lower classes."

The Struggle of Free Workers

> Notice. Those employed at these mills and works will take notice that a store is kept for their accomodation, where they can purchase the best goods at fair prices, and it is expected that all will draw their goods from said store. Those who do not are informed that there are plenty of others who would be glad to take their places at less wages.

> Crompton Mills, Feb. 1843   BENJ. COZZENS[51]

In 1792, Eli Whitney's cotton gin, a machine that separated seeds from the shorter cotton fiber, enabled slavemasters to increase the speed at which they supplied their clients with large volumes of cotton. Other inventions like Whitney's advanced the progress of industry through worker-operated machines. The American Industrial Revolution that began around 1800 is often referred to as bringing a new age of wealth and prosperity; it may have meant prosperous times for manufacturers, but not for workers.

> Perhaps the clearest evidence of this discrepancy between the reward of labor and capital is seen in the statements of the manufacturers themselves in reply to questions sent out by the Treasury Department in 1846 to secure information as to the state of industry under the tariff of 1842. The replies constitute a mine of information as to profits, prices, wages, hours, etc. Under the question as to the cost of production there are occasional indications of respective shares paid in wages and in profits during the four years of operation of the protective tariff of 1842. In these cases wages are seen to have fallen or remained stationary, cost of production declined, while prices were maintained and profits increased.[52]

As water- and steam-driven machinery began to modernize the factories and as Europeans were imported to work for the new industrialists, individual craftspeople such as shoemakers were pushed out of business, unable to compete with the cheap prices of mass-produced goods.

> Aside from a few riots in Pittsburgh, in which the hand-loom weavers destroyed some of the new machines, the American worker was not actively opposed to machinery. He was opposed to the method of its introduction, for exploitive purposes, as he conceived it, in the hands of a group alien to the producer. For every protest against machine industry, there can be found a hundred against the new power of capitalist production and its discipline.[53]

By the 1840's, industrialism gained an edge over other means of producing goods and services. Corporations grew from the profits of low wages. Those workers who resisted exploitation found themselves out of work. On October 16, 1846, the *Voice of Industry,* a weekly labor newspaper published in Massachussetts by workers, reported:

> Hundreds of honest laborers have been dismissed from employment in the manufactories of New England because they have been suspected of knowing their rights and daring to assert them. [54]

The spirit of the era changed from liberalism to exploitation. A Fall River, Massachusetts, labor leader remarked on this change, saying, "The first lesson a boy is taught on leaving the parental roof is to... gain wealth...forgetting all but self."[55]

Between 1840 and 1860, the population density of the North Atlantic states increased by 57 percent. Poverty increased also, at an alarming rate as wages steadily decreased. In 1814, one in 300 Americans were considered paupers; 30 years later, one in seven persons in New York City were reported destitute. Philadelphia and New York City more than doubled their populations in the two decades that followed 1840, and it was reported that the average life span of the Irish in Boston was 14 years.[56]

As Dr. Henry Clark's report of a tenement house in Boston in 1849 testified, the working class poor lived in congested, unhealthy homes and neighborhoods:

> The first cellar from the street was occupied in one corner by a bar for the sale of refreshments, and served as a kitchen and a parlor. The second, into which two beds were crowded, served as family sleeping-room, whilst a third, a dungeon six feet square and the same in height, with no aperture for the admission of air save the narrow door, which was closed at night, served to accomodate the boarders.
>
> The landlord said the tide came through the floor of his rooms but rarely! One cellar was reported by the police to be occupied nightly as a sleeping-apartment for thirty-nine persons. In another, the tide had risen so high that it was necessary to approach the bedside of a patient by means of a plank which was laid from one stool to another; while the dead body of an infant was actually sailing about the room in its coffin.[57]

Landlords were reported to be making 100 percent profits from their rentals.[58]

While the influx of immigrant workers contributed to crowded urban conditions, a good deal of the impoverished population also included those who had lost their jobs, such as apprentices who, once they learned a trade, were dismissed only to be replaced by new apprentices. Even employed workers struggled to survive; wages earned during 11- to 13-hour working days did not provide the essentials for living. Philadelphia carpenters went on strike for a 25¢ increase in daily wages which would have brought their weekly salary to $10.50. On May 21, 1851, the New York *Daily Tribune* published "A Budget for Family of Five for One Week" totaling $10.37, thirteen cents less than the carpenters were striking for. The *Tribune's* calculations did not, however, include medical insurance, educational, or recreational expenses. Father, mother and child sought employment.[59]

Exploitation of workers by their bosses was justified by either a philosophy of laissez-faire or of paternalism. One laissez-faire industrialist expressed his position this way:

> As for myself, I regard my work people just as I regard my machinery. So long as they can do my work for what I choose to pay them, I keep them, getting out of them all I can. What they do or how they fare outside my walls I don't know, nor do I

consider it my business to know. They must look out for themselves as I do for myself. When my machines get old and use-
less, I reject them and get new, and these people are part of
my machinery.[60]

The Lowell factories of Massachusetts provide a good example of a
paternalistic philosophy in action. Corporations controlled the town
of Lowell, Massachusetts, planting their advocates among the
ministers and leaders of the city and regulating practically every
aspect of the worker's life:

Aside from the printed rules, which were copious enough, it
was said by one of the agents, in 1852, that not one tenth of
the regulations were printed. Their operatives were told when,
where, how, and for how much they must work; when and
where they were to eat and sleep. They were ordered to attend
church, for which they had to pay pew rent. They were dis-
charged for immoral conduct, for bad language, for disrespect, for attending dancing classes, or for any cause that
the agents or overseers thought sufficient. When thus dis-
charged, they were blacklisted and could obtain no employment in any corporation in Lowell or nearby towns. They were
required to work one full year before receiving an 'honorable
discharge' and to give two weeks' notice of intention to leave.
The contract was entirely one-sided, however. The corporations accepted no responsibility as to the length of employment and reserved the right to change the conditions as to
wages, hours, speed and effort as they saw fit. Thus a girl employed at two dollars a week might be reduced to one dollar a
week and still she must serve her full twelve months before
she was entitled to an 'honorable discharge.'[61]

By 1850, workers throughout the northeast were organizing for a ten-
hour day. They petitioned Congress and the President to regulate
work hours, but in order to affect private corporations, they had to go
through state legislatures. In 1840, President Van Buren ordered that
all government employees work only ten hours a day. In 1848, the legislatures of New Hampshire and Pennsylvania passed ten-hour work
laws. New Jersey followed in 1851 and Rhode Island in 1853. The
struggle was more difficult in Masssachusetts, however, where corporations like Lowell wielded tremendous power over the "people's"
delegates. In 1851, Boston machinists got a ten-hour day, and, beginning in 1852, the movement to curb working hours spread through
Massachusetts. After several work strikes, Lowell gave its workers an
eleven-hour day and other companies followed. By 1855, the movement for a ten-hour day impressed the legislature enough that a special committee approved a ten-hour work law. When, however, the bill
came to a vote:

> There the men who, for years, had clamored for a ten-hour law and whose pockets had been lined with corporation gold, were seen "doing the heavy standing round" and suggested to members that, as the operatives were satisfied with the eleven-hour rule, it was not worthwhile to carry the matter further. Accordingly, the bill failed.[62]

Money wielded the vote and manufacturers continued their "moral policing" with the blacklist. Those who asserted their rights often found themselves on the street with no other company willing to hire them. The prospects were not good for "free" workers under the free enterprise system. Even moving west was an unrealistic alternative. Striking workers in the jeans factories of Ohio remarked that travel was expensive for someone earning fifty cents a day. One explained:

> Suppose we had the means, we know nothing about the cultivation of land - we have all our lives worked in a factory and we know no other employment. . . . Besides which, we have always been used to live in a town where we could get what little things we want if we have the money, and it is only those who have lived in the wilderness who know what the horrors of wilderness life are.[63]

Industrial workers were experiencing the beginning of a struggle that remains unresolved today. The northern capitalist, like the southern slavemaster, was gaining power. The right to private property, through chattel slave labor in the South or through worker wage slavery in the North, became the symbol of the right of the ruling to pursue their own happiness.

Two arenas of struggle evolved for American masters: control of their labor force at home and expansion of their territorial boundaries westward. Both found sanction in government control. The northern capitalist had like-minded friends in government to control labor legislation and in prisons to train rebellious workers into submission as convict slaves; the southern slavemaster had state and national laws to protect his claim to supremacy over others and a permissive slave trade policy to assure his continued acquisition of slaves. Animosity was growing between these two masters in their hunger for power.

A Manifest Destiny

A call went out for the government to extend its boundaries from coast to coast:

> The *untransacted* destiny of the American people is to subdue the continent - to rush over this vast field to the Pacific Ocean - to animate the many hundred-millions of its people. . . . to unite the world in one social family - to dissolve the spell of

tyranny and exalt charity - to absolve the curse that weighs down humanity, and to shed blessings round the world![64]

While Congress diplomatically let the slave trade continue, the tactics of the slavemaster permeated the institutions of business and justice in America's "free" sector. As Southern plantations depleted the soil quickly and more land was needed to maintain profits, the influence of the South weighed heavily in determining the "free" or "slave" status of the incoming states. After one portion of the Louisiana Territory became the state of Louisiana in 1812, the rest of the territory was renamed Missouri. A great debate ensued over the fate of the remainder of the Missouri territory when the state of Missouri applied for admission. In the Missouri Compromise, an agreement was reached whereby Missouri would enter the Union as a slave state, the rest of the territory would remain "free," and Arkansas would be a slave territory. States would thereafter be admitted alternately under a banner of slave or free.

The laws within all the "free" territories contained a bargain with slavery: fugitive slave clauses prevented the Afro-American's flight to freedom and slavery and involuntary servitude was reserved for all workers duly convicted of crime. The compromising precedent set by Article 6 of the Northwest Territory Ordinance was also found in the Missouri Enabling Act of 1820:

> Sec. 8. . . . in all that territory ceded by France to the United States under the name of Louisiana, which lies north of 36 degrees and 30 minutes north latitude, not included within the limits of the state, complemented by this act, slavery and involuntary servitude, OTHERWISE THAN IN THE PUNISHMENT OF CRIMES WHEREOF THE PARTIES SHALL HAVE BEEN DULY CONVICTED, shall be, and hereby is forever prohibited. *Provided always,* That any person escaping into the same, from whom labour or service is lawfully claimed in any state or territory of the United States, such a fugitive may be lawfully reclaimed and conveyed to the person claiming his or her labour or service as aforesaid.

During the 1830's, Georgia began to push its Native American populations out by claiming jurisdiction over all tribal lands and by raiding villages. Slavemasters wanted more land to replace the soil they had already depleted. Settlers infiltrated Cherokee land, the federal government refused to honor its treaty obligations, and Cherokees were tried and punished for crimes in Georgia courts without being allowed to give testimony. Supreme Court Justice Marshall ruled in favor of the Cherokee right to land granted them by U.S. treaty. President Jackson, however, retorted with, "John Marshall has made his decision, now let him enforce it!" and forced tribal nations to move to lands west of the Mississippi.[65]

Then began the "Trail of Tears." The Choctaw left first, in 1831. The Creeks managed to delay for four years and were finally removed by force; those who resisted made the journey in chains. The Chickasaws left in 1837. The Cherokees... continued to resist. Once more they appealed their removal to the Supreme Court, and once more the Court ruled in favor of the Cherokees.... But President Jackson sent troops to force the Indians to leave their homes.... At last the Cherokees agreed to go in peace, since to remain was suicide.[66]

On foot, wagon, boat and prodded onward by the military, nearly one fourth of the Cherokee people died from lack of supplies, cold, and disease along the westward path.[67]

Many thought bickering over new territory was finally settled by the Missouri Compromise. The expansion of slave territory became a real threat, however, when, in 1836, through a conspiracy to expand the southern slavocracy, Texas obtained independence from Mexico and sought annexation to the United States as a slave state. The South told the North that it wanted Texas in order to balance slave and free power. Henry Clay was among those who disagreed, arguing: "For if today Texas be acquired to strengthen one of the Confederacy, tomorrow Canada may be required to add strength to another..."[68] Clay's response was timely, for in 1845 an article entitled "Re-annexation of Canada" which defended reuniting the continent while giving a greater market to the slave power appeared in the *Baltimore American:*

It will still better secure and perpetuate the peculiar institution, the protection of which is a main argument in favor of other measure [the annexation of Texas]; for it would cut off the intercourse of England with all our part of this continent, and remove the refuge which has long existed in Canada for fugitive slaves.[69]

The philosophy of territorial expansion was not unique to nineteenth century America. Cecil Rhodes, builder of the British Empire in South Africa, and Adolf Hitler, whose "compelling destiny from which none can escape our life's destiny in the world," would also adhere to their own doctrines of Manifest Destiny.[70] The likeness of American expansionism to Hitler's designs becomes frightening when one examines the following from an article on Manifest Destiny reported in the *Niles National Register* on January 22, 1848:

Now we ask, whether any man can coolly contemplate the idea of recalling troops from the territory we at present occupy ...and thus, by one stroke of a secretary's pen, resign this beautiful country to the custody of the ignorant cowards and profligate ruffians [the Mexican government] who have ruled it for the last twenty years? Why, humanity cries out against it.... the aborigines of this country have not attempted and cannot attempt to exist *independently* alongside of us. Providence has so ordained it; and it is folly not to recognize the fact. The Mexicans are *aboriginal Indians,* and they must share the destiny of their race.[71]

Slavemasters were intent upon extending their boundaries beyond Mexico. Advocates of territorial expansion found a friend in President Polk, who took office in 1844, and dispute over the unsettled southern boundaries of Texas led to war with Mexico in 1846. The new land the United States acquired from the Mexican war embraced another form of servitude - peonage.

In New Mexico, the peonage of Mexican Indians had been enforced since the seventeenth century. Some called the peonage of the Mexican even worse than chattel slavery, since the system was "without the obligations of rearing him in infancy, supporting him in old age, or maintaining his family."[72] A form of debt slavery, peonage often continued from generation to generation. Fugitive slave laws authorized the return of runaway peons to their masters, since emancipation required that the servant first repay all debts to his master.

> This the poor peon is unable to do, and the consequence is that he and his family remain in servitude all their lives. Among the proprietors in the country, the master generally keeps a store where the servant is obliged to purchase every article he wants, and thus it is an easy matter to keep him always in debt. The master is required to furnish the peon with goods at the market value, and may advance him two thirds the amount of his monthly wages. But these provisions, made for the benefit of the peon, are in most instances disregarded, and he is obliged to pay an enormous price for every thing he buys, and is allowed to run in debt beyond the amount of his wages, in order to prevent him from leaving his master.[73]

Before the Mexican War, the boundaries of Mexico reached as far north as the line that extends from the Colorado River to the Pacific. With the signing of the Treaty of Guadelupe-Hidalgo in 1848, Mexico gave all its territory north of the Rio Grande to the United States. The dispute over the destiny of the newly acquired land - slave or free - did not end. Texas wanted slavery and the Territory of California had expanded southward to meet the population requirements to apply for statehood. The Compromise of 1850 put an end to the Mexican controversy with a bargain that covered five areas of agreement: California would be admitted as a free state; territorial governments would be established in New Mexico and Utah with no immediate decision as to whether they would be slave or free; a stricter fugitive slave law would be enacted to guarantee the return of escaped slaves to their masters; slave trade would be abolished in the District of Columbia; and dispute between Texas and New Mexico over territorial boundaries would be settled by federal government liquidation of any debts incurred by Texas.

Seventy-two years after the signing of the Declaration of Independence, the United States had almost reached its present expansion to the Pacific Ocean, the South was reaching the height of its power, and Article I, Section 18 of the Constitution of California prohibited slavery, except, of course, "for the punishment of crimes."[74]

Notes

1. Samuel Sillen, *Women Against Slavery* (New York: Masses & Mainstream, 1955), p. 91.

2. Thomas E. Drake, *Quakers and Slavery in America* (Gloucester, Mass.: Peter Smith, 1965; reprint ed. Yale University Press, 1950), pp. 1-84.

3. Ibid., p. 114.

4. Du Bois, pp. 195-196.

5. Ibid., p. 132. Du Bois refers to the abolitionist work of Granville Sharpe, William Clarkson, and William Wilberforce in England.

6. Ibid., p. 150.

7. Woolman, p. vii.

8. Ibid., p. 56.

9. Ibid., pp. 180-181.

10. Ibid., p. 132.

11. Ibid., pp. 224-249.

12. Ibid., p. 134.

13. Ibid., p. 146.

14. Ibid., p. 212.

15. Ibid., p. 211.

16. Ibid., p. 249.

17. Ibid., p. x.

18. Ibid., p. xiii.

19. Ibid., p. 87.

20. Ibid., p. 227.

21. David Brion Davis, *The Problem of Slavery in the Age of Revolution, 1770-1823* (Ithaca: Cornell University Press, 1975), p. 460.

22. Ibid., p. 84.

23. Ibid., pp. 381-382.

24. Blake McKelvey, *American Prisons: A History of Good Intentions* (Montclair, N.J.; Patterson Smith, 1977), p. 3; W. David Lewis, *From Newgate to Dannemora: The Rise of the Penitentiary in New York, 1796-1848* (Ithaca: Cornell University Press, 1965), p. 2.

25. McKelvey, p. 8.

26. W.D. Lewis, p. 6.

27. McKelvey, p. 8.

28. Ibid.

29. Ibid., p. 9; W.D. Lewis, pp. 33-35.

30. Cynthia Owen Philip, ed., *Imprisoned in America: Prison Communications 1776 to Attica* (New York: Harper & Row, Publishers, 1973), pp. 24-25.

31. See W.D. Lewis, pp. 41, 43-46.

32. Ibid., p. 46.

33. Ibid., pp. 91-92.

34. O.F. Lewis, p. 333.

35. Rusche and Kirchheimer, p. 131.

36. McKelvey, p. 29.

37. W.D. Lewis, pp. 68-70.

38. McKelvey, pp. 20-21; W.D. Lewis, pp. 227-228; David Donald, *Charles Sumner and the Coming of the Civil War* (New York: Alfred A. Knopf, 1960), pp. 120-128.

39. W.D. Lewis, p. 47.

40. Clara Bell Hicks, "The History of Penal Institutions in Ohio to 1850," *Ohio Archaeological and Historical Publications,* 33 (1924): 370.

41. Ibid., pp. 378, 380-382. Hicks reports the actual building of the prison used "1,113,462 days of convict labor" and lasted from March 1833 to 1837.

42. Ibid., pp. 412-413.

43. Jessica Mitford, *Kind and Usual Punishment* (New York: Alfred A. Knopf, 1973), p. 32. See also W.D. Lewis, pp. 87-88.

44. Rusche and Kirchheimer, p. 107.

45. See Appendix, "No Proviso Constitutions." Maine used the solitary system until the mid-1830's, when it adopted the Auburn plan. (McKelvey, pp. 29, 49.)

46. Hart, p. 78; c.f. Alice Dana Adams, *The Neglected Period of Anti-Slavery (1808-1831)* (Gloucester, Mass.: Peter Smith, 1964; reprint ed., Radcliffe College, 1908), p. 9. Adams says that slaves were reported in every existing state in 1830 except Vermont.

47. McKelvey, pp. 43-50. Adoption of the Auburn system also expanded westward to Michigan, Ohio, Indiana, Iowa, Illinois, Wisconsin and other "free" states during this period. (Ibid.)

48. Hart, p. 10 and cites George Thompson, *Prison Life* (Hartford: A. Work, 1854), *passim.* Thompson was imprisoned for his attempt to aid three fugitive slaves cross the Mississippi River.

49. Hart, p. 54.

50. Davis, p. 242.

51. Norman Ware, *The Industrial Worker, 1840-1860* (Boston and New York: Riverside Press, Houghton Mifflin Company, 1924), p. 35.

52. Ibid., p. 9.

53. Ibid., p. xi.

54. Ibid., p. 110.

55. Ibid., p. 25 quoting *Voice of Industry,* April 3, 1846.

56. Ibid., pp. 12, 27, 14.

57. Ibid., p. 13.

58. Ibid., p. 14 from an 1853 report by the Society for the Improvement of the Condition of the Poor.

59. Ibid., p. 33.

60. Ibid., p. 77 as quoted from Mass. Senate Doc. no. 21, 1868, p. 23.

61. Ibid., p. 107.

62. Ibid., p. 162 as quoted from Chas. Cowley, History of Lowell (Boston: 1868), p. 149.

63. Ibid., p. 37 as quoted from John R. Commons, *A Documentary History of American Industrial Society* (Cleveland: 1910), 7: 54-55.

64. Excerpted from Allan O. Kownslar, *Manifest Destiny and Expansionism in the 1840's* (Boston: D.C. Heath and Company, 1967), p. 5 quoting William Gilpin, close adviser to President James K. Polk and Senators Thomas Hart Benton and James Buchanan, in a message to the Senate dated March 2, 1846.

65. Richard B. Morris, ed., *Encyclopedia of American History* (New York: Harper & Row Publishers, 1976), pp. 204-205. Jackson's response was to Marshall's March 3, 1832, decision in *Worcester v. Georgia* (6 Peters, 515).

66. Jayne Clark Jones, *The American Indian in America,* vol. 2 (Minneapolis: Lerner Publications Company, 1973), p. 21.

67. Ibid., pp. 21-22.

68. Kownslar, p. 50.

69. Ibid., p. 65.

70. Ibid., pp. 1-3.

71. Ibid., p. 117.

72. Lieutenant W.H. Emory, an army officer on duty in New Mexico during 1846, quoted by Loomis Morton Ganaway, *New Mexico and the Sectional Controversy, 1846-1861* (Philadelphia: Porcupine Press, Inc., 1976; reprint ed. University of New Mexico Press, 1944), p. 9.

73. William H. Davis, *El Gringo; or, New Mexico and Her People* (New York: Arno Press, Inc., 1973; reprint ed. Harper & Brothers, 1857), pp. 232-233.

74. Article I, Section 18 of the 1849 California Constitution stated:
     Neither slavery nor involuntary servitude, unless for the punishment of crimes, shall ever be tolerated in this State.

Chapter 4:
Movement for Abolition

> I pictured myself a bloated, swaggering libertine, trampling on the Bible · its own Constitution · its treaties with the Indians · the petitions of its citizens: with one hand whipping a negro tied to a liberty pole and with the other dashing an emaciated Indian to the ground...Every person who is...a citizen of the United States, i.e., a voter, politician, etc., is at once a slave and slaveholder · in other words a subject and ruler in a slaveholding government.
>
> · John Humphrey Noyes[1]

Quakers and Abolitionists

The abolitionist movement that began to shock this nation into greater international embarrassment three decades before civil war rested its case on issues of moral conscience and yet, in spite of its Christian roots, few churches initially stood behind it. American churches reflected the attitudes of their respective states' populations on slavery. Abolitionists like Stephen Foster and James Gillespie Birney called churches the bulwarks of slavery, especially criticizing Southern congregations where slavemasters weighted church ruling bodies.[2] The national exceptions were Quakers, Mennonites and Brethren who were particularly conspicuous for their antislavery sentiments, regardless of geographic location. In the South, however, abolitionist visibility was limited by law and most advocates of the cause gave quiet testimony by refusing to hold slaves. More radical advocates used their homes to help slaves escape to freedom by the Underground Railroad.

For several, it was difficult to belong to a church and be an abolitionist too. Brought up in Charleston, North Carolina, sisters Sarah and Angelina Grimké faced religious ostracism for their abolitionist beliefs. Sarah, the older, was disowned by the Charleston Presbyterians for speaking out against the practices of her congregation's slaveholders. She left for Philadelphia where she soon joined a Quaker meeting. The following, written by Sarah Grimké in 1827, expresses the effect that chattel slavery had on those who dedicated their lives to its abolition:

> From early childhood [I] long believed their bondage inconsistent with justice and humanity...after being for many months in Pennsylvania when I went back it seemed as if the sight of their condition was insupportable, it burst on my mind with renewed horror...[I] can compare my feeling only with a canker incessantly gnawing · deprived of ability to modify

> their situation, I was as one in bonds looking on their suffer-
> ing I could not soothe or lessen. . . . Events had made this
> world look like a wilderness. I saw nothing in it but desolation
> and suffering. . . .[3]

Angelina soon joined Sarah as a Quaker in Philadelphia, but dissen-
sion began to divide Quakers in the 1820's:

> The early simplicity of their way of life had been affected by
> the commercial success and growing political influence of
> the leading Quakers, especially in Philadelphia. A subtle rift
> began to divide city and country Quakers, with the former
> holding almost all the influential positions of leadership, the
> latter feeling themselves at a disadvantage and highly critical
> of what they considered the corruption of wealth and position
> among city Quakers.[4]

A final split occurred in 1828. Orthodox or city Quakers adhered to a
traditional Quaker style of worship and the new group, Hicksites, following the teachings of Elias Hicks, focused on a less rigid style of
worship stressing "inner light" and adherence to John Woolman's
boycott of slave-made products.

The Grimké sisters continued to speak out against slavery and were
criticized not only for their staunch abolitionist perspectives but also
for stepping beyond passive roles as women. When Angelina married
Baptist minister and abolitionist Theodore Weld, their Quaker
meeting took the opportunity to disown both outspoken abolitionist
sisters - Angelina for marrying outside of meeting and Sarah for attending the ceremony.[5]

The 1830's witnessed the rise of an abolitionist movement criticized
by organized churches. Advocacy of gradual emancipation among
Quakers and those of like-minded faiths was displaced by a growing
demand for immediate emancipation which found outspoken leadership in William Lloyd Garrison. The time for radical abolitionism had
come and most Quakers were not ready. Abolitionist Quakers criticized their brethren: slavery should be destroyed and the gradualism of
past decades could no longer suffice. Meetings throughout the country
differed in their positions. Orthodox Quakers were particular recip-
ients of abolitionist appeal, as the following message from British
Quakers to American Friends in 1834 indicates:

> In the warmth and freedom of brotherly love. . . we entreat
> you fearlessly. . . to take your stand upon the uncompromis-
> ing righteousness of the law of Christ, to suffer no considera-
> tions of expediency, no apprehension of commercial or polit-
> ical difficulties, to divert you from your purpose: to assert that
> freedom, political and religious liberty to their full extent, are
> the unalienable rights of slaves and free people of color, equal
> with the white men; that they have an undoubted right to en-

joy their freedom in the place where Providence has given them birth.[6]

Orthodox Quakers resisted the appeal and decided to wait for lawful action on slavery from the separate state legislatures. Even Baltimore Hicksites took steps to discipline members who joined the ranks of the American Anti-Slavery Society. Gradually, Northern Yearly Meetings of the Society of Friends forbade use of their meeting houses for outside lecturers on temperance, women's rights and abolition, and warned their members against joining the worldly ranks of radicalism.[7]

Many American churches suffered internal division over abolition that resulted in conflict and ostracism. Because of their longstanding testimony against slavery, Quakers provide a special example of church struggle; however, dedicated abolitionists within their ranks made their voices heard. For instance, when Quaker Susan B. Anthony, hearing a Virginia Quaker defend the silence of conservatism on slavery by saying "Christ was no agitator, but a peacemaker," Ms. Anthony responded with all her abolitionist fervor:

> "I came into this world not to bring peace but a sword. . . .
> Woe unto you, scribes and Pharisees, hypocrites that devour
> widows' houses!" Read the New Testament, and say if Christ
> was not an agitator! Who is this among us crying, "Peace,
> peace, when there is no peace"?[8]

Immediate, Not Gradual Emancipation

In 1829, the Afro-American publication *Freedom's Journal* printed David Walker's *Appeal. . . to the Coloured citizens of the world, but in particular and very expressly to those in the United States* to throw off the yoke of slavery. On August 21, 1831, Nat Turner led his famous slave revolt in Virginia, during which 60 whites were killed and which resulted in a reactionary massacre of 100 blacks. During this time, New York philanthropist Arthur Tappan rescued William Lloyd Garrison from a Baltimore jail. Garrison had been sued for libel for an editorial in the *Genius of Universal Emancipation* newspaper in which he named some local slave traders "highway robbers and murderers. . . enemies of their own species." With Tappan furnishing financial assistance, Garrison published the first issue of his *Liberator* in Boston.[9]

Garrison's was not the first call for immediate emancipation, but many Northern abolitionists saw him as their new leader. In 1831, the same year Nat Turner's slave rebellion was suppressed and the first issue of the *Liberator* published, a committee in Columbia, South Carolina offered a $1,500 reward for anyone distributing the newspaper and the Georgia legislature offered a $5,000 reward for Garrison's arrest.[10]

Within a few months, the Tappans and other New York reformers gathered to discuss forming an abolitionist society based on "immediate abolition gradually accomplished" and held their first convention in Philadelphia in 1833. They chose the "city of brotherly love" in order to draw on the old and substantially Quaker Pennsylvania Abolition Society. That Society, however, refused the invitation to participate in convention but, regardless of the lack of support from abolitionist traditionalists, several Quakers attended. The Anti-Slavery Society was formed, and by the end of the '30's there were 250,000 members in 1,350 state and local chapters throughout the nation.[11]

Northern capitalists did not want to hear the call to immediatism. They fought the slavemaster over new territory, using the moral banner of "free soil," but they did not want to challenge the Southerner's claim to his "personal" property because doing so would hit at the same foundation of private property upon which Northern capitalists were building their empires:

> Immediatism challenged the Northern hierarchy of values. To many, a direct assualt on slavery meant a direct assault on private property and the Union as well. Fear for these values clearly inhibited anti-slavery fervor (though possibly a reverse trend operated as well - concern for property and Union may have been stressed in order to justify the convenience of "going slow" on slavery).[12]

Women's Rights in Abolition

Labeled "fanatics" and "communists," radical abolitionists' sole purpose was abolition of chattel slavery and their call for human equality reinvoked the best spirit of the American Revolution. In that spirit was women's rights. Many women came out of their homes to join the abolitionist movement. In 1837, the first women's Anti-Slavery Convention was held in New York with representatives from free and slave states alike, 100 in all. Ex-slave and abolitionist Frederick Douglass wrote in his autobiography:

> When the true history of the antislavery cause shall be written, women will occupy a large space in its pages, for the cause of the slave has been peculiarly woman's cause. Her heart and her conscience have supplied in large degree its motive and mainspring. Her skill, industry, patience, and perseverance have been wonderfully manifest in every trial hour. Not only did her feet run "willing errands," and her fingers do the work which supplied the sinews of war, but her deep moral convictions, and her tender human sensibilities, found convincing and persuasive expression by her pen and her voice.[13]

Due to their own second-class citizenship, some women had a unique understanding for the plight of the slave, but those who spoke out were criticized for "scandalous" and "immoral" behavior. Fighting women refused to be censured from participation, and so began the women's movement in America which, as Angelina Grimké wrote to brother abolitionist critics, belonged to Abolitionism:

> This invasion of our rights was just such an attack upon us, as that made upon Abolitionists generally when they were told a few years ago that they had no right to discuss the subject of Slavery. . . . The time to assert a right is the time when that right is denied. We must establish this right for if we do not, it will be impossible for us to go on with the work of Emancipation. . . . If we surrender the right to speak to the public this year, we must surrender the right to petition the next year and the right to write the year after and so on. What then can woman do for the slave when she is herself under the feet of man and shamed into silence?[14]

Not only were women denied the right to vote, admonished for public speaking and forced into accepting substandard wages, but they were also denied the right to manage family property without their husbands' permission, the right to inherit property and guardianship of their children. Their garments were frivolous harnesses from which their only recognized social value - prettiness - emerged.

Struggle

Important leaders in the cause of people's rights belonged to the nineteenth century movement for abolition - Susan B. Anthony, Frederick Douglass, James Forten, Lucretia Mott, Wendell Phillips, Charles Sumner, Sojourner Truth, Harriet Tubman, John Brown, David Walker, William Lloyd Garrison, Sarah and Angelina Grimké, Nat Turner, Dred Scott, and so many others. The real Abolitionist Movement was just beginning and remains uncompleted today. No matter what the time, place, or specific focus of struggle, Abolition has never been easy. Nineteenth century abolitionists met with planned opposition, insults, and even violence. In 1834, a Boston meeting of clergymen voted to refuse to announce abolitionist meetings in church and they were followed by like-minded ministers in Massachusetts and Connecticut.[15] Beginning with a pro-slavery riot in Boston in 1835, opposition to abolitionism became more violent. The press usually "prepared the ground for violence with a barrage of distorted interpretations of abolitionist views or outright lies," and mobbings and beatings of anti-slavery speakers were not infrequent.[16] In 1837, an abolitionist newspaper editor in Alton, Illinois tried to rescue his shop after it was set afire by an angry mob. Elijah Lovejoy was shot and killed while attempting to put out the flames.

Despite such obstacles, abolitionist societies increased greatly by 1839 - 2,000 in all, with 14 abolitionist newspapers bringing their arguments against slavery to the nation's readers.[17] Throughout the few decades before Emancipation, abolitionists collected thousands of signatures on anti-slavery petitions.

> One gets an idea of their efforts from the fact that during one five-month session of Congress petitions were sent to it for the abolition of slavery in the District of Columbia, signed by more than 400,000 people. In two years, more than two million signatures were obtained to these petitions.[18]

The courts continued to defend the rights of property of the slave owner. In 1842, the Supreme Court declared in *Prigg v. Pennsylvania* that the Fugitive Slave Act of 1793 remained constitutional and "somewhat gratuitously, held that the common-law right of recaption was thereby guaranteed to each slaveholder and that all state laws or processes which had to do therewith were unconstitutional and void."[19] As a term of the Compromise of 1850, Congress passed a new and more repressive fugitive slave law. Slavemasters were assured of their right in human property by the stipulation that forbade the testimony of any alleged runaway claimed by a master.

In 1854, the famous Kansas-Nebraska Act was passed which left the decision of "slave" or "free" up to the voters of the two states. "It was the secret understanding of the promoters of the bill that Kansas would become slave territory and Nebraska free."[20] The rush to tip the vote was on as settlers moved in, sent by "free soilers" and abolitionists in the North and by slavemasters in the South. Violence spread across Kansas and John Brown organized abolitionist guerillas to fight incoming slaveholders. Daniel and J. Merritt Anthony, brothers of Susan B. Anthony, moved to Kansas to help - Merritt as a soldier in John Brown's band.[21] The South won, so the blood shed in Kansas was temporarily lost to slavery.

In May 1856, Senator Charles Sumner took two days of Congressional time to deliver his "Crime Against Kansas" speech which attacked the slave conspiracy in Kansas. "A crime has been committed," he said, "which is without example in records of the past.... It is the rape of virgin territory, compelling it to the hateful embrace of slavery..."[22] Among the senators he attacked for their positions on slavery was Senator Butler from South Carolina who, he said, "has chosen a mistress to whom he has made his vows, and who, though ugly to others, is always lovely to him; though polluted in the sight of the world, is chaste in his sight...the harlot, Slavery..."[23] While Sumner's speech brought abolitionist praise, it incurred slavemaster venom. Butler's nephew Preston Brooks, a Congressman from South Carolina, avenged his uncle's honor. Choosing a gold headed cane for his weapon, a few days after that speech he went up to Sumner on the emptying Senate floor and mercilessly beat him. The injuries to his head Sumner sustained were so severe that he was unable to return to the Senate seat for three years.[24] During the years of Sumner's absence, Massachusetts kept his Senate seat vacant, the Dred Scott Decision was handed down, and John Brown raided Harper's Ferry.

The 1857 Dred Scott Decision declared that blacks were not citizens and that the Missouri Compromise was therefore unconstitutional, since the court could not deprive slaveholders of their right to take slaves in any part of the Union. The battle over Scott's freedom had begun several years before. Dred Scott, born Sam Blow, slave of Peter Blow, chose his new name after receiving a terrible beating from fugitive slave hunters who returned him for the promised bounty. Scott was sold to Dr. John Emerson in Missouri who took him to an army post in the "free" state of Illinois. There Dred Scott married Harriet, a slave of the local Indian agent, and together they spent the next seven years of bondage in places where chattel slavery was forbidden by law.[25]

When they returned to Missouri, Scott asked his master for his freedom but was refused. In 1843, he was leased to an officer who took him into Mexico as the Mexican war began. There he contracted malaria and, upon being returned to Missouri, Dred and Harriet Scott obtained legal counsel to sue their master for freedom. Their suit claimed that the Scotts were legally free since their master had taken them into a territory where slavery was forbidden. The freedom granted to them by the Missouri court lasted only from January 23 to February 14, 1850. On appeal to Missouri's higher court, the majority of the justices decided that the Scott family should be returned to their old master.[26]

Then began a long legal battle which resulted in a retaliatory beating of the Scott family by their master's agent and a final appeal to the Supreme Court in 1856. Five of the Court's nine justices, including Chief Justice Taney, were from the South. *Harper's Weekly* reported the decision on March 14, 1857:

> This long-expected judgement has been delivered. Chief Justice Taney, expressing the views of the majority of the Court, decided that as the legal condition of a slave in the State of Missouri is not affected by the temporary sojourn of such slave in any other State, but on his return his condition still depends on the laws of Missouri, and as the plaintiff was not a citizen of Missouri, he therefore could not sue in the Courts of the United States. The suit was dismissed for want of jurisdiction.
>
> Incidentally, the following points were also decided:
>
> *First,* Negroes, whether slave or free, that is, men of the African race, are not citizens of the United States by the Constitution.
>
> *Second,* The Ordinance of 1787 had no independent constitutional force or legal effect subsequently to the adoption of the Constitution, and could not operate of itself to confer freedom or citizenship within the Northwest Territory on negroes not citizens by the Constitution.
>
> *Third,* The provisions of the Act of 1820, commonly called the Missouri Compromise, in so far as it undertook to exclude

> slavery from and communicate freedom and citizenship to, negroes in the northern part of the Lousiana cession, was a Legislative act exceeding the powers of Congress, and void, and of no legal effect to that end.
>
> Judge Curtis dissented in part, and Judge M'Lean in *toto,* from the decision.[27]

Despite such setbacks, abolitionists continued to help blacks escape to freedom through the Underground Railroad and found various means to lawfully attack slavery.

> Faced with defeat at the national level of government, the anti-slavery forces. . . . waged a continuous struggle at the state level. . . . in five free states (Massachusetts, New York, Pennsylvania, Ohio, and Wisconsin). . . . "Personal Liberty Laws" were passed. These laws variously guaranteed a jury trial to a person who claimed to be free; extended habeas corpus to cover the claims to freedom of fugitives; required state procedures in addition to, or as an alternative to, the federal fugitive rendition procedures; punished state officials for performing duties under the federal fugitive slave acts, or withdrew jurisdiction from state officials in such cases; denied the use of jails to house alleged runaways; provided counsel for blacks or persons claimed as slaves; and provided punishment for persons convicted of kidnapping.[28]

Although some of the Personal Liberty Laws faced eventual repeal, they nevertheless threw a wrench into pro-slavery attempts to kidnap free blacks and find fugitive slaves.[29]

These were frustrating times. The slavemaster was gaining ground, Congress refused to take action to suppress slavery, the Supreme Court was stacked in favor of slaveholding interests and the cruelties of chattel slavery continued without check. John Brown had had enough. On October 16, 1859, Brown and his army of abolitionists and ex-slaves took Harper's Ferry in Virginia, the first step in Brown's grand plan to free the slaves. On October 18, wounded and having lost two sons in battle, he was captured. Before he was hanged for treason on December 2, 1859, John Brown wrote these prophetic last words:

> I, John Brown, am quite certain that the crimes of this guilty land will never be purged away but with blood. I had, as I now think vainly, flattered myself that without very much bloodshed it might be done.[30]

Disunity and Unclearness

While we are grateful for its successes, the old Abolitionist Movement could have been more effective; we must learn from its failings to avoid similar mistakes. While the charismatic leadership of William Lloyd Garrison provided a popular focus for abolitionism, the movement fell short of what it should have been. This failure cannot be attributed to one man, but reflected the failure of an era to perceive the real roots of slavery in America - economic exploitation.

Early divisions in the movement foreshadowed its weaknesses. "Immediate emancipation gradually achieved" grew to mean different things to different factions. While some adhered to the design of complete equality and political representation for the ex-slave, others were not as willing to confer absolute equality: some thought a form of apprenticeship should be required of the freedman first, and others talked of sending ex-slaves to African colonies, thereby preserving segregation of the races.[31]

In 1840, abolitionists were divided on the woman question. The World Anti-Slavery Convention refused to seat women in their ranks while the American Anti-Slavery Convention, under the sway of Garrison, included women. Garrison also argued that those against slavery should divorce themselves from any political activity. A government that permitted slaveholding, he said, did not deserve recognition. He refused to consider the irresponsibility of such a policy, for the slave was still oppressed by government mandates. Among those dissenting were Joshua Leavitt, Elizur Wright, and Myron Holley who left the Society to join the Liberty Party in order to challenge lukewarm politicians failing to take a staunch stand against slavery.[32]

While the Liberty Party unsuccessfully ran James Gillespie Birney for President in 1840 and 1844, abolitionists scored a clear victory when former President John Quincy Adams campaigned for a seat in the House of Representatives and won. As Congressman, Adams stopped the "Pickney gag" House rule that violated people's right to petition their government by ordering all anti-slavery petitions to be accepted and laid aside for no further action.[33]

Frederick Douglass, who joined the Garrisonians after escaping to freedom in 1838, soon abandoned them. Criticized for the eloquent speeches he gave, the self-taught man was considered by some of his upper class abolitionist colleagues to be an unrealistic representative of an ex-slave. Douglass tolerated their short-sightedness and continued to speak as he wished, but when Garrison declared that abolitionists should refrain from political activity, Douglass withdrew from the Garrisonians and continued his work as an independent. Garrison, said Douglass, hated him because he rejected "Garrisonism - an 'ism' which comprehends opposition to the Church, the ministry, the Sabbath and the government. . . apart from the question of Slavery."[34]

As today, those who knew oppression best were the last to achieve recognized leadership. Elimination of the oppression of women, debased as long as there had been slaves, would be seen as a separate issue, rather than part of the universal emancipation that abolition demands. The slave, like today's convict, might be recognized for his or her suffering but not for understanding what abolition requires. When 1800 of the original 2300 subscribers to the *Liberator* in 1834 were black, but history speaks little of the dedicated abolitionists who came up from the ranks of slavery, we face ignorance of what abolition must stand for - empowerment of and leadership from those who have been most oppressed.[35] Harriet Tubman, who escaped from slavery, returned again and again to lead people to freedom. The Moses of her people and "General Tubman" to John Brown, she died in poverty in 1913 still fighting for equality in Auburn, New York. Many have deserved the eulogy that Frederick Douglass wrote for Tubman:

> Most that I have done and suffered in the service of our cause has been in public, and I have received much encouragement at every step of the way. You on the other hand have labored in a private way. I have wrought in the day - you in the night. I have had the applause of the crowd and the satisfaction that comes of being approved by the multitude, while the most that you have done has been witnessed by a few trembling, scared and foot-sore bondmen and women, whom you have led out of the house of bondage, and whose heartfelt "God Bless you" has been your only reward. The midnight sky and the silent stars have been the witnesses of your devotion to freedom and of your heroism. Excepting John Brown - of sacred memory - I know of no one who has willingly encountered more perils and hardships to serve our enslaved people than you have. Much that you have done would seem improbable to those who do not know you as I know you.[36]

After his trip to Ireland in the 1840's, Douglass remarked on the victimization of poor people throughout the world, exploited by investors in slavery under other names:

> The open, uneducated mouth - the long, gaunt arm - the badly formed foot and ankles - the shuffling gait - the retreating forehead and vacant expression. . . all reminded me of the plantation, and my own cruelly abused people.[37]

Sources of the movement's weakness can be found in the superficial understanding that directed some of its influential members. The abolition movement ignored and covered over less obvious forms of bondage which would replace chattel slavery unless quickly uprooted. The attack on the slavery of Afro-Americans could have revealed other forms of servitude that rendered so many unequal before the law, but for nineteenth-century American abolitionists the situation was no different than the British movement of 50 years earlier: "It was unthinkable that an attack on a specific system of labor and domination might also validate other forms of oppression and test the boundaries of legitimate reform."[38] To them, the boundaries of legitimate reform ended with abolition of chattel slavery. In a January, 1831, edition of the *Liberator,* Garrison criticized labor leaders for trying "to inflame the minds of our working classes against the more opulent, and to persuade men that they are condemned and oppressed by a wealthy aristocracy." Five months later, however, the *Liberator* contradicted its editor's earlier statement by claiming "there is a proud aristocracy in the north, sympathizing with and publicly approbating the still more haughty aristocracy at the south; and together, it is their aim, if possible to degrade and defraud the workingmen of all classes, irrespective of color." Garrison's abolitionist campaign failed to act on these words.[39] Since abolitionists failed to consider the labor question as a whole and to support struggling workers who so desperately needed support, labor hesitated to lend its support to the abolition movement until right before the war. The northern worker also demanded emancipation:

> That the factory system contains in itself the elements of slavery, we think no sound reasoning can deny, and every day continues to add power to its incorporate sovereignty, while the sovereignty of the working people decreases at the same ratio.[40]

> It is the monopoly feature that we have opposed.... It is the divorce of labor and capital in the repartition of dividends - the fact that labor is not represented in these companies.... They who work in the mills ought to own them.[41]

William West said of northern workers that it was that "they do not hate chattel slavery less, but that they hate wage slavery more."[42]

In 1845, the National Industrial Congress adopted the following resolution in an astute criticism of abolitionism:

> The Abolition movement, sincere, ardent, heroic with attacks upon chattel slavery, has not succeeded, because those engaged in it have not perceived that it was only one of the many modes of oppression that productive labor has to endure, which everywhere condemn him to ignorance and want.[43]

Blind to this unity of oppression, Garrison and his followers opposed people like Wendell Phillips and Frederick Douglass when they wanted to keep the abolitionist movement alive after certification of the Thirteenth Amendment. While most freedom fighters closed up shop and went home, Wendell Phillips joined the labor movement, Frederick Douglass kept up his work for the quickly forgotten blacks and Susan B. Anthony continued her work for equal rights for women.

Frederick Douglass made the following observation on the disbanding of the American Anti-Slavery Society:

> The American Anti-Slavery Society under the lead of Mr. Garrison had disbanded, its newspapers were discontinued, its agents were withdrawn from the field, and all systematic efforts by abolitionists were abandoned. Many of the society, Mr. Phillips and myself amongst the number, differed from Mr. Garrison as to the wisdom of this course. I felt that the work of the society was not done and that it had not fulfilled

its mission, which was, not merely to emancipate, but to elevate the enslaved class. But against Mr. Garrison's leadership, and the surprise and joy occasioned by emancipation, it was impossible to keep the association alive, and the cause of the freedmen was left mainly to individual effort and to hastily extemporized societies of an ephemeral character, brought together under benevolent impulse, but having no history behind them, and, being new to the work, they were not as effective for good as the old society would have been, had it followed up its work and kept its old instrumentalities in operation.[44]

Different struggles continued, seemingly unaware of their inherent unity of interest but growing closer to needed unity with each year. The plight of women has always been a matter of slavery; racism has always been a lie used to defend imperialism and to divide people in the face of their mutual oppression; and the labor movement has always been a fight against bondage. But to several influential abolitionists, content with the social order that afforded them the luxury to participate in social reform, there were standards of "legitimacy" to abide by. Had abolitionists been free from such a narrow vision, they could have related the slavery of the Afro-American to the sufferings in the northern ghettos; they could have recognized sexist and racist prejudices as symptomatic of their own victimization; they could have looked behind prison walls for the antebellum cruelties in their own back yards and could have worked against the quiet prison movement that was institutionalizing slavery for all poor and working class people. They could have embraced the cause of northern workers who, struggling to survive under industrial servitude, could not, alone, extend their energies any further.

A Silent Admission of Guilt

While abolitionists were struggling to free the chattel slave, a significant change in the constitution of Iowa foreshadowed future attempts to cover over the embarrassing sore of prison slavery. A *prison slave state,* Article 1, Section 23 of the Iowa 1846 Constitution stated:

> 23. Neither slavery nor involuntary servitude, UNLESS FOR THE PUNISHMENT OF CRIMES, shall ever be tolerated in this State.

In 1857, Iowa amended its constitutional status to that of an *involuntary servitude state* by changing Section 23 to:

> There shall be no slavery in this State; nor shall there be involuntary servitude, UNLESS FOR THE PUNISHMENT OF CRIME.

This state constitutional change can be regarded as an admission of guilt, an attempted erasure of that guilt, and no more.

Charles Cook, in his autobiographical *Ways of Sin,* published in 1894 to convey his experiences as an Iowa prisoner, reported conditions uncomfortably reminiscent of the old Auburn plan. Upon entering prison with hands and feet in shackles, the prisoner was made to wear a black and white striped suit, had all his hair cut off in the old slavish style that prevented him from combing it, was marched to and fro with other convicts in lock-step, worked twelve hours every day in the boot and shoe shop without being allowed to leave for a sip of water and lived in unsanitary, rat-infested conditions. Cook described the brutal punishments which were meted out to prisoners who did not meet their keepers' demands.[45]

Iowa had prohibited prison slavery and yet retained involuntary servitude for crime. While the repugnant connotation of the word "slavery" was avoided, close examination of the two conditions shows little actual difference between them. Involuntary servitude is the labor relation of slavery and the ancient reason for slavery's existence.

Webster's New World Dictionary of the American Language defines "servitude" as "the condition of a slave." Add the word "involuntary" and you have "involuntary servitude," a ridiculous, redundant attempt to convey a more humanitarian flavor than "slavery." Our Congressional delegates did not use the word "servitude" unconsciously. A notable insight occurs in a speech by Representative Kasson of Iowa on January 10, 1865, in the U.S. House of Representatives:

> For example, quoting from the third volume of the Madison Papers, when the very question of the action of the [Constitutional] Convention upon this subject was referred to and was under consideration, Mr. Madison declared that he "thought it wrong to admit in the Constitution that there could be property in man"; and Mr. Randolph moved that the word "servitude" be stricken out and the word "service" inserted; and then follows the reason, as given in the Madison Papers, for the change:
>
> "The former [servitude] being thought to express the condition of slaves, and the latter [service] the obligation of free persons."
>
> It was so done.[46]

Emancipation of the slave would be the banner under which thousands of Americans would sacrifice their lives in the 1860's. The next century of lawful bondage called upon sophisticated labels to disguise and protect slavery's continuance. As will be later discussed, "involuntary servitude" proved a convenient change.

As the country moved closer to Civil War, the states were divided in the following ways:

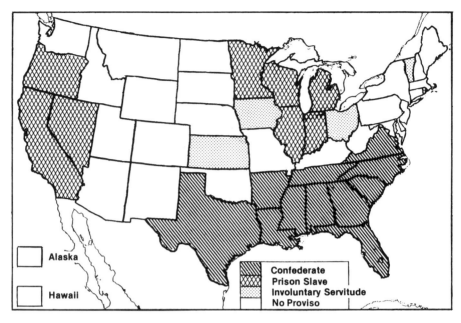

PRE CIVIL WAR STATES

Not Merely a Moral War

As W.E.B. DuBois wrote, the war that freed the chattel slave resulted from a combination of moral, political, and economic forces.[47] The North wanted to neutralize the profits of the South. Secession of the South meant losing America's collateral in cotton for international trade. Furthermore, big northern commercial interests "were using the South's great white harvest to offset the enormous quantity of goods that the nation, especially the West, was importing."[48] The "free" states participated in and profited from the slave trade and its tariffs. New York City became the hub of the slave trade, but the North bickered with the South over annexation of new territories: additional "free" states would enable new industrial masters to expand and profit from skilled wage labor while additional slave territory would enable the slavocracy to expand and profit from slave labor. Chattel slavery stood in the way of the financier-industrialists, and northern money-makers manipulated the moral protests against slavery into a convenient smoke screen for their ultimate gain.

The South stood at the height of its power in 1860: it influenced Congress, controlled the ruling majority in the Supreme Court, and substantially achieved its ends. Despite restrictions on the slave trade, importation of slaves to the South greatly increased between 1850 and 1860. Before the chattel slavemaster fell, he had crushed 250 slave rebellions. Until secession of the southern states, Congress attempted to appease the South. At the opening of the December 1860 Congressional session, President Buchanan

> ...recommended in his annual message three explanatory amendments to the Constitution on the subject of slavery. The first of these was an express recognition of the right of property in slaves; the second declared the duty of protecting this right in the Territories, and the last, recognized the validity of the fugitive slave law.[49]

Congress could not agree on any of the several amendments proposed to settle the slavery question. The Corwin amendment however, did receive Congressional approval in March 1862. It stated:

> No amendment shall be made to the Constitution which will authorize or give to Congress the power to abolish or to interfere, within any State, with the domestic institutions thereof, including that of persons held to labor or service by the laws of said State.[50]

The amendment did not achieve state ratification, for many thought it would not prevent remaining southern states from seceding. The North needed the South and war became the solution to this dilemma.

That same year, 1862, an editorial by abolitionist Horace Greeley, the "Prayer of Twenty Millions," elicited President Lincoln's response:

> If there be those who would not save the Union unless they could at the same time save slavery, I do not agree with them. If there be those who would not save the Union unless they could at the same time destroy slavery, I do not agree with them. My paramount object in this struggle is to save the Union and is not either to save or destroy slavery. If I could save the Union without freeing any slaves, I would do it; and if I could save it by freeing all the slaves, I would also do that. What I do about slavery and the colored race, I do because I believe it would help to save the Union....[51]

Slavery was an obscenity that had caused the United States international as well as national embarrassment. Fighting for preservation of the Union alone could not win international support and the situation of the black became strategic:

> His was the only appeal which would bring sympathy from Europe, despite strong economic bonds with the South, and prevent recognition of a Southern nation built on slavery.... Slowly but surely an economic dispute and a political test of strength took on the aspects of a great moral crusade.[52]

1862: The Final Punishment of Prisoner Toole and The Emancipation Proclamation

While plantation slavery provided a moral smoke screen for the political and economic motives of the Union, the slaves in the North were kept at hard labor behind prison walls. One such prisoner was Irish immigrant Gerald Toole. Despite a credible denial that he set fire to his own business, Toole was serving a life sentence at Wethersfield Prison in Connecticut.

> From the first week that I entered the prison walls, to the month of March, 1862, was characteristic of brutality and audacious hardship never before witnessed. The storm was a long time coming, but could be seen hovering in the distance - a long, dark cloud, that at no distant day was sure to burst asunder. Threats came to me every week, but not to me only, for these same threats were extended to the other prisoners. It was one continual strain from morning till night, "every where and in all places," whether at hard, laborious work, or at dinner, or in the lonely cell - it was everywhere. The emissaries were everywhere to be found. There was no peace, no comfort; in fact, nothing that could be desired. These continual threats and cuffs were now about coming to an end.[53]

Toole worked in the prison boot shop and could not meet his supervisor's demands for a case of boots, twelve per day.

> I told him [the supervisor] plainly, in language not to be misunderstood, that more work I could not do, and follow it up for any length of time. I asked him to look at the big drops of sweat that came running down my brow. On one occasion, while engaged in wiping the perspiration from my face, I was hailed by Buck, with all the airs he was capable of assuming, and in all the bitterness of his nature, (which, I may here add is of the first water,) who shouted at the top of his voice: "If I ever catch you again killing time this way, we'll lick you every day!" (Here I was working in a close shop, without any fresh air, from morn until night, in a state of stupidity half of the time from the effects of physical labor and mental weakness, working as hard as I could, and using all the muscular powers that kind nature had bestowed on me).[54]

The warden promised to beat Toole if he failed to complete a case of boots. That next day Toole strained to complete twelve pair but only finished ten. After "doing all in my power to avoid this disgraceful usage,"[55] he was taken to the dungeon.

> I held up my head, and walked with a quick pace. On entering the dungeon, the doors had all been closed. With a sullen aspect and a flash of the eye, [Warden] Webster told me to

"strip off." This demand I did not anticipate, and I ventured to ask my persecutor what he meant to do. The response was the same as before, but somewhat sharper and more authoritative. I yielded, remarking that this was the first time I had ever been so treated. Deputy Fenton stood by, with his mounted cane in his hand; Webster also had his in the same position. I had no means of defending myself, so I was obliged to leave myself to the mercy of my cruel masters. Having my coat and shirt off, Webster ordered me to turn round and place my hands on the wall, holding them up high as possible. This done, he drew out the piercing and cutting "cat," and laid it on to my shoulders with all the dexterity and force of an enraged barbarian who has long had practice in the same school. . . . Again and again the poisonous lash cut up my flesh, and then the unmerciful tyrant, still thirsting for my blood, drew the bloody cords and sunk them on my back! The pain was excruciating; it was piercing beyond conception. I had never before conceived of the horrid nature of the "cat-o'-nine-tails."I had read of instances where the surgeon looked on, to see if the victim was capable of bearing more; in my case there was not a surgeon, but a *butcher* in his place. . . . Ere the last two blows fell, Webster exclaimed, in all the bitterness of his heart, "Now will you make a case of boots to-morrow - now will you make a case of boots?" I answered in the affirmative, adding, "I have this day done all that I am capable of doing." I also remember having several times begged his pardon while the hellish "cat" fell on my naked shoulders. "Now," he said, "if you don't make twelve pairs to-morrow, I will take you over here again in the evening, and give you twice the number you have now got."[56]

The following day, Toole again did all in his power to avoid another beating.

The hour was now fast approaching for the catastrophe! I found at four o'clock that I could do no more than ten pair of boots, and dreaded the awful punishment that was to take place, - yes, in another hour, with more severity than had yet been inflicted. My yet bleeding and trembling shoulders crept at the very thought. My life at the time became wearisome. Yes, death then would be a relief - that "dreamless sleep, that knows no awakening."

In this distracted state of mind, I placed my knife in my pocket, took another to work with from the bench in front, and continued up to twenty minutes to six, when Buck paid me the first visit for the day. . . . Boss Buck now inquired of me how many pairs I had done. I told him the same as yesterday, - on the last boot of the tenth pair, - adding, "you have seen me here all day, in a state of perspiration, endeavoring to do all my strength would allow; and I now find out, as I said yesterday, that twelve pair I can not do." Not a sentence more he uttered, save the words, "Go off to the space." I went off on

> the moment, as required, for experience taught me remon-
> strance with Buck would only get me kicked about the shop,
> and in the state of mind I was then in I might draw the knife I
> had thus concealed for self-defense. Here I had been remain-
> ing for near ten minutes, awaiting the moment of being pulled
> and dragged away to that ever to be remembered dungeon.
> Oh, God! when thus standing in that space during that ten
> minutes, what awful fleeting thoughts flashed across my
> mind! I even thought the other degraded prisoners that
> caught my eye were happy to me beyond measure. No living
> being could ever be in so awful a state of mind, broaching on
> insanity. I became maddened! The shop appeared rolling
> around! I could scarcely hold my feet, from terror, excitement
> and horror! Indeed, at the time I would have faced daggers
> and swords, for all I wanted was a death-blow that would
> send me out of pain![57]

When Warden Webster appeared and pushed Toole toward the dungeon, Toole grabbed his knife to defend himself against another
beating, and in the scuffle that followed, stabbed Webster three times
before being dragged off to the dungeon by four men and beaten far
worse than before, with eight men holding him down.[58]

Webster died the next day and Toole was put on trial for murder.
Convicted of Webster's murder, Toole suffered death by hanging on
September 28, 1862, eleven days before his twenty-fourth birthday.[59]
Gerald Toole suffered the slavemaster's final punishment - death - and
the cries of others like him were muffled in the North by the quietly en-
forced institution of slavery as a punishment for crime.

A few days after Toole's death, and as a tactic of war, President Lincoln issued the Emancipation Proclamation:

> That on the 1st day of January, A.D. 1863, all persons held as
> slaves within any State...in rebellion against the United
> States shall be then, thenceforward, and forever free.[60]

Freeing all the chattel slaves in the rebel states, the edict served two
strategic functions. It defended the position of the Union by giving
moral purpose to the war, thereby encouraging support from Europe,
and it hit the Confederacy at its economic foundation - slavery. By setting Confederate slaves free, the President encouraged 4 million
blacks to fight on the side of the Union for their emancipation.[61]

> [Lincoln] delayed it as long as he could. He twice overruled
> field commanders who had issued edicts of abolition in their
> war zones. He pondered the obviously troubling matter of con-
> stitutional authority for the step. The Constitution had left the
> lawfulness of slavery up to the separate states. The only legal
> ground Lincoln could plausibly stand on in issuing the Eman-
> cipation Proclamation was that of war-emergency power in
> his role as commander-in-chief, and so he used it on the first
> day of the year 1863. Technically, it is true, it did not free any-

body within Lincoln's territorial command. It applied only to those slaves in rebel states, excluding parts of Virginia and Louisana then under Union control. It did not mention the rest of the Union, for there would have been no military justification for such a step. But it did confirm what was happening in the battlefield: it formally invited free slaves to join the Union army - a step they had taken right along.[62]

War

Slavery reached beyond its chained victims by reducing the number of available jobs to free labor and forcing workers to accept lower wages. Many working people recognized that the struggle of the Afro-American was also their struggle. The *Voice of Industry* declared:

> The question of slavery is in truth the question of labor. Wherever the rights of laborers are discussed or upon whatever department of labor reform we insist, the influence of slavery is arrayed against us. Do we ask for a Free Soil, a land limitation law, or any other measure which looks to the protection and elevation of the laboring classes, we are told by the McDuffies and the Calhouns that slavery is the natural and necessary condition of the producing classes....[63]

And the November, 1862 edition of the *Iron Platform* read:

> There is one truth which should be clearly understood by every working man in the Union. *The slavery of the black man leads to the slavery of the white man.*[64]

More than 50 percent of the nation's workers left for the battlefield, leaving their families to carry on the struggle to survive without them. In the South, men and women with long-cherished aspirations for freedom also joined Union ranks, for, as Lincoln had counted on and as W.E.B. DuBois would later confirm, the black

> became in the first year contraband of war; that is, property belonging to the enemy and valuable to the invader. And, in addition to that, he became, as the South quickly saw, the key to the Southern resistance....[65]

The wage slave and the chattel slave won the war for the Union. The poor Southern white followed the action of the slaves by abandoning the slavemaster, whose losing war became too much of a burden to bear. Some became "recalcitrant, some went into active opposition; and at last it was more desertion and disunion than anything else that brought about the final overthrow."[66] Before the final overthrow of the Confederacy, more than 600,000 died and more than 400,000 were injured on the four-year battle front. The cost to the fighting troops of workers, farmers, slaves and ex-slaves was high. And, as Harriet Tubman, then scout for the Union army, reported after one of the bravest assaults of the war, fought by black Union troops at Fort Wagner,

> And then we saw the lightning, and that was the guns; and then we heard the thunder and that was the big guns; and then we heard the rain falling and that was the drops of blood falling; and when we came to get in the crops, it was the dead men that we reaped.[67]

While men and women were dying for freedom, J.P. Morgan, John D. Rockefeller, Philip Armour, James Hill, Andrew Carnegie, Jay Gould and Jim Fisk were building empires out of war. Avoiding the draft of 1863 by paying the going price of $300 to young men who took the rich men's places in battle, young capitalists reaped their harvest of war in greenbacks. Morgan sold previously condemned government rifles back to the government at lucrative profits; banker Jay Cooke earned $20,000,000 from commissions that the government paid war industries; Armour made $2,000,000 selling pork to the army at inflated prices; Rockefeller initiated his plan to monopolize the oil industry; and 10,000 Chinese and 3,000 Irish were suffering casualties as they labored for pittance to build the transcontinental railroad. Investigations into the war dealings of J.P. Morgan led a Congressional committee to conclude: "Worse than traitors are the men who, pretending loyalty to the flag, feast and fatten on the misfortunes of the nation.[68]

By the end of the Civil War, these robber barons gained unforetold control over the industrial capital of the reunited nation.

> The young men who were to form the new nobility of industry and banking had, most of them, reached their prime of youth or manhood when Lincoln issued his first call for volunteers. Jay Gould, Jim Fisk, J.P. Morgan, Philip Armour, Andrew Carnegie, James Hill and John Rockefeller were all in their early twenties: Collis Huntington and Leland Stanford were over thirty, while Jay Cooke was not yet forty. In the ensuing years all the members of this band of youth would meet their first "windfalls": sure-footed they... would take their posts in the economic revolution which rose to a climax in the war; and the end of the war would see them masters of money, capitalists equipped to increase their capital. In the hour of danger it was as if *they alone were prepared.* It was as if the Second American Revolution had been fought for them.[69]

These men represented monied interests that then exploited the war-torn South using agents known as carpetbaggers and fought the rising labor movement with deceit, sabotage, control of government officials and agencies, and called in American troops to stop worker protests for higher wages. In their propagandized cry for "law and order," they continued to suppress suffrage, civil rights, labor leaders;

victimized workers and the poor met with slavery as a punishment for their crimes of resistance.

Notes

1. Gerda Lerner, *The Grimke Sisters from South Carolina* (New York: Schocken Books, 1967), p. 174.

2. See James Gillespie Birney, *The American Churches, the Bulwarks of American Slavery* (New York: Arno Press and The New York Times; reprint ed. 1842); Stephen S. Foster, *The Brotherhood of Thieves* (New York: Arno Press and The New York Times; reprint ed. 1886). Foster's book is taken from an 1843 letter which was prepared for the press to criticize churches for supporting slavery, "exposing the deep and fathomless abominations of those *pious* thieves, who gain their livelihood by preaching and stealing babies" (p. 8).

3. Lerner, p. 52.

4. Ibid., p. 61.

5. Ibid., p. 255.

6. Drake, p. 142.

7. Ibid., pp. 142-148.

8. Katharine Anthony, *Susan B. Anthony: Her Personal History and Her Era* (New York: Russell & Russell, 1975; reissue ed. Doubleday & Company, Inc., 1954), p. 134.

9. Francine Klagsbrun, *Freedom Now!* (Boston: Houghton Mifflin Company, 1972), pp. 25-29, 36-39.

10. Ibid., p. 41.

11. Ibid., p. 53.

12. Martin Duberman, "The Northern Response to Slavery," Martin Duberman, ed., *The Antislavery Vanguard: New Essays on the Abolitionists* (Princeton: Princeton University Press, 1965), pp. 398-399.

13. Frederick Douglass, *Life and Times of Frederick Douglass,* intro. by Rayford W. Logan (New York: Collier Books, 1962; reprint of 1892 revised ed.), p. 469.

14. Lerner, p. 201.

15. Ibid., p. 171.

16. Ibid., pp. 127-128.

17. James J. Green, *Wendell Phillips* (New York: International Publishers, 1964; reprint ed. 1943), p. 11.

18. Ibid., p. 13.

19. Wyeth Holt, "The Myth of Civil Liberties in America" (book review of *Free Men All: The Personal Liberty Laws of the North* by Thomas D. Morris) *Vanderbilt Law Review,* 27 (1974): 1065.

20. W.E.B. DuBois, *John Brown* (New York: International Publishers, 1972 printing of 1962 ed.; first ed., 1909), p. 135.

21. Anthony, p. 135.

22. Donald, p. 283.

23. Ibid., p. 285.

24. Ibid., pp. 288-312.

25. Charles Morrow Wilson, *The Dred Scott Decision* (Philadelphia: Auerbach Publishers, Inc., 1973), pp. 7-10. Harriet and Dred Scott spent their first five years together as slaves where slavery was prohibited by law, four years while Emerson was buying Harriet from her owner, which "was in double violation of the prevailing territorial laws that also prohibited the *buying* and selling of slaves," and another year as "hire-outs" in Minnesota while Emerson was in Missouri (pp. 9-10). Wilson's "A Chronology of the Life and Times of Dred Scott" lists 1831 to 1838 as years during which "Dred Scott began his seven-year tenure as a slave held in places where slavery was forbidden by state or territorial laws." (p. 114).

26. Ibid., pp. 14-21, 116.

27. Ibid., p. 57.

28. Holt, pp. 1066-1067.

29. Ibid., p. 1067.

30. DuBois, *John Brown,* p. 365.

31. See Larry Gara, "Who Was an Abolitionist?" *The Antislavery Vanguard,* pp. 3-31.

32. See Foner, *Frederick Douglass,* pp. 42-45.

33. Klagsbrun, pp. 125-135.

34. Douglass, pp. 217-218; Foner, *Frederick Douglass,* pp. 59, 136-154; Douglass on "Garrisonism" in Philip S. Foner, *The Life and Writings of Frederick Douglass,* vol. 2 (New York: International Publishers, 1950), letter "To the Secretary of the Edinburgh New Anti-Slavery Association," p. 425.

35. Klagsbrun, p. 40, for subscribers to the *Liberator.*

36. Foner, *Frederick Douglass,* p. 135; see also Sillen, pp. 52-53.

37. Foner, *The Life and Writings of Frederick Douglass,* vol. 2, "The Claims of the Negro Ethnologically Considered, an address delivered at Western Reserve College, July 12, 1854," p. 305; see also James M. McPherson, "A Brief for Equality: The Abolitionist Reply to the Racist Myth, 1860-1865," *The Antislavery Vanguard,* p. 171.

38. Davis, p. 350.

39. William Lofton, "Abolition and Labor", *The Journal of Negro History,* 33 (1948): 250-253. Garrison's defense of his failure to give more support to the labor struggle is explained in this way:

> The great eastern abolitionist, Garrison, recognized the cogency of the argument [for a strong coalition of labor and abolitionists] but felt that it was wise not to adopt the proposed appeal [to give more support to the labor movement] because "we are already staggering under the load of responsibilities connected with what we deem to be, for the time being, the most radical movement on the American soil."

40. Ware, p. 78, quoting *Voice of Industry,* October 9, 1846.

41. Ibid., p. 79, quoting *Voice of Industry,* March 28, 1848.

42. Lofton, p. 272.

43. Ibid., pp. 270-271.

44. Douglass, p. 378.

45. Charles A. Cook, *The Ways of Sin or Experiences of Convict Life* (Des Moines: Patterson-Brown Printery, 1894), chaps. 3-10.

46. *Congressional Globe,* 38th Congress, Second Session, p. 190.

47. DuBois, *Suppression of the African Slave Trade,* pp. 195-196.

48. Kluger, p. 41.

49. Herman V. Ames, *Proposed Amendments to the Constitution of the United States During the First Century of its History* (New York: Burt Franklin, 1970; reprint ed. 1896), p. 194.

50. Ibid., p. 196. The Corwin amendment bears the name of its prime sponsor, Congressman Corwin from Ohio.

51. W.E.B. DuBois, *Black Reconstruction* (Millwood, New York: Kraus-Thomson Organization Limited with permission of Russell and Russell, 1963; reprint ed. Harcourt, Brace and Co., 1935), p. 85.

52. Ibid., pp. 79-80.

53. Gerald Toole, *An Autobiography of Gerald Toole, the State's Prison Convict, who Murdered Daniel Webster, Warden of the Connecticut State Prison on the 27th of March, 1862* (Hartford: Press of Case, Lockwood and Company, 1862), pp. 21-22.

54. Ibid., p. 22.

55. Ibid., p. 25.

56. Ibid.

57. Ibid., p. 29.

58. Ibid., pp. 30-32.

59. Ibid., pp. 42-43.

60. *Encyclopedia Americana,* International ed. (1981), s.v. "Emancipation Proclamation."

61. DuBois, *Black Reconstruction,* p. 57. DuBois reports that of the 4.2 million blacks in the South, 3,953,740 were slaves and 261,918 were "free."

62. Kluger, pp. 42-43.

63. Ware, p. 225.

64. Richard O. Boyer and Herbert M. Morais, *Labor's Untold Story,* 3rd ed. (New York: United Electrical, Radio & Machine Workers of America, 1975), p. 14n.

65. DuBois, *Black Reconstruction,* p. 80.

66. Ibid., as quoted from Campbell, *Black and White in the United States,* p. 165.

67. Boyer and Morais, p. 23.

68. Ibid., p. 19.

69. Ibid., p. 20, quoting Matthew Josephson.

Chapter 5
The Thirteenth Amendment and Beyond

That slavery has *begun* its fall is plain, but. . .its fall will be resisted by those who cling to it. . . . The end will be slow. Woe to abolitionists, if they dream that their work is well nigh done.

- Theodore Weld, 1852[1]

The most piteous thing amid all the black ruin of war-time, amid the broken fortunes of the masters, the blighted hopes of mothers and maidens, and the fall of an empire, - the most piteous thing amid all this was the black freedman who threw down his hoe because the world called him free. What did such a mockery of freedom mean? Not a cent of money, not an inch of land, not a mouthful of victuals, - not even ownership of the rags on his back. Free!

- W.E.B. DuBois[2]

Charles Sumner's Lonely Battle

Charles Sumner embarked on his long career as representative for Massachusetts in the Senate with a unique statement of commitment:

Whatever I am or may be, I freely offer to this cause. I have never been a politician. The slave of principles, I call no party master.[3]

Sumner enraged the slaveholding interests by his intruding commitment to abolition. He served with Senators Howard, Pomeroy, Brown, Buckalew, Carlile and Conness on the Senate Select Committee on Slavery and the Treatment of Freedmen.[4] With Sumner as its outspoken chairman, that committee was charged "to take into consideration all propositions and papers concerning slavery and the treatment of freedmen."[5] The Committee on the Judiciary was the more powerful committee, to which all Senate proposals for amendments to the Constitution were submitted for consideration.

On February 8, 1864, Sumner submitted a joint resolution (S.B. 24) to the Senate to amend the Constitution:

Everywhere within the limits of the United States, and of each state or Territory thereof, all persons are equal before the law, so that no person can hold another as a slave.[6]

Not only would passage of Sumner's proposal have ended all slavery, but it would have secured equality for all persons before the law. Its consequences would have been far-reaching for all people, regardless of race, sex or condition of servitude.

Senator Henderson from Missouri had also proposed a joint resolution (S.B. 16) almost one month earlier, on January 11, 1864, for an amendment to abolish slavery:[7]

> Slavery or involuntary servitude, EXCEPT AS A PUNISHMENT FOR CRIME, shall not exist in the United States.[8]

An avowed slaveholder,[9] Senator Henderson's resolution was modeled on the prison slavery proviso of the constitution with which Missouri entered the Union. Derived from the prison slavery proviso of the Northwest Territory Ordinance, both the Missouri proviso and Henderson's proposed Amendment preserved America's slaveholding heritage.

Nearly one month after Henderson submitted his resolution and only two days after Sumner submitted his, the Senate Committee on the Judiciary announced acceptance of Henderson's resolution as the basis for the Thirteenth Amendment. In his report to the Senate, Senator Trumbull briefed the Senate on the proposed amendment:

> I will state that the amendment, as recommended by the Committee on the Judiciary, provides for submitting to Legislatures of the several States a proposition to amend the Constitution of the United States so that neither slavery nor involuntary servitude, EXCEPT AS A PUNISHMENT FOR CRIME, WHEREOF A PARTY SHALL HAVE BEEN DULY CONVICTED, shall exist within the United States, or any place subject to their jurisdiction; and also that Congress shall have power to enforce this article by proper legislation. I desire to give notice to the Senate that I shall at an early day, call for the consideration of this resolution.[10]

Most of the proposals submitted to the Senate to alter the proposed amendment were attempts by slaveholding interests to prevent abolition and were subsequently rejected. These attempts were undoubtedly designed to coerce abolitionist forces into compromise

> Senator Garrett Davis of Kentucky was particulary conspicuous by reason of his long and very fiery speeches against the amendment, and the numerous "singular factious amendments" which he presented from time to time, eight in all.... One of these provided that no negro should be a citizen of the United States or eligible to any office under the United States, the other that New England should be divided into two States. The division proposed was very singular, inasmuch as Maine and Massachusetts were to form the State of East New England, [and] the rest of the States, West New England. Thus the latter State would not be formed of con-

tiguous territory, but of two sections separated by many miles. . . . This was doubtless introduced to show his antipathy to Massachusetts, for he previously remarked that "the most effective single cause of the pending war has been the intermeddling of Massachusetts with the institution of slavery."[11]

Similar to the original compromise made by the drafters of the Declaration of Independence, the Judiciary Committee's wording of the proposed Thirteenth Amendment was an apparent compromise made to protect the slave holding interests of our nation.

On April 8, 1864, Senator Charles Sumner made his final appeal to the Senate to change the wording of the ominous amendment and asked that his proposed joint resolution be accepted as a substitute:

> *Beyond my general desire to see an act of universal emancipation that shall at once and forever settle this great question, so that it may no longer be the occasion of strife between us, there are two other ideas which are ever present to my mind as a practical legislator: first, to strike at slavery wherever I can hit it; and secondly, to clean the statute-book of all existing supports of slavery, so that it may find nothing there to which it may cling for life. To do less than this at the present moment, when slavery is still menacing, would be an abandonment of duty.*
>
> So long as a single slave continues anywhere beneath the flag of the Republic I am unwilling to rest. Too well I know the vitality of slavery with its infinite capacity of propagation, and how little slavery it takes to make a slave State with all the cruel pretensions of slavery. . . .[12]

As well as incorporating the slaveholding principles of the Missouri senator, the proposed amendment closely resembled Article 6 of the Northwest Territory Ordinance of 1787, Section 6:

> There shall be neither slavery nor involuntary servitude in the said territory, OTHERWISE THAN IN THE PUNISHMENT OF CRIMES WHEREOF THE PARTY SHALL HAVE BEEN DULY CONVICTED: Provided always, that any person escaping into the same, from whom labor or service is lawfully claimed in any one of the original States, such fugitive may be lawfully reclaimed and conveyed to the person claiming his or her labor aforesaid.

Sumner then criticized the proposed amendment's resemblance to the old ordinance.

> Let me say frankly that I should prefer a form of expression different from that which has the sanction of the committee. They have selected what was intended for the old Jeffersonian Ordinance [of 1787], sacred in our history, although, let me add, they have not imitated it closely. *But I must be pardoned*

if I venture to doubt the expediency of perpetuating in the Constitution language which, if it have any signification, seems to imply "slavery or involuntary servitude" may be provided "for the punishment of crime." There was a reason for that language when it was first employed, but that reason no longer exists. If my desires could prevail, I would put aside the ordinance on this occasion, and find another form.

I know nothing better than these words:

> All persons are equal before the law so that no person can hold another as a slave; and the Congress shall have power to make all laws necessary and proper to carry this decision into effect everywhere within the United States and the jurisdiction thereof.[13]

. . . . Enough has been said to explain the origin of the words which are now proposed [French Declaration of Rights, 1787]. It will be for the Senate to determine if it will adopt them.

Should the Senate not incline to this form, there is still another I would suggest, as follows:

> Slavery shall not exist anywhere within the United States or the jurisdiction thereof; and that the Congress shall have power to make all laws necessary and proper to carry this prohibition into effect.[14]

Debates in the Senate, April 8, 1864

The following is from the Congressional Globe's report on the Senate debates of April 8, 1864.

> MR. SUMNER. Now, Mr. President, the state of the question is this. The Senator from Missouri [Mr. Henderson] offered a proposition in this form:
>
> > Art. 1. Slavery or involuntary servitude, except as a punishment for crime, shall not exist in the United States. . . .
>
> I make this comment on the proposition which we have before us, that of the Senator from Missouri, in order to explain why I should be against that in the form in which it stands; I am free to say that in some respects I think it better than the article proposed by the committee. It is as follows:
>
> > Slavery or involuntary servitude, EXCEPT AS A PUNISHMENT FOR CRIME, shall not exist in the United States.
>
> It is simpler than the proposition of the committee. . . .
>
> [My] objection to it [the proposition of the committee] is, further, . . . it seems to me the language is not happy . . . I understand that it starts with the idea of reproducing the Jef-

fersonian ordinance. I doubt the expediency of reproducing
that ordinance. It performed an excellent work in its day; but
there are words in it which are entirely inapplicable to our
time. That ordinance I will read. It is as follows:

> There shall be neither slavery nor involuntary ser-
> vitude in the said Territory OTHERWISE THAN IN
> THE PUNISHMENT OF CRIMES WHEREOF THE
> PARTY SHALL HAVE BEEN DULY CONVICTED.

This ordinance, in precisely these words, was reproduced
at a later day, in the very important act by which Missouri was
admitted into the Union, containing the well-known prohibition which afterwards caused such debate.

> *There are words here, I have said, which are entirely inap-*
> *plicable to our time. They are the limitation, "OTHERWISE*
> *THAN IN THE PUNISHMENT OF CRIMES WHEREOF THE*
> *PARTY SHALL HAVE BEEN DULY CONVICTED." Now, unless*
> *I err, there is an implication from those words that men may*
> *be enslaved as a punishment of crimes whereof they shall*
> *have been duly convicted. There was a reason, I have said, for*
> *that at the time, for I understand that it was the habit in cer-*
> *tain parts of the country to convict persons or to doom them*
> *as slaves for life as a punishment for crime, and it was not*
> *proposed to prohibit this habit. But slavery in our day is*
> *something distinct, perfectly well known, requiring no words*
> *of distinction outside of itself. Why, therefore, add "nor in-*
> *voluntary servitude otherwise than in the punishment of*
> *crimes whereof the party shall have been duly convicted?" To*
> *my mind they are entirely surplusage. They do no good there,*
> *but they absolutely introduce a doubt.*[15]

Sumner denied any distinction between slavery and involuntary servitude, saying that the essential nature of slavery was by his time
clear and recognizable and that the ordinance confused matters by
implying that a difference did exist, creating a doubt of their meaning.
His concern was well-founded because, in 1857, before the Civil War,
Iowa made use of that doubt. In an attempt to disguise its practice of
slavery, Iowa changed its constitution to prohibit slavery and permit
involuntary servitude as punishment for crime.

Sumner further argued that

> In placing a new and important text into our Constitution, it
> seems to me we cannot be too careful in the language we
> adopt. We should consider well that the language we adopt
> here in this Chamber to-day will in all probability be adopted
> in the other House, and it must be adopted, also, by three
> fourths of the Legislatures of the States. *Once having passed*
> *this body, it is substantially beyond correction. Therefore, it*
> *seems to me, we have every motive, the strongest inducement*
> *in the world, to make that language as perfect as possible.*[16]

Sumner also understood that the real meaning of the proposed Thirteenth Amendment would be camouflaged by its awkward grammar; that the prison slavery proviso of the Thirteenth Amendment as ratified has gone substantially unchallenged and unrecognized, even by constitutional lawyers, for more than a century testifies to Sumner's foresight:

> I say, therefore, that I object to the Jeffersonian ordinance even if it were presented here in its original text. But now I am brought to the point that the proposition of the committee is not the Jeffersonian ordinance, except in its bad feature. In other respects, it discards the language of the Jeffersonian ordinance and also its collocation of words. The language of the committee is as follows:
>
>> Neither slavery nor involuntary servitude, EXCEPT AS A PUNISHMENT FOR CRIME, WHEREOF THE PARTY SHALL HAVE BEEN DULY CONVICTED, shall exist within the United States, or any place subject to their jurisdiction.
>
> The Senate will observe what to my ear is a discord, the introduction of those two "shalls" so near together; but that is not of great importance.
> MR. DOOLITTLE. They are both in the Jeffersonian ordinance.
>
> MR. SUMNER. But they are further apart, and the whole effect is entirely different. As I have said already, the language of the ordinance is, "There shall be." Mark the beginning as compared with that of the committee. The committee say, "Neither slavery nor involuntary servitude," &c. The ordinance says, "There shall be" - the word of prohibition coming first, at the outset - "neither slavery nor involuntary servitude in the said Territory otherwise than in the punishment of crimes whereof the party shall have been duly convicted"; whereas the committee say, "Neither slavery nor involuntary servitude, except as a punishment for crime, whereof the party shall have been duly convicted, shall exist within the United States, or any place subject to their jurisdiction."[17]

At this point, Sumner urged that if the Senate intended slavery to stand as a punishment for crime, they should state so clearly or remove the proviso entirely. The Senate did neither:

> If Senators desire the Jeffersonian ordinance, I say let us take it in its original form as it appears in that ordinance, and was subsequently reproduced in the Missouri statute; do not let us take it in this modified form, which, while pretending to be the Jeffersonian ordinance, is not the Jeffersonian ordinance except in that feature which I think, if Senators apply their minds to it, they will see is clearly objectionable. I refer to the words "EXCEPT AS A PUNISHMENT FOR CRIMES, WHEREOF THE PARTY SHALL HAVE BEEN DULY CON-

VICTED." I have already said that for myself I should prefer the form which I have sent to the Chair, and on which the question is now to be taken; but I offer it as a suggestion, and if Senators do not incline to it, I have no desire to press it.

MR. TRUMBULL. Mr. President, at an early stage of the session, the Senator from Missouri introduced a proposition to amend the Constitution of the United States so as forever to prohibit slavery. That resolution was referred to the Committee on the Judiciary. At a later day, a month or two afterwards, the Senator from Massachusetts also introduced a proposition to prohibit slavery. The committee had both those propositions before them. They considered them. There was some difference of opinion in the committee as to the language to be used; and it was upon discussion and an examination of both these propositions, the one originally introduced by the Senator from Missouri, and subsequently by the Senator from Massachusetts, that the committee came to the conclusion to adopt the form which is reported here. . . . [18]

In researching the joint resolution of the Senate, we were unable to locate the minutes of the proceedings in the Committee on the Judiciary. Nor was the National Archives in Washington, D.C. able to help us: the minutes are missing from the records. A letter to us from George P. Perros of the National Archives Legislative and Natural Resources Branch, Civil Archives Division, stated:

An examination of the records of the United States Senate in the National Archives has failed to disclose the minutes of the Senate Judiciary Committee for the 38th Congress (1863-1865). Nor is on hand any disposition as to the disposition of that document.

It seems as if the Senate did not wish to state its intentions clearly. In addition to hiding their own intentions, some members of the Senate tried to create new evidence to misrepresent Sumner's position.

MR. DOOLITTLE. If the Senator from Illinois will allow me for a single moment, it is said that men's first impressions are sometimes the best, and it seems that the Senator from Massachusetts when he introduced his proposition used in it the very words of which he now makes such complaint, "otherwise than in the punishment of crime whereof the party shall have been duly convicted."

MR. SUMNER. I beg the Senator's pardon. The first proposition I introduced was a month or six weeks before that; but after the committee made their report, when I examined it and found that they had undertaken to give us the Jeffersonian ordinance, and I saw that it was not the Jeffersonian ordinance, I then prepared that proposition with a view to embody the Jeffersonian ordinance precisely.

MR. TRUMBULL. I was very much tempted to reply to some of the remarks that have been made in opposition to this proposed amendment, and am strongly tempted also to reply to some of the remarks which have fallen from the Senator from Massachusetts, who in an elaborate argument has attempted to show that no amendment of the Constitution is necessary;* but, sir, if we can have a vote on this subject I will forego making any reply to what has been said, and will content myself with the passage of the resolution, which is the object I have in view, to abolish slavery and prevent its existence hereafter. The language as reported by the committee will accomplish these objects....[19]

Misrepresentation of Sumner's efforts included sabotage of his proposed amendment by Senator Howard, a member of his own Committee on Slavery and the Treatment of Freedmen.

MR. HOWARD. I believe the proposition now before the Senate is the amendment offered by the Senator from Massachusetts, and on that question I have one word to say.

MR. SUMNER. The Senator will allow me to make a remark. I cannot resist the appeal of my friend, the chairman of the committee [Committee on the Judiciary], and therefore shall not pursue any of the propositions, and I wish to withdraw them. I merely wish to put myself right with my friends. I offered them sincerely with a desire to make a contribution to perfect the measure. I now withdraw them.

MR. HOWARD. I must object to the withdrawal of the amendment, as I have the floor. I desire, as I said before, to say one word on the subject of the amendment offered by the Senator from Massachusetts. The language of it is this, that all persons are free before the law.

MR. SUMNER. "All persons are equal."

MR. HOWARD. Will the Secretary be good enough to read it?

The Secretary read, as follows:
    Sec. 1. All persons are free before the law, so that
    no person can hold another as a slave, &c.

MR. SUMNER. That is a mistake. It is "equal."

MR. HOWARD. It is written in the handwriting of the Senator from Massachusetts.

MR. SUMNER. It is "equal," and not "free."

MR. HOWARD. I regard it as very immaterial whether the word "free" or "equal" is used in that connection. What I insist upon is this, that in a legal and technical sense that language is utterly insignificant and meaningless as a clause of the Constitution. I should like the Senator from Massachusetts, if

---

* At no time did Sumner try to show that an amendment to abolish slavery was not needed.

he is able, to state what effect this would have in law in a court of justice. What significance is given to the phrase "equal" or "free" before the law in a common law court? It is not known at all.

Besides, the proposition speaks of all men being equal. I suppose before the law a woman would be equal to a man, a woman would be as free as a man. A wife would be equal to her husband and as free as her husband before the law.[20]

Senator Howard, a member of the Committee on Slavery and the Treatment of Freedmen, attempted to dismantle Sumner's presentation by both inserting an incorrect wording of Sumner's Senate Bill 24 and by appealing to the masculine insecurities of those Senators who would not wish to see "a woman...equal to a man, a woman...as free as a man...or a wife equal to her husband and as free as her husband before the law."

Its Passage, and the Slavery Abolition Banner Discarded

On April 8, 1864, the Senate passed the Thirteenth Amendment to the United States Constitution:

Section 1. Neither slavery nor involuntary servitude, EXCEPT AS A PUNISHMENT FOR CRIME WHEREOF THE PARTY SHALL HAVE BEEN DULY CONVICTED, shall exist within the United States, or any place subject to their jurisdiction.

Section 2. Congress shall have the power to enforce this article by appropriate legislation.

Since law requires that a proposed amendment to the Constitution pass Congress with a two-thirds majority in each house before it be submitted to the states for ratification, the next step in the amending process was submission of the Senate's bill to the House. Sumner had warned his colleagues that once the bill passed the Senate, it would be "substantially beyond correction." Again, Sumner's analysis was correct: the long debates in the House over the Senate's proposed amendment did not mention the offensive exception.

On January 31, 1865, the House passed the Thirteenth Amendment with the required two-thirds majority - 119 yeas to 56 nays and 8 abstaining. It was then signed by President Lincoln and submitted to the various states for ratification. On December 18, 1865, the Secretary of State certified that the Thirteenth Amendment had become part of the Constitution.

The Senate's refusal to act on Sumner's appeal to delete the exception from the final document was a tragic mistake that would victimize American justice for more than 100 years to come. Slavery remained the destiny of those imprisoned for crime.

The Black Codes

Both the spirit and institution of slavery were far from dead in the war-ravaged and poverty-stricken South. This period of new freedom witnessed marginal enforcement of chattel slavery prohibition measures and full exploitation of the Thirteenth Amendment's special redemption of prison slavery.

At the close of the Civil War, the Bureau of Refugees, Freedmen and Abandoned Lands, better known as the Freedmen's Bureau, was established to provide food, clothing, housing and land to the millions of refugees from slavery. It was given one year and meager funding, little more than $5 million, or $1.25 per capita, to heal the deep wounds of more than two centuries of chattel slavery.[21] The reconstructed states of the South rallied by passing the Black Codes, laws designed to restrict freedmen's opportunities, movement and employment. They penalized the black refugee at every turn by criminalizing vagrancy and defining new crimes to trap the destitute and jobless of the South.

Just as the vagrancy laws of fourteenth through sixteenth century Europe were designed to forestall inevitable socio-economic changes from feudalism to capitalism by incriminating the poor and exploiting their labor through convict slavery, so post-Civil War Black Codes were designed to restore power to former slavemasters. Vagrancy and other violations of hundreds of petty laws recently added to Southern statutes was unavoidable for millions of free, homeless, uneducated and desperately poor blacks confronting a broken and evolving economy which forced both them and the masses of already poor whites into increased competition for fewer jobs. Conviction of vagrancy or any of the other of a growing list of crimes subjected a person to fines or imprisonment.

> To seek more attractive work terms, a freedman would of course have had to leave his old plantation in search of a new arrangement, but the moment he did so, he was liable to charges of vagrancy and a fine. The fine might be paid by any landholder, who could then command the alleged vagrant's services - a form, that is, of involuntary servitude proscribed by the newly effective Thirteenth Amendment. In Florida, any Negro failing to fulfill his employment contract or who was impudent to the owner of the land he worked was subject to being declared a vagrant and punished accordingly.... South Carolina, as usual, set the standard of vehemence for the South. No "person of color" was permitted to enter and reside in the state unless he posted a bond within twenty days after arriving, guaranteed by two white property owners, for $1,000 "conditioned for his good behavior, and for his support." Any Negro who wished to work in the state at an occupation other than farmer or servant had to be especially licensed, had to prove his or her fitness for the work, and pay

> an annual tax ranging from $10 to $100. To do farm work, a
> Negro in South Carolina had to have a written contract, at-
> tested to by white witnesses; failure to obtain one before
> commencing to work was a misdemeanor punishable by a
> fine from $5 to $50. Contracting Negroes were known as "ser-
> vants" and the contractors as "masters."[22]

Most ex-slaves who avoided conviction were forced to sign contracts they could not read obliging them to labor as sharecroppers or
peons for former slavemasters.

> [The freedman's] access to the land was hindered and limited;
> his right to work was curtailed; his right of self-defense was
> taken away, when his right to bear arms was stopped; and his
> employment was virtually reduced to contract labor with
> penal servitude as a punishment for leaving his job.[23]

Harsh penalties for misdemeanant crimes were included in the long
list of crimes added to state statutes. Mississippi's famous "pig law"
for example

> ...declared the theft of any property valued at more than ten
> dollars, or of any kind of cattle or swine, regardless of value,
> to be grand larceny, subjecting the thief to a term of up to five
> years in the state penitentiary. This [law]...was largely re-
> sponsible for an increase in the population of the state prison
> from 272 in 1874 to 1,072 at the end of 1877.[24]

With passage of the Thirteenth Amendment in Congress and the
many Black Codes throughtout the South, prisons in the South began
to fill with recently emancipated slaves. Newly crowded prisons leased
out their slaves to contractors who worked them in plantations, lum-
ber camps, swamps, mines and road construction. Prisoners were
literally worked to death thereby increasing the effective frequency of
execution, the slavemaster's ultimate punishment. In Alabama alone,
the prisoner death rate rose to 41 percent in 1869.[25] No longer was it
necessary to consider the capital investment in human property since
prison slavemasters had a continuous reserve of poor convicted
Americans to draw from. Instead, business sense now dictated swift
and final punishments to keep the massive labor supply in line.

The Thirteenth Amendment rendered all people free from slavery,
except any person convicted of a crime. Prison slavery replaced chattel slavery and, again, oppression reigned in the South. "Slavery...as
a punishment for crime," for the poor and friendless of all races, re-
rooted itself in the traditions of southern slavemasters.

The Convict Lease System

Big business thrived in prisons where slave labor abounded; prison
slavery proved more profitable than chattel slavery, since no financial

loss to the master resulted from the illness or death of a slave. There was no need to buy another slave to make up for the lost labor or procreative power of a disabled slave, as laborers from the new class of offenders refilled the slave vaults of the State.

The postbellum South was ripe for full implementation of the convict lease system. Because the pre-war economy had been rooted in chattel slavery, no labor movement had grown to protest the unfair competition of prison slave products in the free market and there was as yet no free industrialized southern market. The labor movement of the South lagged more than 50 years behind the progress of the already established campaigns of northern workers.[26] Since the impoverished conditions of the war-torn South, coupled with the vindictive Black Codes, crowded southern prisons, the leasing of prisoners to businessmen helped relieve the pressures to build more and costly prisons and provided a new source of cheap labor for former slavemasters and speculating businessmen. At the agreed leasing fee, prisoners were handed over to their new masters to be worked, cared for and discipline ' as the lessee saw fit.[27]

The convict lease system was established throughout the South shortly after passage of the Thirteenth Amendment. Both the state and its contracting lessee profited enormously from their convenient business arrangement, while convicts labored heavily for long hours with insufficient food and provisions, subject to the maiming discipline of corporal punishments. There was such

> indifference toward the often shocking neglect and brutality of the lease camps, the cause of such abnormally high death and morbidity rates that official investigators in several states concluded that a convict who survived five to seven years in the camps, or two years in some of the lumber camps, could consider himself fortunate.[28]

The brutal transformation from chattel slavery into prison slavery in the South combined the northern tradition of penal slavery developed under the Auburn plan with prized practice of two centuries of chattel slavery in the South.

The Prison Slave State of Mississippi

There are three basic categories of state constitutional rulings regarding prison slavery: prison slave, involuntary servitude, and no proviso states. *Prison slave states* have specific constitutional rulings which mirror the Thirteenth Amendment; *involuntary servitude states* prohibit slavery and permit involuntary servitude to punish crimes; and *no proviso states* make no mention of slavery in their specific state constitutions and therefore fall under the federal authority of the Thirteenth Amendment.

On the eve of the Civil War, Mississippi could boast that 55.1 percent of its population were slaves.[29] When Mississippi rejoined the Union in August 1865, it agreed to abolish slavery but during the first session of its renewed government rejected the chattel slavery prohibition mandated by the Thirteenth Amendment and adopted measures that indicated "strong sympathy with the former state of affairs."[30] Soon after, Mississippi became part of the Fourth Military District under reconstruction and adopted a new constitution. In Mississippi's Constitution of 1868, Section 15 of Article I abolished slavery except to punish crimes:

> There shall be neither slavery nor involuntary servitude in this State, OTHERWISE THAN IN THE PUNISHMENT OF CRIME, WHEREOF THE PARTY SHALL HAVE BEEN DULY CONVICTED.

Section 15 reaffirmed the federal ruling on slavery and thereby transformed the constitutional status of Mississippi to that of *a prison slave state,* and Mississippi dutifully carried out its prison slave proviso. As Thorsten Sellin's *Slavery and the Penal System* tells us:

> Mississippi's penitentiary, which had been partly destroyed by Sherman's army, was sufficiently repaired in 1866 to permit the leasing of it to J.W. Young and Company for a period of fourteen years; but within a few months the prison was so overcrowded and the convict population increasing at so rapid a rate that the lessee was authorized to employ prisoners lacking mechanical skills and serving relatively short sentences "at any work, public or private, upon railroads, levees, dirt roads, or other works." In 1868, this arrangement was cancelled by the military commander of the Fourth District and the lease given to a rich planter, Edmund Richardson, who, instead of paying for the use of convicts, received $18,000 annually from the state, which also assumed costs of transporting the prisoners to and from Richardson's plantations. "There is little wonder that he came to be known as the greatest cotton planter in the world, with a crop that in one year reached the amazing total of 11,500 bales." Profits persuaded the legislature, in 1872, to establish a system of prison farms operated by the state and ready for occupancy in 1876. In the meantime, the lessee would not be allowed to work the prisoners outside the penitentiary except on public roads, a limitation which was removed in 1876, when a new lease was granted, the farm idea having been scuttled. The new lessee was J.S. Hamilton and Associates, who subleased the prisoners to "planters, speculators, and railroad and levee contractors.... Out over the state, in great rolling cages or temporary stockades, on remote plantations or deep in the swamps of the Delta, the convicts were completely at the mercy of the sub-lessees and their guards." From time to time, the press carried reports of the flagrant abuses to which the convicts were subjected in the camps, but it was difficult

to stir the conscience of a white public that knew that no tax dollars were spent on prisons and that the camps were almost entirely populated by Negroes. "Of the few white men who went to prison at all, a remarkably large percentage... [had] sentences of more than ten years" which had to be served in the penitentiary. In the camps, the few white men were used mostly in clerical jobs or as straw bosses.

Critics of the lease system finally aroused the legislature in 1884. Prodded by a press report that "eighteen convicts, being returned to prison as disabled, proved to be in such a terrible condition from punishment and frost-bite that they had to be smuggled through Vicksburg in a covered wagon," a legislative committee made an inspection of the camps. Its blistering report, partly reproduced in the Raymond *Gazette* of March 8, 1884, stated that the prisoners on

> farms and public works have been subjected to indignities without authority of law and contrary to civilized humanity. Often...sub-lessees resort to "pulling" the prisoner until he faints from the lash on his naked back, while the sufferer was held by four strong men holding each a hand or foot stretched out on the frozen ground or over stumps or logs - often over 300 stripes at a time, which more than once, it is thought, resulted in the death of a convict. Men unable to work have been driven to their death and some have died fettered to the chain gang.... When working in the swamps or fields, they were refused pure water and were driven to drink out of sloughs or plow furrows in the fields in which they labored. One instance of this being on the N.O.N.E.R.R., where owners were unable to get contractors to work at a given point known as Canay Swamps. They hired from sublessees the labor of convicts at $1.75 per head per day. They were placed in the swamp in water ranging to their knees, and in almost nude state they spaded caney and rooty ground, their bare feet chained together by chains that fretted the flesh. They were compelled to attend to the calls of nature in line as they stood day in and day out, their thirst compelling them to drink the water in which they were compelled to deposit their excrement.[31]

Early in 1887, the Gulf and Ship Island Railroad became the sole lessee. Its camps were no better than those of the sublessees. This lease was terminated the following year and, until 1894, the state leased individual convicts to private planters for eight dollars a month for blacks and seven dollars for whites. The death rate of eleven percent in 1888 dropped to three percent in 1889. Mounting public protest finally led the constitutional convention of 1890 to abolish the lease system as of 1894. The legislature was authorized "to establish a prison farm" and also to employ convicts "on levees, roads and other public works under state supervision, but not under private contractors." The reason for this action was well-stated by a legislative committee in 1888. "The leasing system under any form is wrong in principle and vicious. . . . The system of leasing convicts to individuals or corporations to be worked by them for profit simply restores a state of servitude worse than slavery; worse in this that it is without any of the safeguards resulting from the ownership of the slave."[32]

Alabama - from Prison Slave to Involuntary Servitude

Like Mississippi, the Confederate State of Alabama rejoined the Union after approving the Thirteenth Amendment and changing its state contitution to prohibit slavery. Article I, Section 34 of the 1865 Constitution of Alabama gave that state *prison slave* status. Section 34 read:

> That hereafter there shall be in this State neither slavery or involuntary servitude, OTHERWISE THAN FOR THE PUNISHMENT OF CRIME, WHEREOF THE PARTY SHALL HAVE BEEN DULY CONVICTED.

Two years later, in 1867, Alabama wrote a new state constitution which appeared somewhat progressive in its ruling on slavery - all slavery was prohibited and only involuntary servitude was permitted to punish crimes. Section 35 replaced the old Section 34 and read:

> That no form of slavery shall exist in this State, and there shall be no involuntary servitude, OTHERWISE THAN FOR THE PUNISHMENT OF CRIME, OF WHICH THE PARTY SHALL HAVE BEEN DULY CONVICTED.

By replacing prison slavery with involuntary servitude, Alabama became an *involuntary servitude state.* However, Alabama did not differ in its slaveholding practices from *prison slave states.* Ironically, the timing of this "progressive" constitutional change corresponded with its enlarging the scope of its convicts lease system. As Professor Sellin wrote:

> In 1866, the governor of Alabama leased the penitentiary to a contractor who was charged the sum of five dollars and given a sizeable loan. The legislature granted him permission to work the prisoners outside the walls; they were soon found in Ironton and New Castle mines. Appalling treatment and working conditions there and at railroad construction camps were reflected in the mortality rate of the convicts, which rose to 41 per cent in 1869, an all-time high. Envious of the financial profits enjoyed by the lessee, the legislature, in 1874, decided to of-

fer railroads, iron and coal mining corporations, and planters the opportunity to lease convicts for short terms of from one to five years. . . . Entrepreneurs quickly took advantage of the offer and numerous camps were established at various work sites. . . . Most males worked in the mines, while females, children, and infirm males were "leased to lumbering companies, turpentine industries and agricultural operators, whose work was not reckoned to be as 'dangerous' or 'arduous' as that in the mines." The deplorable conditions in some of these camps led the Mobil *Register* of February 15, 1875, to report that the convicts "laboring with manacled limbs in swamps and sleeping in the unwholesome atmosphere. . . died like cattle in slaughter pens."[33]

Alabama's involuntary-servitude-only ruling attempted to mask its harsh implementation of "slavery. . . as a punishment for crime". As demonstrated by the following 1882 report, prison slavery in Alabama met with criticism reminicent of the fervor of antebellum abolitionist:

I found the convicts confined at fourteen different prisons controlled by as many persons or companies and situated at as many different places. . . . [The prisons] were as filthy, as a rule, as dirt could make them, and both prisons and prisoners were infested with vermin. . . . Convicts were excessively and, in some instances, cruelly punished. . . . They were poorly clothed and fed. . . . The sick were neglected, insomuch that no hospital had been provided, they being confined in the cells with well convicts. . . . The prisons have no adequate water supply, and I verily believe there were men in them who had not washed their faces in twelve months. . . . I found the men so much intimidated that it was next to impossible to get from them anything touching their treatment. . . . The system is a disgrace to the State, a reproach to civilization and Christian sentiment of the age, and ought to be speedily abandoned.[34]

The *involuntary servitude state* of Alabama managed to keep the deplorable practice of the convict lease system lawfully employed longer than any other state.

Alabama abolished the lease in 1928, following the exposure of the death of a young white convict named Knox, who was deliberately scalded to death in a laundry vat at the Flat Top mine operated by the Sloss-Sheffield Steel Co. Prior to the scalding he had been brutally whipped with a steel wire the thickness of a man's finger. After his death the warden who witnessed his death had bichloride of mercury pumped into the body to simulate suicide. He was murdered because he could not perform the amount of work required.[35]

While the prison slave state of Mississippi ended its convict lease system in 1894, it took the involuntary servitude state of Alabama another 34 years to abolish its lease system.

Mirrors of Punishment in Spite of Changes in State Constitutions

When the Thirteenth Amendment became law, no state could legally practice slavery except to punish crimes. The Tenth Amendment of the U.S. Constitution specifically granted each state the power to grant more, but not fewer, rights to its respective citizens than the national document granted. States outside the Confederacy had already implemented rulings against slavery before the Civil War but all practiced some form of prison slavery as permitted by the Northwest Territory Ordinance of 1787 and as later stipulated by the Thirteenth Amendment.

While barbaric conditions faced prison slaves throughout the nation, several states were changing their separate state constitutional provisos regarding prison slavery.

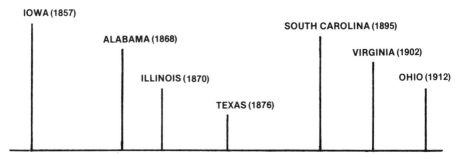

The attitude of all state governments towards the conditions of their prisoners during the decades following the Civil War is illustrated by the following statement of a former Governor of the *no proviso state* of Kentucky:

> Possession of the convict's person is an opportunity for the state to make money. The amount to be made is whatever can be wrung from him, without regard to moral or mortal consequences. The penitentiary which shows the largest cash balance paid into the state treasury is the best penitentiary. In the main the notion is clearly set forth and followed that a convict, whether pilferer or murderer, man, woman or child, has almost no human right that the state is bound to be at any expense to protect.[36]

Illinois: 1870

By prohibiting chattel slavery, Illinois's original state constitution conferred more rights on its residents than existed at the federal level. Nevertheless, slavery and involuntary servitude were permitted as punishments for crime. Article VI, Section I of that state's 1818 Constitution stated:

> Neither slavery nor involuntary servitude shall hereafter be introduced into this State, OTHERWISE THAN FOR THE PUNISHMENT OF CRIMES, WHEREOF THE PARTY SHALL HAVE BEEN DULY CONVICTED.

Illinois was therefore a *prison slave state* until 1870, when, five years after certification of the Thirteenth Amendment, it dispensed with any specific position on slavery, withdrawing Section I of Article VI and becoming a *no proviso state.*

During the intervening years, Illinois had developed its prison system and was contracting the labor of its prisoners to private businesses. In his book *American Prisons,* historian Blake McKelvey noted of this period that Illinois "failed to bring its state prisons within the scope of its board of charities [for inspection and regulation], and its citizens remained ignorant of many evils in these supposedly model institutions."[37] Deleting constitutional reference to prison slavery could only augment public indifference to treatment of prisoners.

Texas: 1876

The 1869 Bill of Rights prohibiting slavery and involuntary servitude, except as a punishment for crime, made Texas a *prison slave state.* Article I, Section 22 of the 1869 document stated:

> Importation of persons under the name of "coolies" or any other name or designation, or the adoption of any system of peonage, whereby the helpless and unfortunate may be reduced to practical bondage, shall never be authorized, or tolerated by the laws of this State; and neither slavery nor involuntary servitude, EXCEPT AS A PUNISHMENT FOR CRIME WHEREOF THE PARTY SHALL HAVE BEEN DULY CONVICTED, shall ever exist within this state.

The complete text of Section 22 was omitted from the Constitution of 1876, thereby changing the constitutional status of Texas from *prison slave* to *no proviso.* While the revised Constitution of Texas made no reference to slavery, that state's treatment of its prisoners celebrated exploitation of the exception to slavery within the Thirteenth Amendment. In 1910, the Prison Reform League condemned Texas prison slave practices citing "the following special dispatch to the *Los Angeles Times* from Galveston, Texas, under the date of November 6, 1900:

> 'The legislative committee's investigation of this state's penal institutions and treatment of convicts on the farms, as well as in the prisons, reveals the fact that more than fifty convicts have been killed by cruelties and whippings within a period of three years or less.

'The record may be much larger, and presumably is, but the board of inquiry finds it almost impossible to wring the evidence from the convicts whom they examine.

'The majority of the convicts who could give positive evidence of specific cases are afraid to tell, because they fear they will incur hatred of the guards at the penitentiaries, and on the convict farms and plantations. As illustrating this point, a long term convict with an excellent prison record, before the committee today admitted he witnessed at least three whippings, the victims of which lived but a few days after the punishment, but he begged piteously not to be forced to give the evidence.

'"I have a long time to serve here, and if I testify I must lead a dog's life, and I know I shall be given the limit."'

'When a guard beats a convict into insensibility the guard's word goes with the superintendent, when the guard merely explains that the convict showed fight or refused to obey orders. The whipping of convicts until their bodies were a mass of bleeding wounds, with leather straps two feet long and three inches wide, numbers more than 400 that the commission has positive evidence of, and the inquiry is not completed.'"[38]

Denials of freedom of speech, imposition of forced labor, and brutal punishment for cooperating with official investigators constitute slavery in its most reprehensible form. While Texas withdrew its specific authorization for prison slavery, the ploy was to defer such authorization back to the Thirteenth Amendment, which sanctions inhuman treatment for prisoners.

Careful examination of the old Section 22 of Texas' 1869 Constitution shows the prohibition of peonage missing in the 1876 Constitution, but, as the following excerpt from an article in the February 13, 1910 edition of the *San Antonio Express* indicates, the practice of peonage continued:

[Young] white men from different parts of the United States were brought to Austin...to give testimony... in regard to the peonage that they have been made to suffer upon a Texas plantation. Most of these witnesses are under 20 years of age. Some of them only 17 years old when they were subjected to the most horrible cruelties...and when they were permitted to leave the place they were physical wrecks. In most instances these boys are of good families and when they fell into the alleged clutches of the agent of the plantation they were guilty of no offense that would mark them as criminals.[39]

Besides the travelers tricked and stolen into bondage, generations of Mexican-Americans were chained to the land by debts owed to the growing ring of farm lords. Texas had good reason to cover over its practices of peonage for the free but poor and slavery for its poor but convicted citizens.

The *no proviso state* of Texas has fully exploited its protected authority to make slaves of convicted citizens. In 1870, there was one prisoner for every 1,519 Texans and by 1900 there was one convict slave for every 702. By 1907, Texas had the largest prison population in the country, and in 1981, its prison population passed the 30,000 mark.[40] The following testimony, taken from a letter written by a Texas prison slave in 1980, shows that the slaveholding policies of Texas prison-keepers have not changed significantly:

> Sprawled serpentinely in the rural Gulf Coastal Plains of eastern Texas, between the Blacklands Belt and the Coastal Prairies, lies the megalithic Texas Department of Corrections (T.D.C.), a neo-slavocracy that adamantly refuses to bridge the psychological chasm separating it from the twentieth century.
>
> Dispersed over eight Texas counties and headquartered in Huntsville, T.D.C. comprises 17 maximum security units, with the Ellis Unit (where so-called "hardened criminals" and prisoners sentenced to die are confined) being the most maximizing secured of the maximum security system.
>
> Each prison stands out like a redoubtable monument in the stark country-side surrounding. The brick and glass structures give testament to modern man's attempt to gain total control of the fabric of other human lives.
>
> Each prison was built to accomodate approximately 1,000 prisoners. But with a prison population of 26,832, the largest in the U.S., T.D.C. is overcrowded....
>
> The prison system embodies the naked power and the most brutal policies of the state, and since Philadelphia opened its Walnut Street Jail in 1790, prison officials have been overzealous in their single objective of reducing men and women to animals. Thus, it is important to be firm believers in the Thirteenth Amendment to the United States Constitution: "Neither slavery nor involuntary servitude, *except as a punishment for crime*...shall exist within the United States". It acts as the "patriotic" lever to poison the atmosphere of reform on the one hand, while numbing the senses to the savagery of prison reality on the other.
>
> In manifold ways T.D.C. has instituted profit making methods for draining human energies with mechanical exactness. It bleeds society in general during its yearly begging ritual before the Texas legislature for the appropriation for more and more funding. T.D.C. had recently added a cost of living demand to offset inflation. On the other hand, T.D.C. does not compensate its prisoners for the labor mandatorily demanded of them....Moreover, from the voluntary participation of its slaves in the annual (five Sundays) October prison rodeo, T.D.C. realizes in excess of $500,000 per year on the well-publicized pretension that rodeo profits are spent on "prisoner rehabilitation."

On a larger and far more profitable scale, T.D.C. has gained a monopolistic hold, nationally, over diverse penal industries by drastically underbidding other state institutions and filing more and more lucrative contracts in its bulging portfolio - a prime example of the fundamental benefit of having a free labor pool readily accessible....

T.D.C. has long been hailed as the "model" institution every prison administration would aspire to head. T.D.C. is emerging yearly as one of the most profitable enterprises (on a small scale, of course) under capitalistic relations, and its books are free of state audits.

And a contract with T.D.C. is more appealing because its docile, but productive labor force is guaranteed and work stoppages are practically nonexistent.... Moreover, T.D.C. has officially instituted the [most] elaborate warning snitch system in the nation, and its inmate collaborators are not only condoned as an "unofficial" guard system, but they are fully sanctioned, protected, and roam unrestrainedly within the prison of their assignment. The inmate collaborators, infamously known as "building tenders," are relegated to a privileged class higher than the slaves they lord it over.

But the calm of T.D.C. is misleading, and stability under fascist relations is a surface phenomenon at best. T.D.C. is headed for a social meltdown because, basically, its authoritarian repressiveness is the profound negation of human rights; and the myriad contractions it spawns manifest in the authoritarian concavity of its odiously primordial repressivism.

When will we regain our humanity?

South Carolina: 1895

Of particular interest in the postbellum period of state constitutional changes is the former Confederate State of South Carolina. In 1895, South Carolina followed Texas in withdrawing its ruling on prison slavery and also becoming a *no proviso state.*

South Carolina's 1869 state constitution attempted to cover over prison slave practices by prohibiting all slavery and only permitting involuntary servitude to punish crimes. That state's earlier *involuntary servitude state* status was conferred by Article I, Section 2 of its Constitution of 1869. Section 2 stated:

Slavery shall never exist in this State; neither shall involuntary servitude, EXCEPT AS A PUNISHMENT FOR CRIME.

Until 1866, there was no state penitentiary in South Carolina and punishment rested with the counties.[41] The eventual building of its first prison relied on the rationale used in the rest of the reconstructed South.

> According to one state official, the reason for establishing it was that "after the emancipation of the colored people, whose idea of freedom from bondage was freedom from work and license to pillage, we had to establish means for their control. Hence came the penitentiary."[42]

Due to overcrowding and political efforts to turn punishment into a lucrative state venture, the *involuntary servitude state* of South Carolina enforced its constitutional proviso through the convict lease system.

> A few prisoners were leased as early as 1873, but in 1877 the legislature authorized large-scale leasing. One hundred convicts were handed over to the Concord and Augusta Railroad. "By 1878 South Carolina had 221 prisoners working on railroads, in phosphate mines, and on private plantations. In two years' time, 153 prisoners had died - the death rate on the Greenwood and Augusta being 52.52 percent - 82 had escaped, and many of those returned to state custody were so disabled that they could not walk. An investigation showed the prisoners to be suffering from malnutrition, vermin, and beatings, and from living in indescribable filth.[43]

The leasing system in South Carolina ended in 1885.[44] Ten years later, in 1895, the text of Article I, Section 2 was removed from the state constitution. The new document made no mention of slavery or involuntary servitude and South Carolina's status changed from an *involuntary servitude state* into a *no proviso state*. Perhaps, with abolition of the convict lease system, the state government no longer felt the need to justify slavery under the lease system by calling it another name. In constitutional terms, South Carolina abandoned a brutal definition of punishment by calling it involuntary servitude and then returned in 1895 to an accurate definition of its slave punishments by deferring state authority to the federal Thirteenth Amendment.

Virginia, 31 Years After the Case of Woody Ruffin

Virginia, the state which housed the capitol of the Confederacy, abolished chattel slavery in Article I, Section 19 of its 1870 constitution. Section 19 stated:

> That neither slavery nor involuntary servitude, EXCEPT AS LAWFUL IMPRISONMENT MAY CONSTITUTE SUCH, shall exist in this State.

In 1902, Section 19 was omitted from the state constitution and slavery and involuntary servitude were not mentioned, thus transforming the constitutional status of Virginia from *prison slave* to *no proviso.*

When, in 1900, the United States Industrial Commission strongly endorsed abandonment of leasing or contracting prison labor, the State of Virginia was not ready to let go its arrangements with private businesses using convict labor.[45] Virginia's constitutional change to a *no proviso state* may have reflected a hopeful attempt to maintain anonymity to avoid criticism. Virginia's position on prison slavery was made unmistakably clear, however, in the precedent-shaping 1871 decision in the case of *Ruffin v. the Commonwealth.*

During the period of the convict lease system, prison slaves were leased to railroad companies in Virginia, including one Woody Ruffin. Ruffin was leased to the Chesapeake and Ohio Railroad in Bath County, Virginia, but attempted to escape, allegedly killing a company guard. "For this offence he was tried in the Circuit court of the city of Richmond, by a jury selected from a *venire* of said city, and was found guilty of murder in the first degree, and was sentenced by said court to be hung on the 25th day of May 1871."[46]

Ruffin's attorney appealed the decision of the case to a higher court, arguing that the recently incorporated Bill of Rights in Virginia declared, "among other declarations of personal and political rights, 'that in all capital or criminal prosecutions, a man hath a right to a speedy trial by an impartial jury of *his vicinage,* without whose unanimous consent he cannot be found guilty.'"[47] In a sweeping decision, the court gave no credit to Ruffin's claim of having his right to due process violated and declared that

[1] For the time, during his term of service in the penitentiary, he is in a state of penal servitude to the State. He has, as a consequence of his crime, not only forfeited his liberty, but all his personal rights except those which the law in its humanity accords to him. He is for the time being a slave of the State. He is *civiliter mortus;* and his estate, if he has any, is administered like that of a dead man.

[2] *The bill of rights is a declaration of general principles to govern a society of freemen, and not of convicted felons and men civilly dead.* Such men have some rights...but not the rights of freemen. They are the *slaves of the state* undergoing punishment for... crimes committed against the laws of the land. While in this state of penal servitude, they must be subject to the regulations of the institutions of which they are inmates, and the laws of the State whom their service is due in expiation of their crimes. [Emphasis added.][48]

The Virginia Court of Appeals decision in *Ruffin v. The Commonwealth* transformed prison slavery from the *spirit* of U.S. Constitutional law into literal practice as it confirmed slavery as a legal punishment for crime.

And Into the 20th Century

In the first half of this century, very little changed in the reading of state constitutions regarding slavery. Three states changed their status as already mentioned: Virginia took out its proviso for slavery in 1902 and joined the ranks of *no proviso* states; Ohio joined the ranks of the *involuntary servitude* states in 1912; and Missouri, formerly a *prison slave* state, withdrew its provision for slavery and had *no proviso* to replace the authority of the Thirteenth Amendment.

Ohio, in the seemingly most significant state constitutional change of this period, altered its constitution to authorize involuntary servitude only:

> There shall be no slavery in this state; nor involuntary servitude, UNLESS FOR THE PUNISHMENT OF CRIME.

Ohio changed its label for punishment in 1912 but the brutality which stems from institutionalized slavery continued in that *involuntary servitude state.*

> Dear CAPS,
> I am writing to ask you to please consider investigating guard brutality and racist practices at [this prison].
> I have personally seen guards beat a man who was already handcuffed and in what represents a continuing practice of brutality, guards savagely beat and injured inmates on [date withheld]. Prisoners Doe, Smith and Jones [names changed] were all beaten so badly that they had to be examined by outside physicians. Doe and Smith were rushed to the hospital on the outside. One man is reported to have sustained a broken neck...The beatings were administered after the men had been escorted to "the hole" area and after they were already in restraint. There is no excuse for the criminal conduct of those who are paid to represent the State of Ohio as caretakers of prisoners. Must the prisoner suffer murder and violence in cruel and unusual punishment? Each fruit bears its own kind and so does brutality.
> President Carter has spoken out on Human Rights abroad but what about having it right here in Ohio. The prisoners here suffer inhumane treatment by a staff of all white guards who are both unprofessional and reactionary, in my opinion. Use of Force Reports are security matters not to be reviewed by the public or even outside departmental officials. Even the Ohio Legislative Institutional Inspections Committee cannot gain ready access to the Use of Force Reports and investigate the severity of them without department of corrections road-blocks.
> And double celling (forced) is still being used as a daily practice despite a two year old federal court decision holding the practice unconstitutional, but this double celling based

on race continues while the public is barred from examining the goings on inside its prisons though they must pay the taxes to fund them. Your attention would be a god-send.

Prisoner in Ohio

Regardless of state constitutional provisos and changes in those provisos, every state in this country practiced - and still practices - "slavery...as a punishment for crime."

Notes

1. Lerner, p. 305.

2. W.E.B. DuBois, intro. by Herbert Aptheker, *The Souls of Black Folk* (Millwood, N.Y.: Kraus-Thomson Organization Limited, 1973; reprint A.C. McClurg & Co., 1953), p. 111; see also Kluger, p. 51.

3. Carl Schurz, *Charles Sumner* (Urbana: The University of Illinois Press, 1951), p. 48.

4. *Congressional Globe,* 38th Congress, 1st Session, vol. 1, p. 8.

5. Ibid., p. 197.

6. Ibid., p. 521.

7. Ames, pp. 214-215.

8. *Congressional Globe,* vol. 2, p. 1313.

9. Ibid., p. 1461, Henderson concludes a long argument in the slavery debates with:
> There are but two sides to the question. The one is Union without slavery; and another is the immediate and unconditional acknowledgment of the southern confederacy.... For the expression of this sentiment I may be called a fanatic.... It results not from any sudden abhorrence of slavery, for I have been in its midst all my life. It does not spring from hatred of slaveholders, for, whether in honor or shame, I am a slaveholder to-day.

10. Ibid., vol. 1, p. 553.

11. Ames, pp. 215-216.

12. *Congressional Globe,* vol. 2, p. 1482.

13. Ibid.

14. Ibid., p. 1483.

15. Ibid., pp. 1487-1488.

16. Ibid., p. 1488.

17. Ibid.

18. Ibid.

19. Ibid.

20. Ibid.

21. Kluger, p. 51.

22. Ibid., pp. 45-46.

23. DuBois, *Black Reconstruction,* p. 167.

24. Vernon Lane Wharton, *The Negro in Mississippi, 1865-1890,* (Chapel Hill: University of North Carolina Press, 1947), p. 237; see also Sellin, p. 147n.

25. Sellin, p. 151.

26. DuBois, *Black Reconstruction,* p. 131.

27. See Sellin, pp. 145-146.

28. Ibid., p. 162.

29. Ibid., p. 134.

30. Franklin B. Hough, *American Constitutions: Comprising the Constitution of Each State in the Union, and of the United States...,* vol. 1 (Albany, N.Y.: Weed, Parsons & Company, 1872), p. 743.

31. Sellin, pp. 147-148.

32. Ibid., p. 149.

33. Ibid., pp. 150-151.

34. John W. Bankhead, shortly after he became the Alabama state prison warden, as quoted by George W. Cable, "The Convict Lease System in the Southern States," *The Silent South* (Montclair, N.J.: Patterson Smith Publishing Corporation, 1969; reprint ed. 1889, Charles Scribner's Sons), p. 168; see also Sellin, pp. 151-152.

35. Walter Wilson, *Forced Labor in the United States* (New York: International Publishers, 1933), p. 41.

36. Prison Reform League, *Crime and Criminals* (Los Angeles: Prison Reform League Publishing Company, 1910), pp. 128-129.

37. McKelvey, p. 97.

38. Prison Reform League, pp. 48-50.

39. Clarissa Olds Keebler, *American Bastilles* (Washington, D.C.: Carnahan Press, 1910), p. 26.

40. Clarissa Olds Keebler, *The Crime of Crimes or the Convict Lease System Unmasked* (Washington, D.C.: Pentecostal Era Company, 1907), pp. 22-23; U.S. Department of Justice, *Bureau of Justice Statistics Bulletin,* Prisoners at Midyear 1981 (September 1981), p. 2.

41. Sellin, p. 258; McKelvey, p. 204.

42. Sellin, p. 158.

43. John Samuel Ezell, *The South Since 1865* (New York: Macmillan Company, 1963) p. 367; see also Sellin, p. 158.

44. Sellin, p. 158.

45. McKelvey, pp. 205-206, 249-250.

46. *Ruffin v. the Commonwealth,* 62 Va., 792.

47. Ibid.

48. Ibid., p. 796.

Chapter 6:
Twentieth Century Justice

I know from actual experience what the auction block means....I know from actual experience that the only difference between Cassie [of *Uncle Tom's Cabin*] and me was that Cassie was sold to the highest bidder and I was sold to the lowest.

- Kate Richards O'Hare[1]

Before the Civil War, blacks were rarely imprisoned in the Southern slavocracy because jailing bondservants deprived the master of profits from the labor of their chained human property. Northern cages, already sites for exploitation of labor by private businessmen through the contract labor system, were teaching poor and rebellious workers the submission that competing capitalists demanded. Following certification of the Thirteenth Amendment, this state-administered slavery, developed in the North to punish poor white convicts, was almost exclusively applied against emancipated freedmen in the South. Now lower-class citizens of every color filled slave vaults of punishment while laws continued to incriminate the poor and veil their exploitation by the wealthy.

The Great Abandonment

The United States government made great strides by prohibiting chattel slavery in the Thirteenth Amendment; guaranteeing due process and equal protection to all citizens by the Fourteenth Amendment in 1866 and mandating that no one be denied the right to vote because of race, color or previous condition of servitude by the Fifteenth Amendment of 1869. The Constitution also gave Congress power to enforce these new amendments "by appropriate legislation."[2] From that authority came the Civil Rights Act of 1875, asserting the right of all people, regardless of color, to "the full and equal enjoyment of accomodations...of inns, public conveyances on land or water, theaters and other places of amusement...." When, however, Senator Charles Sumner tried to amend the bill to desegregate schools, Congress refused.[3] The reluctance of government to enforce constitutional rights for ex-slaves was foreshadowed in 1870 when the Freedmen's Bureau was shut down.

It was the most extraordinary governmental effort at mass uplift in the nation's history; not until the New Deal would its like be tried. Yet only a little more than $5 million - $1.25 per capita - was spent to compensate for 200 years of ignorance enforced on a whole transplanted people. It was a pitiful amount for a cause of such urgency and magnitude. True, the Freedmen's Bureau schools [4,000 throughout the South, with an attendance of nearly 250,000] had inspired the Reconstitution legislatures of the South to provide for public education programs, but there would be little local or state money to pay for them for decades, and white property owners, hard pressed to hold on, were disinclined in the extreme to be taxed in behalf of their late bondsmen, whose need for learning they found dubious in the first place.[4]

The planter rallied; former slavemasters became new entrepreneurs in the "free market" by renting slave labor from crowded prisons. Many emancipated slaves who avoided falling into imprisonment were bound in some other form of servitude. Some became sharecroppers chained to the land through deepening debts owed the landlords' stores, with their deliberately inflated prices.

Previously unable to compete with the wageless labor of chattel slavery, poor whites could not compete any more successfully with the reinforced servitude of "emancipated" slaves and were now more destitute than before the war. Although exploitation of black workers contributed again in the powerlessness of white workers, many lower-class Southerners still failed to recognize that their best interests lay in complete equality for their black brethren. Racism continued to serve masters well, preventing poor whites from recognizing the true roots of their impoverishment. As they had for more than two centuries before, many southern whites idealized the planter, identifying him as their mentor. W.E.B. DuBois explained:

> It seemed after the war immaterial to the poor white that the profit from the exploitation of black labor continued to go to the planter. He regarded the process as the exploitation of black folk by white, not of labor by capital. When, then, he faced the possibility of being himself compelled to compete with a Negro wage worker, while both were the hirelings of a white planter, his whole soul revolted. He turned, therefore, from war service to guerrilla warfare, particularly against Negroes. He joined eagerly secret organizations, like the Ku Klux Klan, which fed his vanity by making him co-worker with the white planter, and gave him a chance to maintain his race superiority by killing and intimidating "niggers"; and even in secret forays of his own, he could drive away the planter's black help, leaving the land open to white labor. Or he could murder too successful freedmen.
>
> It was only when they saw the Negro with a vote in his hand, backed by the power and money of the nation, that the poor whites who followed some of the planters into the ranks of the "scalawags" began to conceive of an economic solidarity between white and black workers.... But before all this was so established as to be intelligently recognized, arm-

ed revolt in the South became organized by the planters with
the cooperation of the mass of poor whites. Taking advantage of an industrial crisis which throttled both democracy
and industry in the North, this combination drove the Negro
back toward slavery. Finally the poor whites joined the sons
of the planters and disenfranchised the black laborer, thus
nullifing the labor movement in the South for a half century
and more.[5]

The industrial crisis which DuBois spoke of was the depression of
1873-76. The decade preceding the industrial crash was prosperous
for the capitalist; fortunes were made in oil, copper, timber, beef, gold
and silver and the railroad stretched from coast to coast.

[At] the same time millions lived in abject poverty in densely
packed slums.... They struggled merely to maintain their
families above the level of brutal hunger and want...the
great majority [working] such long hours for such little pay
that their status was a tragic anomaly in the light of the prosperity generally enjoyed by business and industry.[6]

Money for the farmer and the worker was scarce. Union leader William
Sylvis appealed to the need for unity among all workers. Labor needed
the black worker, he said:

The line of demarcation is between the robbers and the robbed, no matter whether the wronged be the friendless widow,
the skilled white mechanic or the ignorant black. Capital is
not the respector of persons and it is in the very nature of
things a sheer impossibility to degrade one class of labor
without degrading all.[7]

Through Sylvis's leadership the National Labor Union was formed and
women and blacks were admitted as delegates on a strong platform of
unity for workers. The demise of the N.L.U. came after six short years
and Sylvis's untimely death at age 41. While wages continued to fall to
a dollar a day, the union's leadership turned to influencing the government to print more currency rather than working for better wages and
benefits for workers.[8]

By 1877, there were three million unemployed workers and only
eight or nine trade unions remaining. Union members were blacklisted, charged with conspiracy and locked out of work. As blacklisted
workers roamed from city to city and state to state in search of work,
men like Andrew Carnegie reaped gold from the suffering nation. "The
man who has money during a panic," said Carnegie, "is a wise and
valuable citizen." J.D. Rockefeller, Henry Frick and Andrew Mellon
were among those "wise and valuable" citizens gobbling up their
competitiors to secure the growth of their own burgeoning monopolies.[9]

Workers gathered to demand their just due in demonstrations in Chicago, New York and other great cities, only to meet the flying clubs of armed police.[10] The growing voice of angry workers began to worry industrialists, and, as historians Richard Boyer and Herbert Morais reported, "individuals working within the Republican Party began preparing for a new offensive against the trade union movement."

> [The Republicans'] first move was to gain a new ally for themselves while denying it to labor. They lived in fear that labor, making a common cause with restive farmers, would resurrect the Democratic Party and, in alliance with the South's planters, turn all Republicans out and, worse still, reverse their profit-breeding policies. To avert this they decided to make the Southern planters, stalwarts of the Democratic Party, their allies instead of their opponents. Since 1867 they had given support, however vacillating, to the Negro people in their fight against reenslavement.... They had backed, in short, a revolutionary upsurge in the South that had scored great democratic gains but now, pressed by the new threats of the depression, they were in a mood to make allies of their old opponents to prevent the formation of a new and radical Democratic Party. This they were soon to do in a fundamental realignment of political forces that increased the dangers facing labor.
>
> The army that had garrisoned the South was soon to be withdrawn and thrown against Northern workers on strike against depression wage cuts. The Negroes in the meantime were left to the mercies of their ex-masters. Under the new alliance the Democratic Party in the South became to a large extent an appendage of the Republican Party in the North, at least economically, its platforms usually as conservative and as lacking in menace to the wealthy as those of the Republicans themselves.[11]

Abandoning the cause of freedom in the South took four or five years, climaxing in the Presidential election of 1877. Twenty electoral votes stood between Republican candidate Rutherford B. Hayes and the Presidency. The formal agreement which gave Hayes the White House let conservative southern Democrats do as they wished to blacks in return for support of Hayes and a pledge to aid Northern big businessmen suppress rebellious farmers and workers:

> The Republicans had abandoned the Negroes in the South the better to deal with rising protest in the North - as they did so they took effective action to prevent the Democratic Party from developing into a farmer-labor vehicle of protest. Thus it was that Negroes were being murdered in Columbia and Spartanburg, S.C.; in Livingston, Ala., and Greggs County, Tex., as troops were being called out against Massachusetts textile workers and Pennsylvania miners fighting through the country's severest depression.[12]

Disfranchisement, Murder, and Peonage

The Fourteenth and Fifteenth Amendments now had little practical value based on their original purpose to guarantee due process and black suffrage. At the turn of the century, eight southern states passed poll tax laws depriving nearly 10 million people of their right to vote "either because of their color or because they were too poor to pay for the privilege."[13]

"Due process" is a hollow term to describe the court procedures which sentenced thousands each year into prison-administered slavery. For decades, it would not be uncommon to report a southern court's sentencing a starving worker convicted of stealing a ham to twenty years' hard labor. Racist atrocities grew out of the ignorance and fears of impotent people seeking power in crucifying others even more powerless. The National Association for the Advancement of Colored People (N.A.A.C.P.) in 1911 reported a typically grotesque mob murder:

> *Whereas* the Press Dispatches show that one M. Potter, a colored man, charged with killing a white man, was taken from the jail at Livermore, Ky., last week, and taken to the town Opera House, and tied on the stage, and that an admission fee was charged to witness the lynching, the prices ranging from those usually charged for orchestra and gallery seats, and that a feature of the lynching was that the audience was allowed to shoot at the suspended body of the victim, and, as in the words of the Press reports, "Those who bought orchestra seats had the privilege of emptying their six shooters at the swaying form above them, but the gallery occupants were limited to one shot. . . ."[14]

A decade later, it was reported that of the 2,522 lynchings of black men over a thirty-year period studied by the newly formed American Civil Liberties Union, less than 19 percent of the victims had been even *charged* with a crime.[15]

In New York City during the summer of 1917, a silent march of thousands of Afro-Americans protested these mass killings and demanded justice. The following statement made by the Parade Committee and distributed in leaflet form throughout the city explained that

> We march because we want to make impossible repetition of [the lynchings in] Waco, Memphis, East St. Louis, by rousing the conscience of the country and to bring the murderers of our brothers, sisters and innocent children to justice.[16]

Georgia-born black minister Richard R. Wright, Jr., told the National Conference on Social Work in June of 1919 that local governments could not be expected to protect blacks against mob violence when black citizens were robbed of the power to vote their allies back into office. He said:

There have been over 3,500 [lynchings] in our country; many of them have been for causes more or less trivial; such as "talking back to a white person," disputing about money, theft, resisting arrest, etc., for which the offender would have received a light sentence if convicted in a court by trial. But a democracy which disfranchises a part of its citizens may expect lynching. Sheriffs are slow to protect those who do not vote for them.[17]

The government officially disapproved of these mob murders but did little to stop them. When government fosters attitudes and policies that encourage oppression of a minority, resulting exploitation of that part of the labor force helps keep all workers at odds with one another, reducing their effectiveness by undermining their unity.

Fostering racist divisiveness made it simple to depress wages. Several decades passed before southern workers crossed racial boundaries to organize effectively for their mutual benefit. Meanwhile, vagrancy laws not only kept government cages filled but also helped provide free laborers through peonage, a form of debt slavery which had been outlawed by an 1867 federal law. In spite of the Supreme Court upholding the constitutionality of that law in 1911, peonage continued for another 30 years.[18] During the early 1900's, W.E.B. DuBois's newsletter, *The Crisis,* was the voice of the young N.A.A.C.P., an organization which has served throughout this century as an effective agent in the protracted struggle for equal rights for blacks. In 1911, *The Crisis* printed a revealing letter about peonage in the South:

I am not an educated man. I will give you the peonage system as it is practised here in the name of the law. . . .

I am brought in a prisoner, go through the farce of being tried. The whole of my fine may amount to fifty dollars. A kindly appearing man will come up and pay my fine and take me to his farm to allow me to work it out. At the end of a month I find that I owe him more than I did when I went there. The debt is increased year in and year out. You would ask, "How is that?" It is simply that he is charging you more for your board, lodging, and washing than they allow you for your work, and you can't help yourself either, nor can anyone else help you, because you are still a prisoner and never get your fine worked out. If you do as they say and be a good Negro, you are allowed to marry, provided you can get someone to have you, and of course the debt still increases. This is in the United States, where it is supposed that every man has equal rights before the law, and we are held in bondage by this same outfit.

Of course we can't prove anything. Our word is nothing. If we state things as they are, the powers that be make a different statement, and that sets ours aside at Washington and, I suppose, in Heaven, too. . . .

What I have told you is strictly confidential. If you publish it, don't put my name to it. I would be dead in a short time after the news reached here.

> One more word about peonage. The court and the man you work for are always partners. One makes the fine and the other one works you and holds you, and if you leave you are tracked up with bloodhounds and brought back.[19]

In 1907, another newspaper reported on debt slavery in Florida:

> Northern capitalists come South to develop the resources of the country... It is a part of the commercialism of the country, and is a convenient method utilized by capitalists in exploiting labor.
> More than three-fourths of the lumber and turpentine operators in the state are Northern men. Most of the camp foremen are Northern men.... In the rush for the almighty dollar all distinctions of creed and color are obliterated.[20]

Eighty-three peonage complaints were pending at the U.S. Justice Department in 1907; in 1908, an investigating committee reported finding a "complete system of peonage in the logging and lumbering industries of Maine"; and a few years later, the Immigration Commission reported that immigrants were in debt slavery throughout the South. Forced labor for unpaid debts turned up at the camps of free labor participating in the building of Attica prison. Even the government was indicted for the practice in December 1931, when it was discovered that the War Department was using forced labor for levee work along the Mississippi River. Throughout the West, Mexicans were in debt slavery on ranches, road construction sites, irrigation jobs and in the salmon canning industries of the Pacific Northwest. At a Congressional Committee hearing, the general solicitor of the Santa Fe Railroad, E.E. McKinnis, admitted hiring over 75 percent of their workers through a California agency supplying free Mexican laborers. The agency furnished the work site commissary where the Mexicans had to buy their supplies at inflated prices from the employment agency to whom they were already in debt.[21]

Tenant farmers often organized to demand fair labor practices. As in earlier labor struggles in this country, it was a slow uphill battle and the courts afforded them little protection. In 1919, a tenants' farm union in Phillipes County, Arkansas, determined to end peonage, was attacked by an armed band of planters and businessmen. The battle resulted in two hundred dead and hundreds of tenant farmers arrested on murder charges. After a 45 minute trial, 67 farmers were sentenced to death. In 1931, a similar attack was made on Alabama tenant union members and resulted in the arrest of 35 sharecroppers.[22]

Exploitation and Rebellion

It took 50 years for workers in the South to begin organizing effectively against exploitation. Northward in industrialized states, organized workers were also victims of unequal protection before the law. Like slavery abolitionists before them, labor leaders were called communists by their powerful opponents. This charge, aimed at arousing public patriotism, was proliferated by large newspapers owned by rich businessmen having big profits at heart.

As Republicans sold out Reconstruction, the Pinkerton Detective Agency began a lucrative business serving the best interests of corporate clients. Its founder, Allen Pinkerton, had such a flourishing business that he was able to devote much of his time to a writing career:

> My extensive and perfected detective system has made this
> work easy for me where it would have been hardly possible for
> other writers; for since the strikes of '77, my agencies have
> been busily employed by a great railway, manufacturing and
> other corporations, for the purpose of bringing the leaders
> and instigators [of strikes] to the punishment they so richly
> deserve. Hundreds have been punished. Hundreds more will
> be punished.[23]

Coal and railroad boss Franklin B. Gowen orchestrated one of the earliest post-war attacks on labor unions, paying Pinkerton a $100,000 retainer in 1873 to spy on coal miner organizers. The Irish Americans proved a particular source of inconvenience for Gowen after 179 of their number died in an 1869 mining accident caused by unsafe working conditions. In 1870, the miners forced Gowen to sign a union contract, much to the vociferous dismay of his stockholders. The Pinkerton spy failed to turn up any incriminating evidence against the strikers and Gowen initiated a new campaign against the miners, spreading the story that their leaders belonged to a communist band from Ireland called the "Molly Maguires." These "Molly Maguires" were nothing but the product of the financier's gifted imagination.[24]

After six years of unrelenting war on the miners, Gowen proved his conviction that "it was sufficient to hang a man to declare him a Molly Maguire." In 1875, the miners went on strike to protest the company's 25 percent cut in their wages. Gowen's campaign of lies alleging arson and murder by the "Molly Maguires" brought public opinion to his side. After six weeks of starvation, miners were forced back to work at a 20 percent wage cut and two of their leaders went to prison for conspiracy to raise prices of vendible comodities in Pennsylvania. His final revenge came a year later, when he had the Pinkerton spy testify in court that union leaders committed several murders. In spite of testimony conflicting with that of Gowen's witnesses, 19 union members were convicted of murder and executed.[25]

While the government sent no troops to protect innocent citizens from mob lynchings, it did not hesitate to send soldiers to shield businessmen from the demands of organized labor. After World War I, the National Association of Manufacturers began a red-bating campaign aimed at convincing the public that labor was Bolshevik, although only one tenth of one percent of all Americans were Communists. In 1919, steel workers went on strike in 50 cities for higher wages and better working conditions. The U.S. Army, detectives, police, the newly formed American Legion and the U.S. Department of Justice moved to stop them. Many workers were killed, hundreds seriously wounded, beaten and several thousand jailed. Newspapers were filled with reports on Moscow and on America's nationwide search for Communists.[26] As Boyer and Morais's *Labor's Untold Story* reports:

> On the night of Jan. 2, 1920, 10,000 American workers, both aliens and citizens, most of them trade union members and many of them union officials, were hauled from their beds, dragged out of meetings, grabbed on the streets and from their homes, and thrown into prison by the federal police under the direction of Attorney General Palmer and his aid, J. Edgar Hoover. . . . In Boston 400 workers were led through the streets, manacled and handcuffed, clanking with chains. . . .
>
> Almost everywhere prisoners were manhandled and beaten while in Philadelphia, where 200 were arrested, the third degree was used on almost all. In Hartford, Conn., scores of workers were tortured by fierce, unbearable heat in "punishment rooms" while at least one victim had a rope placed around his neck by Justice Department men who said they would hang him if he did not give them the names of other workers.
>
> In Detroit the raid "marked a peak in brutality." Eight hundred men were packed in a narrow windowless corridor on the top floor of the Federal building. They remained there, many ill and without food, for six full days until Mayor James Couzens said the conditions under which they were being tortured were "intolerable in a civilized city." Then they were moved to a deserted army encampment at Fort Wayne where new methods of torture were devised. The wives and children of those imprisoned there were beaten in the sight of the prisoners.[27]

South, west, east and north, the struggle continued, but the choice to resist or not resist oppression presents grim alternatives for poor and working people. Sharecroppers, labor organizers and minority Americans demanding equality have always risked punishment. Victories, bitterly won, take decades, while political prisoners face special punishment for conviction of the most minor offenses. In the early thirties, a newspaper reporter visiting the Allegheny County Workhouse at Blawnox, Pennsylvania, wrote:

> In the workhouse there are many men sentenced to as high as five years, particularly in the case of class-conscious workers. Ordinarily persons sentenced to two to five years are sent to the Western Penitentiary in Pittsburgh. However, this is considered too easy punishment for striking miners and

they are sent to the workhouse where conditions are much harder and the food much worse.[28]

The vast majority of prisoners have been ordinary people whose primary conscious struggle was day-to-day survival without benefit of sufficient food, shelter, employment, education or opportunities. They, in less careful or thoughful ways, have also rebelled. By reenforcing powerlessness, prison slavery had played an important role in maintaining inequality. Penal philosophy remains as rooted in slave punishments as this previously cited statement implies:

> . . .the necessary condition for the prisoners' reentry into society is unconditional submission to authority, a conclusion which has remained unshaken by reform programs and tendencies up to the present. . . . Obedience is demanded not so much for the smooth functioning of the prison but for the sake of the convict himself, who shall learn to submit willingly to the fate of the lower classes. That is a difficult task.[29]

It remains a difficult task today. The history of slavery includes a history of rebellion in which untold numbers have died. Few slave rebellions have been won without the committed participation of free citizens, but, throughout history, slaves have voluntarily fought for emancipation. In 1933, Walter Wilson wrote:

> Leased or bound-out prisoners were in most of the revolts of indentured servants, convicts and slaves before the Revolutionary War. Since then they have engaged in many fights. In the period from 1881 to 1900, for example, there are 22 recorded strikes against convict labor in coal mines. Most of them have been forgotten as very few records were kept, or because the whole matter was hushed up by the ruling class at the time it occurred.
>
> Perhaps the most significant of all such revolts was the Coal Creek Rebellion of 1891-92 in the coal mines of East Tennessee. Following a combination lock-out and strike, convict strike-breakers were brought in by the Tennessee Coal, Iron & Railroad Co. (now a subsidiary of the United States Steel Corp.), which leased an average of 1,500 to 1,600 convicts from the State of Tennessee. The company paid to the state an average of $42 a year for the use of an able-bodied worker. Naturally with such cheap labor power huge profits were piled up. It may be said that this company was built upon the trade and exploitation of convict slaves.
>
> The president of the corporation at that time was Thomas C. Platt, Republican boss of New York in the 1890's. Members of the New York Legislature and other northern capitalists owned stock in the company. However, the convicts were bound out to Mr. Platt, the Republican, by the southern Democrat legislature and governor of Tennessee.
>
> The miners, Negro and white, aided by the farmers of East

Tennessee, drove out the guards, burned the prison stockades throughout East Tennessee and released the convicts who escaped to the hills. Governor Buchanan sent in the militia to subdue the workers. After a pitched battle the entire force of soldiers was captured and driven out after being disarmed and after promising never to return to the mining section. The struggle had begun in earnest. It lasted from July 14, 1891 (Bastille Day), to November, 1892, with a few skirmishes [occurring] as late as 1893. . . .

Negroes and whites, men who fought for the North and men who fought for the South in the Civil War, farmers and miners, convicts and "free" men, stuck together in the face of the entire armed forces of Tennessee. Approximately 10,000 soldiers and members of businessmen's posses were used to crush the revolt. Workers and convicts stormed the forts and cannons and died together. But they died with the knowledge that they had killed a great many more of the common enemy than the enemy had killed of them. Over 500 miners were arrested after the workers had been disarmed.

Before the lease system was adopted in Tennessee in 1889, convicts were worked under contract to private contractors at Nashville. But after the convicts burned the prison on several occasions and with it all the manufactured goods in the place, the employers repudiated their contracts. It was then that the convicts were leased to the coal mines.[30]

Shared Ownership of the Convict Is Attacked

Although the Thirteenth Amendment was supposed to abolish slavery, it merely transferred ownership of the slave to the State. *Ruffin v. the Commonwealth* confirmed this interpretation of the law in 1871, when the Court of Appeals of Virginia dignified the practice of stripping a human being of all rights following conviction of a crime. "He is," the court said, "a slave of the State."[31]

North and South, businessmen shared in profits from prison slavery. The convict lease system put freedmen back on plantations and in the mines and swamps of the South; while in the North, contractors came into the prison to oversee and profit from convict labor. Because southern industries lagged far behind those in northern states, southern convict slaves produced raw products to sell to northern industries. Northern prisoners did more industrial work.

By the turn of the century, the convict-lease and contract labor systems were being widely criticized for their brutality and exploitation. The following, written by a newspaper reporter in 1908, reinforced growing public outrage:

To see slavery with all its revolting cruelties, it is necessary only to visit one of the convict-operating coal mines. The

Pratt City mine, near this city [Birmingham, Alabama], is one of these.

It was with an air of pride they showed me through. . . . I saw men, their quarters, what they ate, where they worked and slept; the four-foot leather trace-strap with which they were whipped when their armed, keen-eyed taskmasters said they shirked; the rifle-carrying, square-jawed guards with their packs of bloodhounds kept always ready to track men down - I saw it all. . . .

That leather bludgeon keeps coming to my mind. Each man is assigned his daily task; and if he fails he is strung up and whipped. . . .

There were at the Pratt City mines about 1,000 men. About half were convicts of the state - long term men; the others were the county's men, sent here for misdemeanors. The latter class are leased to private mining companies at an average of $18 per head a month. . . .

Probably the worse feature of convict labor is its continued competition with free labor.[32]

The economic consequences of convict slavery affected the free market, resulting in echos of antebellum complaints about the unfair competition of chattel slave products from the South. The focus of organized labor's complaint, as well as the complaints of some businesses, was the shared ownership of convict labor by businessmen. Ever since the beginnings of the Auburn plan, organized labor had been protesting the sale of prison-made products on the free market. By denying the protections of labor and citizenship rights, slavery creates misery for both bonded and free workers by depressing all prices and all wages. Ambitious businessmen could use the cheap labor available throughout the nation by putting their runaway shops in prisons, thereby avoiding the demands of organized labor for better wages and working conditions. By 1900, even national and state government labor commissions condemned the sale of prison-manufactured products on the free market. New York State was among the first to restrict private businesses' use of prison labor.[33]

The National Committee on Prison Labor, seated in New York, influenced the eventual end of the convict lease and contract labor systems. In his book *Penal Servitude,* E. Stagg Whitin, the Committee's General Secretary, reported the following resolution of November 24, 1911:

After one year of study the National Committee on Prison Labor found the preponderance of evidence to be in favor of the state use system; after a second year of study and further investigation, the Committee is in a position to declare as prejudicial to the welfare of the prisoner, the prisoner's family and the public, the contract system of prison labor. The Committee therefore declares itself opposed to the contract sys-

tem of prison labor and to every other system which exploits
his labor to the detriment of the prisoner.[34]

In the preface, dated on Lincoln's birthday, Whitin wrote:

> To the members of the Committee . . . the author makes due
> acknowledgement, and trusts that the work, which has but just
> begun, will be continued in the same broad spirit until it can
> be said with truth that neither slavery nor involuntary servi-
> tude, *not even as a punishment for crime, exists within the
> United States or any place subject to their jurisdiction.* [Em-
> phasis added.][35]

In addition to reporting the barbarities of the contract and lease systems, the study surveyed the use of convict slavery as it existed
throughout the United States. Whitin's illustration of exploitation of
free workers in a small town in northern New York provides an inter-
esting anecdote: "Fred Slaver," so-labeled by Whitin, controlled the
basketweaving industry in Liverpool, New York. Owning the raw material for baskets, Slaver had his willows stripped by prisoners and
payed the state nine dollars for every carload of willows the convicts
stripped. He then shipped the stripped willows to the nearby town of
Salinas, New York, where baskets were woven by his "free" workers.
Slaver's monopoly kept many of the town's willow strippers out of
work while other "men, women and children worked at starvation
wages" weaving baskets. Slaver then shipped his goods westward,
where he sold them at wholesale prices, avoiding penalties for
violating the New York State law prohibiting sale of convict goods on
the free market.[36]

Whitin and the National Committee on Prison Labor made important
contributions by promoting the eventual end of the convict lease and
contract labor systems, but they failed to extend their work to abolishing slavery in prisons. Whitin's suggested alternative to the private
use of convict labor was to place the slave labor of prisoners in the
hands of the state, for state use only. He argued that lessee and contracting businesses cared only about profits but that state-hired correctional officers would have reformation of the convict at heart. As
the following illustrates, Whitin's rationale for his suggested alternative left much to be desired:

> [The] *warden,* or superintendent, within the confines of his
> prison is a *czar,* his word is law, his will is supreme. . . . *The
> warden lives upon the institution,* his personal wants are first
> to be satisfied; he usually has the use of a beautiful house
> connected in some way with the enclosure; his table is sup-
> plied with all the luxuries of the season from the prison com-
> missary, prepared by prisoners often under supervision of an
> accomplished convict chef; convicts serve meals and attend
> upon his wife and his children, anticipating their every want;
> the education of his children is in some cases delegated to

convict tutors, while many of the details of running the institution are deputed to convict clerks, some of whom have executive ability surpassing that of the warden. All reports as to breaches of discipline and the work in the institution are made to the warden on which he is supposed to judge the prisoner, rewarding or punishing. These reports form the basis for the prisoner's release under indeterminant sentence . . . . In the *supreme paternalism* which exists rest infinite possibilities for the real education and development of the convict toward a better and more useful life, and the consummation of all the evil which human nature can foster up in response to the brutality of the tyrant.[37]

As if the good intent of the slavemaster could negate the disabling effects of denying people citizenship, labor, and human rights! Whitin, we assume unknowingly, used the same defense of slavery championed throughout the South by antebellum plantation owners and their spokesmen in Congress. His suggested uses for convicts by the state included roadwork, farming, mining and manufacturing.[38] All these were already implemented, but the state would now take on complete supervision of profit from prison labor rather than sharing that privilege with the contractor or lessee. Contracting and leasing out of prisoners was eventually forbidden and slavery continued as the sole responsibility of the state.

The National Committee on Prison Labor's suggestions were quite radical for its time and some of its ideas for change would be implemented over the next half century. In addition to replacing private business use of prison labor with the state-use system, the Committee suggested abolishing striped uniforms and the old lock-step march, employing a resident prison physician, hiring women to oversee the women convicts and relieving the prison shop foremen of having to tend to the insane and to women convicts' children. Among the reforms not implemented were developing a prison farm "worked by convicts placed on their honor, the guard replacing his gun by a hoe and adding his labor to the labor of the gang," and establishing a neutral organization to oversee the courts and determine the legality of convictions by examining "the effects of politics and race prejudice upon the courts."[39]

And Slavery Continued . . .

The convict lease and contract labor systems died slowly. In 1933, leasing of certain classes of prisoners was still practiced in North Carolina, South Carolina, Arkansas, Louisiana, Florida and Kentucky.[40] As noted earlier, the last state to formally abolish the lease system was the "involuntary servitude" state of Alabama, in 1928.

Because southern industry lagged behind that in the North, state-use systems below the Mason-Dixon Line put their convicts to work on prison farms in the traditional crops of American chattel slavemasters. The following, taken from the July 18, 1908 Atlanta *Georgian* and cited by prison reformer Clarissa Olds Keebler, provides an example of the cruelty which ruled the state prison farms. In the prison farm at Millegeville, Georgia:

> "Guards at the farm receive $25 per month and a house to live in." The *Georgian* tells of the wife of one guard who had to take her children and move away. "She could not allow her children to be reared...where the sound of the cruel lash on the backs of convicts and the screams could be heard. The children would run into the house and tell mother how many licks they counted."
>
> "On one occasion it is recounted that she heard the screams of a convict being beaten, and during the beating she counted seventy-two licks of the lash, and there were some before and after she counted. She begged her husband to go and see if the sudden stopping of the screams meant the death of the convict, but the husband knew that inquiry meant the possible loss of his job."[41]

In Louisiana, there were ten thousand recorded floggings from 1929 to 1940; when, in 1941, the governor ordered floggings stopped he was "simply ignored."[42] The whip, however, could be replaced by other instruments of torture:

> When flogging was abolished in Florida in 1923, another form of disciplinary punishment was invented - solitary confinement - but not as this is ordinarily understood.... The instrument for this punishment was to be a cell with solid walls and "3 feet wide, 6 feet 6 inches long and 7 feet from the floor to the grating over the top" and "so constructed that it can be divided across in two equal parts, and a convict may be confined in one half of the space in the day time, but shall have the full space in the night time." This cell became known as the sweat box. Its effect on those confined in it caused Dr. W.H. Cox, the state prison physician, to report in 1931 that "if within my power to do so, I would change the mode of punishment.... I doubt the constitutionality of the authority to devitalize a man and call it punishment or chastisement."
>
> This observation was dramatized the following year when a New Jersey teenager, Arthur Maillefert, died in the sweat box at the Sunbeam camp in Duval county [Florida]. He was ill and unable to work on the road. The camp captain and his "whipping boss" said he was shamming. After beating him mercilessly, they placed him in the sweat box, locked his feet in clamps, and placed a chain attached to an overhead beam around his neck. He was found strangled to death in the morning. A local justice of the peace pronounced it suicide, but an official investigation led to the indictment of the responsible officers on a charge of murder. They were convicted of manslaughter. The [related] investigation revealed that brutal treat-

ment of prisoners was commonplace in the camp, as it was in many other Florida camps in spite of rules and regulations.[43]

As Thorsten Sellin wrote:

> With the demise of the lease system, one might assume that when states and counties took full control of convicts, its worst features - the lash, the sweat box, the stocks, the shackles, the ball-and-chain, and the intolerable working and living conditions imposed by bosses whose sole concern was maximum financial profit - would also vanish.[44]

The states proved little better than private entrepreneurs in their kindness as convict masters. The chain gang kept convicts at hard labor and close to death building roads for public transportation. Sellin reported that

> Chains were worn constantly. Only a blacksmith could remove them. At night in the more or less permanent, crowded bunkhouses, the belt chain [a three foot long chain which linked the leg iron to the waist iron by means of a hook]... was attached to a metal rod or long chain which ran the length of the lodging at the foot of the beds.... But the worst of the mobile camps, used extensively in the Carolinas, Georgia, and Florida by the smaller rural counties, was the cage on wheels. In his message to the Florida legislature in 1911, Governor Gilchrist, who hoped to see all state convicts placed on the projected state prison farm at Raiford, indignantly described a visit to a Georgia convict road camp where "the men sleep in a moveable car placed on four wheels, with bars, constructed very much [like] ... a car... in which animals are conveyed [by]...the circuses showing throughout the State, with this exception: in the circus cars there are usually only one or two animals. In the convict cars, there are sometimes ten or twelve convicts. They are shackled and connected with a chain at night." In the 1930's, the typical North Carolina cage was about the size of a small moving van, eighteen feet long and seven or eight feet wide and high. Roof, floor, and ends were of solid steel and the sides "a close network of flat steel bars".... The prisoners often had to stay in these cages from Saturday noon to Monday morning and on holidays or when bad weather halted work.[45]

The chain gang continues today, particularly in the South. The symbols of slavery - ball and chain - were removed after World War II[46] but that did not mean that the carnival of inhumanity ended. Like the seventeenth century galley slaves who purposely maimed themselves so they might outlive their punishment, at Angola prison farm in 1951, 37 white convicts cut their heel tendons

> to attract public attention to the conditions under which they lived and worked...being quartered in filthy and overcrowded

barracks known as "jungle camps," where hundreds of men sleeping in double and triple-decked beds were jammed into space barely adequate for a hundred men; work in the fields from dawn to dusk with insufficient food and inadequate medical attention, flogging and other brutal punishments for failure to keep up with one's task as well as for disciplinary infractions; the use of armed prisoners as guards; the generally low quality of paid personnel. . . . Official investigations revealed that these conditions were real, not imaginary. In 1952 the Angola penitentiary was publicized as "America's Worse Prison". . . although it was not without competition for that dubious distiction.[47]

Prison slavery still strives to "break" its victims, training them in the servility which exploitation demands - inside and outside prison walls.

Notes

1. Kate Richards O'Hare, *Crime and Criminals,* booklet No. 4 (St. Louis: Frank P. O'Hare, n.d.), p. 13. Socialist Kate Richards O'Hare was sentenced to five years at the Missouri State Penitentiary for a speech she made in Bowman, North Dakota. Convicted of trying to obstruct enlistment into the armed services during World War I, O'Hare's eighteen months imprisonment made her an outspoken critic of the prison system.

2. The Thirteenth, Fourteenth, and Fifteenth Amendments with their enforcement provisions follow:

Thirteenth Amendment (1865)

Sec. 1. Neither slavery nor involuntary servitude, EXCEPT AS A PUNISHMENT FOR CRIME WHEREOF THE PARTY SHALL HAVE BEEN DULY CONVICTED, shall exist within the United States, or any place subject to their jurisdiction.

Sec. 2. Congress shall have power to enforce this article by appropriate legislation.

Fourteenth Amendment (1868)

Sec. 1. All persons born or naturalized in the United States, and subject to the jurisdiction thereof, are citizens of the United States and of the State wherein they reside. No State shall make or enforce any law which shall abridge the priviledges or immunities of citizens of the United States; nor shall any State deprive any person of life, liberty, or property without due process of law; nor deny to any person within its jurisdiction the equal protection of the law.

Sec. 2. Representatives shall be apportioned among the several States according to their respective numbers, counting the whole numbers of persons in each State, excluding Indians not taxed. But when the right to vote at any election. . .is denied to any of the male inhabitants of such State, being twenty-one years of age, and citizens of the United States, or in any other way abridged, except for participation in rebellion or other crime, the basis of representation therein shall be reduced in the proportion which the number of such male citizens shall bear to the whole number of male citizens twenty-one years of age in such State.

Sec. 3. No person shall. . .hold any office, civil or military, under the United States, or under any State, who, having previously taken an oath [in a federal or state, civil or military office]. . .to support the Constitution of the United States, shall have been engaged in aid of insurrection or rebellion against the same, or given aid or comfort to enemies thereof. But Congress may by a vote of two-thirds of each House remove such disability.

Sec. 4. The validity of the public debt of the United States. . .shall not be questioned. But neither the United States nor any State shall assume or pay any debt or obligation incurred in aid of insurrection or rebellion against the United States, or any claim for the loss or emancipation of any slave; but all such debts, obligations and claims shall be held illegal and void.

Sec. 5. The Congress shall have power to enforce, by appropriate legislation, the provisions of this article.

Fifteenth Amendment (1870)

Sec. 1. The right of citizens of the United States to vote shall not be denied or abridged by the United States or by any State on account of race, color, or previous condition of servitude.

Sec. 2. The Congress shall have the power to enforce this article by appropriate legislation.

3. Kluger, p. 50.

4. Ibid., p. 51.

5. DuBois, *Black Reconstruction,* p. 131.

6. Boyer and Morais, p. 34.

7. Ibid., p. 31.

8. Ibid., pp. 35-36.

9. Ibid., pp. 40-41.

10. Ibid., p. 41.

11. Ibid., p. 42.

12. Ibid., p. 43.

13. Ibid., pp. 141n-142n.

14. N.A.A.C.P. Executive Board Meeting Minutes of November 2, 1911, "The Opera House Lynching," Herbert Aptheker, ed., *A Documentary History of the Negro People in the United States,* vol. 2, (1910-1932) (Secaucus, N.J.: The Citadel Press, Lyle Stuart, Inc., 1973), p. 29.

15. William Pickens, "Lynching and Debt-Slavery," in Aptheker, ed., op. cit., p. 325.

16. "The Silent Anti-Lynching Parade," in Aptheker, ed., op. cit., p. 181.

17. Richard Wright, Jr., "What Does the Negro Want in Our Democracy?" in Aptheker, ed., op. cit., p. 290.

18. "From the South," a May 18, 1911 letter sent to W.E.B. DuBois, in Aptheker, ed., op. cit. In a note on p. 31, Aptheker explains:

> The Supreme Court upheld the constitutionality of the anti-peonage law (219 U.S. 191 [1911]: *Bailey v. Alabama*); nevertheless, peonage remained widespread in the South for another thiry years.

19. Ibid., pp. 31-32.

20. Keebler, *American Bastilles,* p. 55 quoting "a correspondent of a Western paper, writing from Jacksonville, Fla., Nov. 30, 1907."

21. Wilson, pp. 101-102, 107-108, 114-115, 116-117.

22. Ibid., pp. 110-113.

23. Boyer and Morais, p. 50n.

24. Ibid., pp. 43-53. On p. 50 Boyer and Morais explain:

> A good number of historians now concede that there was never any organization in Pennsylvania known as the Molly Maguires - although any militant miner might have been called a Molly Maguire after the newspapers had spread Gowen's charge far and wide. But the Molly Maguires in fact were nothing but a fabrication of Reading Valley's leading and most eccentric citizen. There was only the Ancient Order of the Hibernias' usually called the AOH, its oaths and rituals demanding brotherhood and patriotism.

25. Ibid., pp. 51-58, quotation from p. 53.

26. Ibid., see pp. 204-211. On p. 210 is written:

> The red scare made more money than speed-up, increased profits faster than machinery or labor-saving devices. It was ageless and forever new. It had been used against Americans ever since the middle of the nineteenth century when even the Abolitionists had been called Communists.... It divided workers almost as effectively as using white employees against Negro.
>
> The red scare was valuable in that it could be used with or without a Communist Party.... As...two tiny [Communist] parties were organized [in 1919], it was said louder than ever before that revolution was imminent. The newspapers were filled with stories of Moscow gold and Russian spies. Said the *New York Tribune* on June 4, 1919, "Nationwide Search for Reds Begins,".... On Jan. 2, 1920...the *New York Times* proclaimed, "200 Reds Taken in Chicago. Wholesale Plot Hatched to Overthrow U.S. Government."

27. Ibid., p. 212.

28. Wilson, p. 32.

29. Rusche and Kirchheimer, p. 107.

30. Wilson, pp. 63-64.

31. *Ruffin v. the Commonwealth,* 62 Va., 796.

32. Keebler, *American Bastilles,* pp. 52-53, quoting a reporter from *The Kentucky Post,* September 4, 1908.

33. McKelvey, p. 250; E. Stagg Whitin, *Penal Servitude* (New York: Benjamin H. Tyrrell Press, 1912), p. 7.

34. Whitin, p. i.

35. Ibid.

36. Ibid., pp. 11-18, quotation on p. 17.

37. Ibid., pp. 24-25.

38. Ibid., pp. 45-55.

39. Ibid., pp. 110-115. These suggestions are found in the Appendix of Whitin's book and were specifically addressed to the Jessup Board of Managers in Maryland under the title, "Report on the House of Correction, Jessup, Maryland."

40. Wilson, p. 41.

41. Keebler, *American Bastilles,* p. 35.

42. Sellin, p. 171.

43. Ibid., pp. 169-170.

44. Ibid., p. 163.

45. Ibid., pp. 167-168.

46. Ibid., p. 167.

47. Ibid., pp. 171-172, quoting *Report of a Study of the Louisiana State Penitentiary made by Austin H. MacCormick, Executive Director of the Osborne Association, Inc., in July, 1964, at the Request of Governor John J. McKeithen* (New York: The Osborne Association, 1964; mimeo), p. 2.

Chapter 7:
Slavery, Man...

The perimeter car circles, our bodies are counted again, and as the nurse's tray squeaks down the hall, I see the girl who swallowed gasoline and stabbed herself with a pin - a long one near her heart. What good is it doing her to be locked back here in solitary, I wonder.

- Marianne Hricko Stewart
California Institute for Women, 1979

LABOR RIGHTS VIOLATIONS

"Involuntary Servitude" Is Misleading

Today, a prison slave can no more control his or her "sale" from one prison to another, often hundreds of miles apart, than could an antebellum chattel slave. Cages have replaced cabins, while poor diet and enforced poverty continue. Electric doors and automatically locked passages enforce curfew. Prison watches day and night acknowledge no right to privacy, and prisoners may not convene without the approval or supervision of their keepers. Prisoners cannot assume their rightful responsibilities as parents, since incarceration is most often seen by the courts as proof of "unfitness." Conjugal visits are rarely, if ever, permitted, and the sexual relationship of couples is blighted by the imprisonment of a partner. Prison education programs are inadequate, libaries are skimpily supplied and those captives who teach themselves law and act to protect their rights through the courts are labeled "dangerous" by prison officialdom: A thinking slave is a potentially rebellious slave.

The American prison system combines slavery's three elements: prisoners are held in the complete control and possession of the state; the practices of their citizenship and of their labor rights are denied. As slave punishments have become more sophisticated, so have the arguments that defend and disguise their atrocities. Advocates of contemporary prison slavery call it involuntary servitude - a label which incurs little protest in this enlightened age of "human rights."

Charles Sumner warned in 1864 that the working of the Thirteenth Amendment introduced doubt whether slavery is a condition different and separate from involuntary servitude. On May 18, 1896, a federal court stated in the case of *Plessy v. Ferguson:* "Slavery implies involuntary servitude - a state of bondage; the ownership of mankind as a chattel, or at least the control of the labor and services of one man for the benefit of another, and the absence of a legal right to the disposal of his own person, property and services."[1] Close examination of the legal definitions of both conditions reveal their parallel relationship. *Black's Law Dictionary* defined slavery as "the condition of a slave; that civil relation in which one man has absolute power over the life, fortune, and liberty of another." The same source describes involuntary servitude as "the condition of one who is compelled by force, coercion or imprisonment, and against his will, to labor for another, whether he is paid or not."[2] The condition of slavery results in involuntary servitude; involuntary servitude is slave labor - labor devoid of dignity, choice or just and due compensation to the worker. Involuntary servitude is the *labor* relation of slavery, and slavery is the *civil* relation in which a person's practice of citizenship, labor rights and human rights is negated or denied. The civil relations of this "peculiar institution" are designed to guarantee forced and uncompensated labor. Free labor provides the rights and opportunites for workers to choose their jobs, receive just and equitable wages and organize with other workers for better wages, working conditions, employment security, and benefits. No American prisoner has these rights; every American prison exploits convict labor.

The Bottom Line

While racist and classist myths have sought to justify numan bondage, dollars and cents have built its framework. Clinging to antebellum traditions in servitude, several southern states put convicts to work on plantations. Texas, held by many in corrections to be the "model prison system," keeps many of its 31,000 convicts at farm labor and in the cotton fields.[3] As a prisoner in the Texas Department of Corrections (T.D.C.) wrote,

> The purpose of T.D.C. is not to rehabilitate prisoners, but to work them for the profit of the state. Indeed, it almost seems as though the goal of T.D.C. (if it has any specific goals for prisoners) is to make sure they leave prison sufficiently bitter to be a certain recidivist in the near future. There is no meaningful rehabilitation program; nor will there be so long as the state actually loses money by rehabilitating and paroling prisoners.
>
> The reigning philosophy of T.D.C. is that a man costs nothing, so he is worth nothing. He is a convicted criminal and (in the administration's warped, fanatical minds) he is worth nothing beyond what labors the T.D.C. can extract from him for X number of years. If he is injured, crippled or killed working in unsafe surroundings, so what? There will be a replacement along from courts momentarily. Only the fear of public disapproval has removed the brutality and beatings and murder from open admission into clandestine yet still active processes. Now as in earlier centuries, there is no value attached to that which costs nothing....

To try explaining a system where the dogs are caged in pens with more room per animal than the prisoners, where the cattle have a full time veterinarian while the human prisoner might wait five or six months to receive treatment from a bonafide doctor, where a man [guard] might be fired for whipping his horse, yet only administratively transferred to another unit for killing a human is impossible.

Yet it all has an answer: the bottom line. The profit and loss statement. As long as Texas can realize huge profits from free labor, it will continue building larger and more prisons in order to put to work a larger and larger slave labor force; it will continue to become more and more careless about innocence or guilt in convicting and condemning a person to slave labor, looking only at the bottom line.

As the following statement by the superintendent of a prison in Arizona indicates, involuntary servitude is important prison business:

Hell, this is big industry we have here. We just sell to state institutions and to the children's colony and university. Yes, this is a *big* business. [He smiled!] A *damn big business.* We have four farms within a distance of seven miles, worked by the male population. There are trustees living on ranches under the foreman. I don't know the number. We also manufacture innerspring mattresses and make all license plates for the state and all the street signs. We have a printing company, a cotton gin mill, a dairy farm, a swine farm, beef cattle and a big chicken ranch. . . . We raise all our own food; everything they eat comes from here. Everything they wear comes from here. They even make the mattresses they sleep on.[4]

A Pennsylvania prisoner wrote that Pittsburgh prison industries produce license plates, street and highway signs, and metal cabinets and furniture, which all sell at a profit; license plates alone bring in over $300 million a year for the Bureau of Motor Vehicles. He reported the Camp Hill prison to have a furniture factory as large as the rest of the prison combined; Gratersford produces textiles; Dallas produces mattresses, textile products, and cardboard boxes; and Rockview produces canned food with the trade name "Pencor" flagrantly printed on the labels. These products are sold outside of the correctional system, and many orders go out of state.

Invasion of the free market with the unfair competition of cheaper prison-made products is only one consequence of the more basic evil: forced prisoner labor for little or no pay. A Florida prisoner at Raiford remarked, "This state can truly afford to pay a prisoner (slave) a reasonable wage." Working on the chicken floor where prisoners killed and dressed 2,000 chickens a day, five days a week, the prisoner had no idea where the chickens went because they did not show up as prison fare. He also reported that the Raiford furniture factory made lockers sold throughout the state, requiring a squad to travel around fixing them. He understood that this furniture factory was privately owned and that the largest operation at Raiford was the shoe factory, which mass produced work boots and shoes.

When locked away from family and community, a person's labor is most easily exploited. As Maria Lopez wrote from her jail cell in San Diego,

> There are no activities, no open windows or fresh air and sunshine. "Recreation" consists of a concrete box on the roof with a wire mesh top affording a "view" of a small square of sky. The hour per day on the roof mandated for all prisoners works out in practice to maybe twice a week.
>
> That leaves finding a job to fill the time: the highest wages are paid by Federal Prison Industries (UNICOR/ FPI, Inc.), a separate corporation. The four pay scales range from 31¢ to 85¢ an hour. . . .
>
> The four level pay scale for all jail jobs runs from 8¢ to 18¢ an hour. I work as the Education Department secretary and law clerk, and make 18¢ an hour. On the streets, starting pay for an equivalent secretarial position is $10.50 an hour; and a client in a law firm would pay $12.00 to $20.00 an hour for my services. Although I work two separate jobs, due to a lack of skilled persons to fill the positions, I am paid only 18¢ an hour salary. Slave labor.

In the early seventies, Jessica Mitford's *Kind and Usual Punishment* exposed the workings of the California prison machine, where 70 percent of prisoner workers received no pay for their labor and where those who do receive pay, like Maria, are worth many times their wage.[5]

> Furthermore, prisoners say that when there is a heavy production schedule, key workers in the factory who would normally be eligible for parole find themselves mysteriously denied a release date. (This, they say, is true throughout the prison industries - a man with some particular skill, for whom there is no ready placement, will be out of luck when he comes before the parole board, who will tell him: "You're not ready, come back in a year.")[6]

Slavery is still dictated by profit, and it has always been difficult for slaveholders to give up their most productive captives. Promises of emancipation still lure slaves into working hard to expedite their freedom, only to have it denied them year after year.

> Today, Federal Prison Industries, Inc., is far and away the most profitable line of business in the country. Profits on sales in 1970 were 17 percent (next highest is the mining industry with 11 percent) - the average for all U.S. industries is 4.5 percent. The board of directors' annual report summarizes

the success story: over a thirty-five-year period, 1935 to 1970, the industries grossed $896 million, increasing their net worth by $50 million and contributing $82 million in dividends to the U.S. Treasury - thus, like it or not, we are all shareholders in the proceeds of captive labor. Because the Army is a major customer (the industries supply it with everything from military dress shoes to electronic cable), the war years have been especially good to prison industries. A chart in the report depicts successive peak periods under the headings "WW II," "Korea," "Vietnam," the latter responsible for a spectacular rise in sales from $38 million to $60 million over a seven-year-period.[7]

It seems no strange coincidence that the recent "balancing" of the national budget by cutting social programs for the poor also includes a renewed war on crime and increased military expenditures. Surviving is becoming yet more stressful, government is calling for harsher penalties for crime, and the incarceration rate of people convicted of crime nearly doubled during the first six months of 1981.[8] The National Moratorium on Prison Construction reports that taxpayers collectively pay an average $9,100 a year for each person in prison, in direct costs alone.[9] Where does this money go? Certainly not to pay prisoners decent wages so they can continue to support their families, compensate their victims or receive services that would help them become better citizens. Money which could fund a college education instead maintains human cages. As in attempts to examine the fiscal workings of our well-endowed defense industry, the public is not allowed behind prison walls for "security reasons." While the detailed cost of human bondage is hidden in a maze of red tape, corruption lies but a few layers beneath the public packaging. North Carolina's "showcase prisons," for example, are used to convince the public that taxes are well spent. A North Carolina prisoner told us that state law requires that prison labor help develop skills that will better equip prisoners to return to society. Unlike previous regulations, this law does not restrict prison labor to work not performed by free labor or private industry. He then described how actual prison labor practices misuse public funds:

> The inmates of this camp work forty hours each week. The work done is cutting bushes along the sides of roadways. They use a bush ax. This task involves cutting by hand bushes that are well off the shoulder of the road and, in some instances, which are frequent, erosion controlling growth is cut.
>   This task is done mechanically in other states, if done at all. And the demand for such labor is non-existent in society. This is a meaningless job that pays seventy cents a day. It is a "volunteer" position which if one decides not to participate he is put in punitive segregation and his chances for a better status are at stake.

This camp is not a showcase unit such as Bunn, Smithfield or other camps where the road crew does meaningful work. . . . This Catch 22 situation is indeed slavery and on this camp 32 inmates out of a population of 138 are caught by this trap. On Bunn, the closest "showcase" unit, with over 200 men, only ten inmates participate in this type of task and are better equipped.

Besides the 70¢ each day, the men here receive Number 2 gain time [time off their sentences], or four days each month. Kitchen workers here receive $1 per day and Number 3 gain time at eight days per month. Road work is physically and mentally more demanding.

Each county is charged $16.00 per man for this work, which means the taxpayer pays the prison department approximately $133,120 each year to have this non-productive task performed. $5,824 goes to the inmates at 70¢ per day for each of 32 men. And $127,297 goes to pay for guards, gas and tools? What about the $8,000 plus each year the taxpayer pays for one inmate: do these profits go towards that?

This type of *forced, meaningless* labor is not required on any "non-showcase" camp. Upon inquiry, this information will be denied by the authorities and a very attractive picture painted.

Meager convict earnings are further exploited by prison rules that regulate spending. As peons had to make all their purchases through the company store, so must prisoners. Using California as an example, Jessica Mitford wrote,

[Prison] prices are fixed by the individual canteen manager (there is no central pricing policy), pegged anywhere from 10 to 50 percent higher than those in the supermarket; the canteens realize an average gross profit of over 22 percent and a net of 13 percent, compared with a prevailing 1 percent net that is claimed in the outside market. . . .

Should the prisoner want to order something not in stock, the transaction must go through the canteen, which levies a 10 percent surcharge on a sum compounded of the cost of the merchandise, sales tax, and postage. As one wrote, "When the inmate orders an item (say, a footlocker from Sears for $11.97), he has to pay the initial cost of the item, then add California sales tax, then add the cost of postage from the vendor to the institution, then - and only then - add an additional 10 percent of the entire sum of the above, which purportedly goes to the Inmate Welfare Fund. And the end result of an $11.97 order is in the neighborhood of $15 or $16." What if the prisoner's family wants to make him a present of the footlocker? They are barred from sending it to him, instead must send enough cash, computed as above, through the regular [prison] channels.[10]

An employee of the California Department of Corrections audit division described the Inmate Welfare Fund as "an extortion racket, an illegal use of prisoners' money. It's just another fund for accounting purposes, a euphemism called 'inmate welfare' to make it sound good."[11]

The Texas Department of Corrections is noted for its annual rodeo, advertised as benefiting prisoners. As one prisoner correspondent writes,

> The Modern Gladiatorial Arena is in Texas. Each weekend through the month of October people from around the state flock to Huntsville to watch as convicts are trampled, gored and mutilated for a top prize of around $300. Most of these convicts receive no outside income and this is their only hope of obtaining some money for tobacco and coffee. The prize for the state? A little over one million dollars annually. This money supposedly goes into a "recreation fund" for the prisoners. I will not go into the fraud and embezzlement here or just what happens to the money, but about the only recreation realized is the "recreation" the prisoners get who build the Texas Department of Corrections employees' new party room.

From state to state the corruption continues:

> In New York City, the commissary fund of over $1 million from combined jails somehow filters into the general fund for the city. In San Francisco, [ex-] Sheriff Richard Hongisto said that before he took office, "no one seemed to know where the money had gone to."[12]

Trapped by this mire of exploitive waste are prisoners, who have no means to create change but must continually bow to what is demanded of them. As Pennsylvania prisoner Dorothy Morris writes,

> We, the women at Muncy State Correctional Institution for Women, need all the help we can get. Prison life here is fighting for the right to be treated as human beings. We are forced to work, and if we refuse to work we are threatened with misconducts or solitary confinement. For the work we are forced to do against our will, we are paid ten to twelve or seventeen cents an hour. That is not even enough to buy the personal things we need. We are forced to mop floors, to work on the farm and lift heavy bags of potatoes, etc., and forced to clean the cottages which the prison officials call field day. We are never given a rest. Something must be done. We need all the help we can get. We are worked like runaway slaves. We are put in the fields to pick Massa Hewitt's corn and potatoes; they even force some to pick rocks. We are humans, not slaves, but Massa (Superintendent) treats us like slaves and brings

the whip out when we refuse to be treated like slaves. Slavery must be abolished and the time is now. Massa forces us to work while he sits back in his chair behind his desk where it's cool but Massa does not get out there in the fields when the hot sun is shining. We need all the help we can get. We are pleading for all the help we can get.

Dehumanization, Punishment, and Alienation

From St. Cloud, Minnesota came this declaration from a prison slave:

These people here have a lot of nerve. In the "Graystone Gazette" (the administration's newsletter) they are advertising for the pigs to come into B-House (where they house Prison Slaves): Boots 50¢ and shoes 25¢. The concept is that it will go into the house fund, but it is a brave effort on the pigs' part to downgrade the inmates and promote more slavey ("flaunt it in our faces").

We are in a mini-Unit System here on this plantation so it is almost impossible to school the new inmates to the game. I am in the process of trying to shut down the Shoe Shine Stand for what it stands for psychologically. I just hope I can succeed at it soon.

From Angola, a Louisiana prisoner wrote,

This intitution is programmed through a method that a man MUST work in the fields before becoming classified to a better job; sometimes he may work throughout his sentence in the fields, no matter how lengthy.

A letter from another prisoner states,

I am a prisoner in the state of Georgia. At the time of this writing, Georgia does not pay its inmates any form of compensation for the work they perform. This practice is very harmful to the inmates, to society, and to the whole rehabilitative process. It is harmful to the inmate to live under very primitive, barbaric conditions. There are inmates here who don't even have deodorant to take care of their personal hygiene. And there are others who go around picking up cigarette butts from the floors, ground, and trash cans in order to smoke.

Slavery is distinguished both by the labor expended and by the conditions under which it is expended. Prisoners who refuse to work receive disciplinary write-ups and negative work reports on which basis the parole board frequently denies parole. Continued work refusal may bring loss of "privileges" (additional denial of rights), forced psychiatric treatment or medication, solitary confinement, beatings, and constant harassment from their keepers. As reported by a Terre Haute, Indiana prisoner, convict resistance to inhumane working conditions is tragically common:

> I had a friend who was with me in Jackson State Prison, in Michigan, who was killed as a result of being forced to work with defective equipment. When he tried to quit his job because of this he was threatened with losing his parole. So he continued to work. Within a week, they found him with a broken neck, laying in the mud. Officials tried to keep this from the public but I called the Detroit Free Press which did a fine story. But I was placed in the hole for ten months and transferred to Marquette, and never worked the rest of my time. This is only one incident in many.

No matter how legitimate their excuse, those who refuse to work are punished. One Florida prisoner, suffering such severe back problems that any quick or strenuous movement brings on "undefinable" pain, requested a pass to the clinic during working hours to get his medication refilled:

> ...after threats and a few names which I shall not put down here, I was refused. The exact phrase being, "You're here to do work, not to get sick." So much for that idea. The next day, I decided to commit a great sin here in the Florida Chain Gang: I refused to work. I couldn't get a pass and my back was killing me. Needless to say, the reaction I got from the boss man was instantaneous. I was handcuffed and placed in the "cage" for a period of six and a half hours. Then after being harranged by "officials" for another hour, I was placed on Administrative Confinement where I still am. We are currently putting together litigation concerning the conditions here which are, to say the least, highly unconstitutional. The fetid air is at least 105 to 110 degrees in the cells. The cells themselves are filthy. I could go on for hours, but all you have to do is picture in your mind Slave Punishment quarters....

In addition to work-related injuries, illness, death and the daily degradation of meaningless, wageless labor, involuntary servitude results in alienation which contributes to recidivism. As an Atlanta prisoner put it:

> It should not be necessary to experience slavery (or involuntary servitude) in order to realize its evils and detriments to the subject. Slavery in any manner breeds hatred and contempt for the master and the work performed!
> For anyone to appreciate the necessity of work, he/she must enjoy the fruit of his/her labor. To not be allowed to do so causes one to develop a hatred and contempt for work whenever confronted with it. I am positive that you will agree that this is *not* the attitude most people would like to see our kept returned to the streets with.

Getting Worse...

Recent trends in prison labor policy indicate that forced labor is intensifying. A C.A.P.S. member, imprisoned in Delaware, reported that the second session of that state's 1980 legislature passed a law amending Chapter 65, Title 11 of the Delaware Code Relating to Work by Inmates. The new law allows the Department of Corrections to require physically able inmates to work without compensation. When they work more than eight hours in a day or 40 hours in a week, they receive a credit for that overtime, rounded down to the nearest hour. Inmates receive a reduction of sentence at the rate of two hours for every hour of overtime credited, with the exception that nothing can reduce the sentence of persons serving minimum mandatory sentences without eligibility for parole. Prisoners who refuse to work· under these terms may have their previously earned time credits revoked as well as endure other disciplinary measures.

A Florida prisoner reported that the national leader in reinstituting executions is breaking other new ground in modern slave punishments. His masters have decided that exploiting prisoners for their labor is not enough:

> The thing that is happening now is some bill has been passed requiring prisoners to pay for being in prison. According to Section 944.0265 of the Florida Statutes, anyone who refuses to disclose revenue to classification officers would be removed from eligibility for parole.

In order to qualify for parole, each Florida prisoner must report any savings or assets he or she may have outside prison so that the state may claim further payment before authorizing release.

Prisoner appeals, celebrated writings exposing the debilitative and oppressive nature of involuntary servitude and a long history of human suffering and political embarrassment from past practices of slave labor have all failed to give impetus to needed change. As a C.A.P.S. member wrote from an Indiana prison,

> In 1977 Indiana...made some radical changes in its new penal reform changes which were designed to arrest increasing crime rates through the threat of more severe punishment. These new changes left the concept of forced labor, hard or otherwise, intact, however, and added provisions which delegate to the Department of Corrections (D.O.C.) the administrative prerogative of imposing additional labor, without just compensation, in a purely punitive sense.
>
> For the first time in its history, the State Legislature delegated to the D.O.C. the unbridled power to use forced labor as a means of disciplining unconforming prisoners. It also codified into law the D.O.C.'s authority to punish those prisoners who refuse to perform assigned work within the prison

setting. Any prisoner now, for example, who "encourages others to refuse to work or (himself) participate(s) in a work stoppage" is subject to be confined in detention for up to six months, be demoted one grade in his respective classification, and can lose up to one hundred eighty days of credit time [time earned towards release] previously earned. He is subject to the very same deprivations for even attempting the above infractions! . . .

A prisoner who may choose not to work is subject to be charged with refusing to work, participating in a work stoppage, refusing to obey an order, unexcused absence from work, violating an institutional rule, and attempting to do each of these. He can be punished consecutively for each of these charges and given up to twenty hours of extra work, not to exceed four hours per day, on each of these charges.

The legislature's prohibition against the D.O.C.'s use of corporal punishment, and its authorizing of that Department's use of forced, uncompensated labor as appropriate punishment is an unmitigated contradiction of purpose and intent. While they seek to prevent official tyranny, they create conditions under which tyranny itself exists. Americans have long felt that our individual labor, and its fruits, and our right to govern its use is prerequisite to individual health and well being. Forcing captives into a state of modern slavery entails no worthwhile values to our society, nor will it contribute to the growth and development of prisoners.

HUMAN RIGHTS VIOLATIONS

Fear

People denied the practice of their rights are subjected to cruelty often in violation of rules established to prevent excessive, cruel, and unusual punishment. In the antebellum South, law forebade the killing of slaves, except under the most rare of circumstances, but law did not stop the murders. One need only look at the 1971 prison rebellion at Attica to ascertain the "unusual circumstances" which result in the massacre of people demanding their rights. Prisoners have some rights, say the courts, but their rights must fall within the security standards of the prison,[13] standards that enforce totalitarian rule.

As slaves were tortured and killed on southern plantations and their masters escaped penalty of law, so today prison slaves are subjected to torture and death. From Mississippi came a prisoner report on one of many slave deaths that receive no public notice:

> John Smith [name changed], approximately 48, wakes up just like any other inmate and eats his grits and soured bologna for breakfast. After breakfast, the clean-up equipment comes around and the [jail] guards make him clean up before he can

go back to sleep, which is all there is to do since we have no TV's or recreation of any kind.

We clean up and Mr. Smith waits on his medicine to come around, but he's not sure it will come at all because you can't predict when the trustees might want to take your medicine to get them a "little buzzy." But if you're epileptic like Mr. Smith and you really need your phenobarbitol and Dilantin to keep you alive, you wait and hope that they bring your medicine. Mr. Smith waits until 10:00 a.m., and still no medicine. So he lays on his bunk and reads his Bible and eventually drifts off into an endless sleep.

At noon it is time to eat in the cell-block. I come to cell number 4 in which Mr. Smith is sleeping on his stomach and I shake him to wake him for lunch, but it is as I have expected all along. Mr. Smith will never wake up again because he had an epileptic fit and died and the main reason for his death is not receiving his proper medication. The guards turned on the radio to quiet the confusion and the radio announcer informs the world that one John Smith was "unable to make lunch" because he died of natural causes. Since no one challenged it, you will probably go and join "John Smith of natural causes"!

I was an eyewitness to this murder of a prison slave and nothing was ever done about it. Also, Mr. Smith left a "To whom it may concern" in his Bible. It stated that Mr. Smith was being held against his will . . . his time was up and he was not being treated properly. This man knew he was going to die and yet there was nothing he could do about it. Isn't it unreal that such cruelty still exists right here in the U.S. of America. I'm beginning to believe that "U.S.A." stands for the Underprivileged Slaves of America, don't it seem so to you?

Prisoner deaths are common, rarely made public and usually passed off as unexplained, "suicides" or attributed to the criminally violent "nature" of state captives. The ethic of violence, however, belongs within the nature of a system that confines and exploits convicted citizens. The brutality of modern punishment became briefly apparent in the recently publicized testimony of an enforcing slave of the Florida prison system. On the Columbia Broadcasting System's January 11, 1981 television broadcast of *Sixty Minutes,* Johnny Fort told CBS correspondent Dan Rather that he was ordered to beat up twelve people, including a teacher sympathetic to prisoners. Fort led an elite squad of prisoners who performed routine inmate beatings for the staff at Florida's Union Correctional Institution. Among the rewards for carrying out beatings, U.C.I.'s enforcing slaves received the boys of their choice (prisoners for sexual relations).[14] Any system of tyranny needs informants to maintain complete control. Snitches, or rats, as prisoners know them, are enforcing slaves who trade information about prisoners to prison keepers for favors. Since beatings, now unlawful, are still used to keep rebellious slaves in line, prison keepers often call on enforcing slaves to do their dirty work for them.

The six-foot-one, three-hundred-pound Fort described how he killed sleeping Vertis Graham, found dead in his cell on December 8, 1979. He said that U.C.I. Sergeant Buzz Snyder took Fort across the prison to another dormitory and pointed out the victim through the window of the bunk where he lay sleeping. Fort went into the prisoner's cell, turned to the watching guard and pointed to make sure he had the right victim, and with the guard's renewed assurance, struck Graham on the side of the head with a heavy lead pipe, killing him with one blow. The next day, the sergeant informed Fort that he had killed the wrong man, that Vertis Graham was sleeping in the intended victim's bunk.[15]

A former U.C.I. guard has confirmed goon squad practices, the newly promoted Lieutenant Snyder denies Fort's story, and the Florida Department of Corrections denies all related allegations. In the July 26, 1981, rebroadcast of "Goon Squad", *Sixty Minutes* reported that subsequent official investigation into Johnny Fort's allegations asserts that Johnny Fort did not kill Vertis Graham. Johnny Fort is sticking to his story while the Florida Department of Corrections claims that it has one of the best prison systems in the country.[16]

The "best prison system," a title claimed by several states, usually refers to a prison system that is "secure," safe from prisoner resistance. One such acclaimed state recently lost a federal civil rights case suit to prisoners in *Ruiz v. Estelle.* As reported in the November 11, 1978, *New York Times,* Corrections Department surgeon Dr. Luke Nigliazzo testified at a federal hearing that

> he had examined "hundreds" of inmates who were beaten or otherwise assaulted. He told of one man, captured after an escape attempt, who had been bullwhipped by guards and mauled by dogs and whose scrotum had been grazed by a bullet. The doctor termed it "the worst case of brutality I have ever seen."[17]

The article reported that David Vanderhoff, a Justice Department attorney working in behalf of the prisoners, asserted in his opening remarks at the hearing that security throughout the Texas system was "obtained by fear."[18]

When your keeper makes the rules, just or unjust, that you must live by; when there is no escape from the guns, chains, and special punishments used to enforce the rules; and when you are unarmed, disenfranchised and isolated from any support systems in the free world, fear is an ongoing visceral response that can keep you alive. A prisoner who sent us a petition with forty prisoner signatures from Sing Sing prison in Ossining, New York, attached this note to one of his letters:

> P.S. The police are watching me as though I were about to start something! I got 18+ years and they can kiss my "ass". But if something does go wrong what can I do? Who will help me?

And from Florida, a prisoner who sent us a newspaper report on Johnny Fort's allegations also wrote:

> A number of things have been witnessed here that fear will not allow them to be mentioned - beatings, killings, contract murder, stabbings, etc., all arranged by the prison administration.
>
> By talking to other inmates here, in order to try to find out why so much fear exists, a number of things were made known; the year of the riot here..., well it was stated and went down in record (and I want you to check on this if you can) that no one was killed in that so-called riot.... I have been told that there was a burial of these inmates [killed in the riot] to cover this! These inmates are down on record as escapees. The problem is getting my source to talk. I understand that all but one body was moved from the original burial place under the prison and reburied in the prison grave yard between other graves.
>
> Fear! This is fear's paradise. You are right, prison slavery has taken a great effect - so great that there is no concern for human life.*

Disregard for Human Life

Slavery anywhere has always been known for its complete disregard for human life. Like the reprieves from punishment offered to convicted British subjects who agreed to have their limbs amputated to test the styptic medicines of scientist a few centuries back, prisoners today are coerced into testing new medicines or becoming the subjects of unprecedented experiments. One contemporary scientist said that "criminals in our penitentiaries are fine experimental material - and much cheaper than chimpanzees."[19] In 1963, for example, prisoners

> in Ohio and Illinois were injected with live cancer cells and blood from leukemia patients to determine whether these diseases could be transmitted; doctors in Oklahoma were grossing an estimated $300,000 from deals with pharmaceutical companies to test out new drugs on prisoners.[20]

In 1971, in what was later described as a "totally pointless study" by Dr. Ephraim Kahn of the California Department of Public Health, Dr. Robert E. Hodges experimentally induced scurvy into five Iowa prisoners:

> Among the effects of the experiment recorded in...Dr. Hodges' publication that could be permanent, Dr. Kahn cited heart damage, loss of hair, damage to teeth, hemorrhage into

---

*We do not know if an investigation has begun or if the purported killings were recorded.

femoral nerve sheaths - the latter is "terribly painful and could lead to permanent nerve damage."[21]

Medical incompetence and negligence is an important reflection of the institutional abuse of human life that typifies the normal running of a prison. In 1980, we received a letter from a Wisconsin prisoner reporting that a case of meningitis had been discovered where he was incarcerated and, despite danger from the extremely contagious nature of the disease, prison officials were attempting to keep the information from prisoners and the public. At the same time, the Governor of the prison slave state of Wisconsin was attempting to exempt the prison system from state law regarding health care facilities. His Budget Review Bill passed the state legislature and, although another provision of law requires the state to follow American Medical Association standards, Section 405, succeeded in releasing prison infirmaries from the more stringent regulations imposed on state hospitals.

"What such an exemption means," wrote the WCI/Waupun Paralegal Program, "is that it will allow the state prison health care facilities and the personnel to continue on in their affliction of pain and misery on sick persons now incarcerated by the inability of those persons to provide adequate levels of health care, because there will be no laws mandating they do so."[22]

Negligence in medical treatment of prisoners was among the conditions that led prisoners at Indiana State Prison to riot on September 1, 1973, stage a peaceful demonstration on December 15, 1977, and riot again on April 27, 1980: a "spontaneous combustion," in the words of the Prisoners' Commission, resulting from the continued failure of the administration to heed prisoner requests for improved conditions. The *Report from Prisoners Inside Indiana State Prison,* released by the Prisoners' Commission to legal services and the press in an attempt to get outside support, listed dangerous physical conditions in the prison: poor heat, rodent and vermin infestation, danger of fire; poor nutrition and unsanitary food preparation; grievance and appeal procedures which brought no satisfactory attention to prisoner complaints; staff violation of their own rules in treatment of prisoners; lack of due process; racist discrimination towards prisoners and in harrassment of visitors; enforced homosexuality through prohibition of heterosexuality; and many more of the same negative conditions which permeate all our nation's prisons. Of improper medical care, the Commission stated:

There is a prisoner here who, but for the lack of medical attention at the time he requested it, will live out the remainder of his life in absolute darkness. Yes, he is blind! Forever blind because a minor problem was allowed to degenerate into a life-long disability. No prisoner at this prison can watch him struggling with his blindness without experiencing personal discomfort, rage, and hatred for a system that refuses to honor our *right* to proper health care. We are all burdened with the knowledge that, but for the grace of God, it could have been me![23]

Complete renovation of medical facilities and an upgrade in personnel will not alleviate the major portion of questionable medical services as long as custody staff are allowed to use questionable security tactics as the cause for inept medical treatment. Overall, adequate medical attention can only come about when society's views/practices on prisons and prisoners has transcended the contemporary stereotyping of "vicious animals who need to be caged...."[24]

Cruel and Usual

Perhaps the most insidious quality of American punishment is how deeply it cuts to the core of its many victims. A young woman imprisoned at the State Correctional Institution at Muncy, Pennsylvania, wrote:

> I'm really upset over the whole thing, cause I was locked behind there [solitary] for nothing. I'm only 19 now, but my nerves are so bad [that] I shake all over when I lay down to sleep. My hands shake constantly. It drives me silly to see my hands shake when I try to do something. I have went through too much hell here. How much longer must I go through this? How can I be sure my mentality will last that long?

The settings of these modern concentration camps can be deceiving, like that of the State Correctional Institutional at Muncy for women, located in Pennsylvania's Pocono mountains, hundreds of miles from any city, and therefore hundreds of miles from most prisoners' families, who are too poor to visit or help. As a Muncy prisoner declared:

> You can have the cleanest spot in the world, but... Hitler was clean in appearance, yet he slaughtered people. When the atomic bomb was dropped on Hiroshima and Nagasaki, the perpetrators of that action were clean in appearance. The KKK is clean in appearance - how many lives have been barbarically taken? The Slavemasters were clean in appearance, but were their actions clean when they raped, beat, chained, killed our people?
>
>   There ain't nothing clean about being locked in a room twenty-three and a half hours every day. There ain't nothing clean about having your meals searched. There ain't nothing clean about frezzing concrete and steel bars. There ain't nothing clean about matrons who work that don't even answer when you call them for an emergency such as sisters

setting themselves on fire, sisters hanging themselves, sisters having seizures, sisters being dragged to the hole where
there is no clothing, no water, no toilet paper, and sisters being sick, screaming in agony, only to have the door slammed
on them. There ain't nothing clean about the treatment of my
sisters under the present conditions.

While cruelty has persisted in slavery's methods throughout history, the most frightening forms of force are found in our scientifically
sophisticated age, where cruelty is more subtly and deeply inflicted.
Unlike the crude punishments of the lash and physical mutilation,
new slave punishments employ refined techniques which force submission through psychological and chemical warfare while the victims serve in experiments for the advancement of "science." Brain
surgery (psychosurgery), behavior-control medication, electric-shock
therapy and behavior modification techniques provide contemporary
methods of mutilation - psychogenocide.

Built to replace the country's maximum security dungeon at Alca-
traz, the long-term Control Unit at Marion, Illinois is an experimental
behavior modification program designed to alter human behavior to
meet modern slaveholding criteria. Proponents of the program mask
their Auschwitz mentality in the behaviorist jargon of Dr. Edgar
Schien, who states:

> I would like you to think of brainwashing, not in terms of
> politics, ethics and morals, but in terms of the deliberate
> changing of human behavior and attitudes by a group of men
> who have relatively complete control over the environment in
> which the captive populace lives.[25]

Prisoners who demonstrate beliefs, attitudes and behavior deemed
thorns in the side of slaveholding practitioners are threatened with being sent to Marion to undergo its mindtwisting programs. Formerly
called the Control and Rehabilitative Effort, or "C.A.R.E.," Program,
Marion's Control Unit Treatment Program is an experimental behavior
modification program based on a system of rewards and punishments. A prisoner who will change his behavior and attitude or give up
his values and beliefs, and conform to what the prison administration
considers acceptable behavior, may be rewarded by being returned to
the general prison population, either at Marion or another prison. As
former Control Unit prisoner Alberto Mares explained, prison officials
use sensory deprivation, or complete isolation in an attempt to
"break" the will of prisoners who do not go along with the program.
Being deprived of cultural and environmental contacts tends to bring
about degenerative changes which can result in death because cultural and environmental contacts are essential to human survival.[26]
Physical and social contact, including contact with families, are min-
imized. Prisoners confined to the Control Unit are compelled to visit

their families via monitored telephones in a special visiting room where a glass partition separates the prisoner from his visitor.[27]

The Control Unit seeks to alienate prisoners from any possible source of support for their beliefs, punishes independent or "uncooperative behavior," rewards subservience or "cooperative behavior," prevents prisoners from writing home about the conditions of their imprisonment, permits only those reading materials which support the program, systematically withholds mail, uses prisoners to exploit and spy on each other, tricks men into making private statements which are then shown to others, destroys trust, works to destroy meaningful emotional ties, and segregates natural leaders and makes those who are cooperative with the program into leaders.[28]

Physical movement of prisoners in the Control Unit is constrained by automatically locked passageways and maze-like corridors in which every movement is dictated by a loudspeaker. Every crevice of the Unit is watched by electronic or human eyes and recorded in a log book. Men confined in the Control Unit are kept in complete solitary confinement and meet only who, where, and when their controllers dictate. The prisoner's perpetual "sanctuary" is a cell, which, described by Marion prisoner Eddy Griffin:

> contains a flat steel slab jutting from the wall. Overlaying the slab is a one-inch piece of foam wrapped in coarse plastic. This is supposed to be a bed. Yet it cuts so deeply into the body when one lays on it that the body literally reeks with pain. After a few days, you are totally numb. There is no longer intercommunication between the sense organs and the brain. The nervous system has carried so many pain impulses to the brain until obviously the brain refuses to accept any more signals. Feelings become indistinct, emotions unpredictable. The monotony makes thoughts hard to separate and capsulate. The eyes grow weary of the scene, and shadows appear around the periphery, causing sudden reflexive action. Essentially, the content of a man's mind is the only means of defense in terms of his sanity.
>
> Besides these methods of torture (which is what they are) there is also extreme cold conditioning in winter and lack of ventilation in summer. Hot and cold water manipulation is carried out in the showers. Shock waves are administered to the brain when guards bang a rubber mallet against the steel bars. Then there is outright brutality, mainly in the form of beatings. The suicide rate in the Control Unit is five times the rate in general population at Marion.
>
> At the root of the Control Unit's Behavior Modification Program, though, is indefinite confinement. This is perhaps the most difficult aspect of the Control Unit to communicate to the public. Yet a testament to this policy was a man named Hiller "Red" Hayes. After 13 years in solitary confinement (nearly six in the control unit), he became the "boogie man" of

the prison system - the living/dying example of what can happen to any prisoner. The more he deteriorated in his own skeleton, the more prisoners could expect to wane in his likeness. He died in the unit in August, 1977.

In essence, the Unit is a Death Row for the living. And the silent implications of Behavior Modification speak their sharpest and clearest ultimatum: CONFORM OR DIE.[29]

One does not have to be confined in a modern hell-hole to be scarred by scientific punishment. As a long-time resident of special punishment wrote from her cell in solitary confinement at the Maryland Correctional Institute for Women:

I've watched women driven mad enough to set themselves on fire, on several occasions; so many women are being sent to the state insane asylums that two hospitals refused to accept any more "victims," victims of a process utilized to extirpate *all* those qualities that distinguish human-kind from animal-kind. Psychological manipulation, all types of negative reinforces, labeling theories, contingent rewards and all other psychological tactics calculated to break, degrade, modify and produce severe anxiety in a human being, and the deplorable living conditions and psychological damage women are suffering here are the end-product of a long, insidious, complicated and persistent behavior modification program... Though many reasons are given, the main causative factors for this treatment are intrinsic strength of any kind, intelligence, outspokenness and being verbally critical of policies and decisions, and any type of political ideas, beliefs and alliances. People who have never been involved in or concerned about prison issues may wonder if I'm only a gifted liar or perhaps a paranoic...the one sure way to find out is to come and "see," even if you never get to the dungeons. Look at the women walking around drugged, dazed, passive, bloated, *Broken,* and then Think...I'm sure the "Truth" of the matter will penetrate your consciousness.

DENIAL OF CITIZENSHIP RIGHTS

As *Webster's New World Dictionary of the American Language* puts it, "civil rights" are "those rights guaranteed to the individual by the Thirteenth, Fourteenth, Fifteenth and Nineteenth Amendments to the Constitution of the United States and by certain other acts of Congress; especially, exemption from involuntary servitude and equal treatment of all people with respect to the enjoyment of life, liberty, and property and the protection of law."[30] Enforcement of citizenship, civil and human rights prohibit stealing the fruits of another person's labor. Involuntary servitude is ineffective without denial of these rights. As prisoners' labor rights are violated, so too are the protections of their citizenship.

In order to deny any person the right to control his or her labor power, a government must also negate rights to free expression, petition, association, political representation: denial of these rights can be considered cruel and unusual punishment. Call it involuntary servitude, the results are the same: slavery. While it is impossible to describe all the oppressions suffered by prisoners, they can all be subsumed under a simple label: the negative conditions of prison slavery. At the root of the abuse and exploitation of prisoners is their powerlessness, powerlessness guaranteed by withdrawal of their practices of citizenship.

Perhaps the most obvious violation of citizenship is found in denial of the American prisoner's right to vote. Shortly after the 1980 national elections, an imprisoned citizen wrote to C.A.P.S. from solitary confinement:

> I am presently in the Federal Pen at Terre Haute, Indiana. Last October I voted in the national election by absentee ballot. My vote was not accepted because I was a convicted felon. I know that the Constitution says a citizen may have representation. I feel that denying my right to vote is denying me representation. I am wondering if you could assist me in steering me to, or advising me who could help me restore my right to vote.
> I am willing to file suit in Federal Court to rectify the situation.

Two years earlier, we received a letter smuggled out of Maryland's Jessup prison from imprisoned Barbara White. In the letter, Ms. White stated:

> Why shouldn't we be allowed to vote into public office those candidates we desire to represent our communities, our families, and ourselves? I feel that we are more apt to choose an uncorrupt individual, or one who is really sincere and has the okay's to help the people. Another very important issue is for residents in correctional institutions to receive at least the minimum wage for work performed on their job. If I earned the minimum wage I would be able to aid in the support of my two children and my mother, if I could.

Like Barbara, we also believe that politicians elected by prisoners might be more responsibly chosen and would be obliged to humanize our systems of punishment. No obligation to prisoners exists on Capitol Hill today, just as there was no political obligation to black Americans before Radical Reconstruction.

Even religious freedom is violated in prison, Muslim prisoners being especially victimized in their attempts to maintain the practices of their faith. In New York, for example, Muslims at Attica have filed a formal complaint of harrassment, citing prison guard disruption of their services, denial of adequate space for worship, administration refusal to let prisoners use traditional prayer mats, administrative surveillance of their services and being thwarted in their attempts to find out if pork, forbidden to Muslims, was in their food.[31]

Whether idle or at labor, today's slaves are given no voice in determining the rules they must live under. Their mail is subject to censorship and confiscation, and prisoners' personal ties to the outside world are destroyed by institutional isolation and restricted visiting privileges. Many families completely disintegrate as divorce proceedings follow imprisonment, which frequently eliminates a person's ability and eligibility to contest. Not protected from undue search and seizure, prisoners must endure cell "shakedowns" which come without warning or reason, respect no right of privacy, and which often result in confiscation and destruction of personal property. Tried on their keepers' allegations in kangaroo courts where they are allowed no legal counsel or due process, prisoners never know when an insignificant statement or act will be deemed grounds for denying parole or prolonging imprisonment. Their access to the courts limited by indigency and confinement, convicts are left to their own resources to write legal writs of complaint that are ignored or which evoke punishment intended to keep writ writers from becoming a threat to the "efficient" running of the prison. Those who pose a threat to the normal management of slavery are transferred to other prisons - "sold South" - as punishment. Prisoners' protest, strikes and rebellions are violently suppressed and, denied freedom of press, they cannot bring their plight to the attention of the outside world. Their exploitation is perpetuated by lack of outside support.

Prisoner attempts to let the public know what is going on inside are especially thwarted by their keepers. One example was found in a "letter" we received from an Attica prisoner: the contents were missing. After informing him that we had received an empty and unsealed envelope, he replied:

> You must help me. I would never send you an open and empty envelope! I am locked up 24 hours per day. I have access to very few resources. The letter you did not get was full of truth! I am afraid that unless I put some "cosmetics" on what I say, I won't be able to write to you at all.

Another letter came from a C.A.P.S. member imprisoned in Huntsville, Texas, dated September, 1979:

> You will be interested and no doubt "appalled" to know that the Texas Board of Corrections has recently made a rule that prohibits Texas inmates from circulating petitions among themselves or from participating in *"unauthorized"* activities, or from forming unauthorized or unapproved organizations or from soliciting membership in such organizations. According to W.J. Estelle (our slavemaster) this ruling is for the protec-

tion of the inmates . . . he wants to take away our right to petition for the redress of grievances for our own protection!

From a July, 1979, letter from Somers prison:

> Your material to this prison is being shortstopped, as was your letter of June 13th until I learned of it this afternoon and demanded that it be given to me immediately or returned to sender without delay. They can do pretty much as they please - withholding mail is probably the least of the "rights" I've had violated in my many years of fighting the prison system. As I said in a recent letter to the newspapers: "Leaving the fate of confined men to those who have built a massive industry around them (and stand witness alone to what they are doing and what they need to do to it) is begging the day when almost everyone in this nation will be one or the other."

For six years, the Committee to Abolish Prison Slavery has been circulating a petition, printed in its quarterly *Abolitionist* newsletter, calling for change of the Thirteenth Amendment. The newsletter has been forbidden in several prisons because of the petition. An August 8, 1979, letter from Warden Carl Robinson of the Connecticut Correctional Institution at Somers provides typical reasoning for the denial of the newsletter:

> The publication was found unacceptable on the basis of Section 3 of the Criteria for Rejection of Publications: "Advocates disruption in that it poses a clear threat to the security, discipline, or order of the institution." The Committee [Library Committee at the Somers Correctional Institution] had no objections to the contents of the booklet. Its primary concern was the petition enclosed and its potential for disruption in its being circulated within the institution.

The Petition to Abolish Prison Slavery provides a rare opportunity for prisoners to peacefully and lawfully redress their grievances in coordination with a growing support base in the outside community. It is an educational tool intended to empower prisoners by increasing their understanding of constitutional law and the relationship of law to their daily lives; it is a means whereby prisoners can help to lawfully reclaim their own lives.* When the "security, discipline, or order" of an institution is, in the words of Warden Robinson, *clearly threatened* by practice of constitutionally ordained rights, that institution is based on denial of democratic practices.

---

* A copy of this petition can be found in the Appendix.

Another letter from Somers prison explained some of the difficulties facing prisoners who wish to join together to work for their rights:

> Your letter of September 17th, clearly marked *Legal Mail* and opened outside my presence in violation of their own rule, was delivered on the 22nd. . . . The administration is afraid that you'll educate us to their program of using prisoners to help them dehumanize and defeat prisoners, as much a part of serving time as the walls and bars.
>
> You can appreciate the problem of organizing where a group. . . is disbanded. Worse, if they see the same men together more than once, they better be gambling, playing sport, talking racial hatred, anything else than trying to become politically conscious. Almost all the men on your mailing list here suffered the harsh penalties meted out following the Sept. '76 sitdown protest and feel, rightly or wrongly, that it served no purpose for 80 men out of 1,000 to demonstrate.

Since slave protest, in any form, is dangerous, it has always been difficult to rally slaves to stand up for their rights in an organized manner. Most prisoner rebellions have been quite, nonviolent attempts to relieve oppression. Those who, in any manner whatesoever, make a stand or express a grievance are seen as threats to the institution to be made an example to others who might follow in their path. For those who file legal complaints or who choose to litigate, there has always been special punishment. Writing from solitary confinement in Texas, where he had been for two years, a prisoner told us that on three separate occasions in nine months

> . . . the Classification Committee told me that if I would promise to stop filing complaints and agitating the inmates into filing the same, I would be let out of segregation. I refused to promise because they keep treating us as if we were animals. (I told them.)

As Willy Carns wrote from Memphis:

> I am a federal prisoner and self-styled jailhouse lawyer. For three years I have fought the Bureau of Prisons because of their policy of disrespecting human rights and the inhuman treatment of federal prisoners, all in the name of justice.
>
> If I had been willing to forsake all my values, overlook injustice and join that special breed of animal that would put fellow human beings in a cage, and keep poking them with sticks for years for no useful purpose other than revenge, I could have been released almost a year ago on this five years I'm doing.
>
> I guess what I am trying to say is that I fully support the Committee to Abolish Prison Slavery. I do not have funds or I would gladly share them toward our goal, but I will assist in any way possible.

As has been true with all forms of slavery, rebellions occur every minute and every hour. No matter how small and private the rebellion, whether it be working slow at an assigned job, sneaking food back to a cell, studying by lit matches after "lights out," or hating with whole heart keepers who harrass and order, rebellion is a quest for self-preservation, for an impossible escape from the chains.

> Dear C.A.P.S.,
>
> Although your letter is clearly marked legal mail it was sliced open at the top...it appears someone had tried to steam it open at first and then maliciously tore it...
>
> On January 3, 1979, a T.D.C. official had brought me before him for disobeying one of his officer's orders of "Not to Eat a Biscuit".... When a man is hungry and there is food available he is going to eat. (I was gotten up at 2:00 in the morning and had to walk outside in bitter cold down-pour rain to get to the dining hall in just shirt sleeves.) All the while I was eating, the window was open and bitter cold wind and rain blowing in on us.
>
> When the Captain saw that I wasn't unnerved he told me that I was lucky that it wasn't him that I disobeyed, that there was more of him than there was of me, and that he would have beat me so bad I would have been in the hospital for six months...I told him that would be a violation of my 8th and 14th Amendment rights to be free from cruel and unusual punishment. His reply was, and I quote, "I'll take that right and then we'll see what you can do about it. I don't give a damn about your right! Now put that down in your little book!" Of course I did, as soon as I got the chance....
>
> On the confiscation of my legal material, I told an official that it was a violation of my 1st, 5th, and 14th Amendment rights of access to the courts, due process of law, equal opportunity, and equal protection of the law. My keeper's reply, and again I quote, "I don't go by Constitutional law, I go by T.D.C. Rules and Regulations." He was referring to a rule and regulation that prisoners could not have books or their legal material in Solitary. When in the 20th Century it is a standard rule with the Federal Courts that prisoners in both State and Federal prisons be allowed to have their legal material in Solitary. Not only are inmates of the T.D.C. denied their legal material in Solitary but they are also denied State administrative remedy from forms I-127 and I-128's.
>
> What it all breaks down to is this, you have civil rights in prison if you have courage to stand up to the prison authorites in the face of death and you can endure this treacherous, savage and brutal retaliation.

Even with "the courage to stand up to prison authorities in the face of death," claiming civil rights is a dangerous game in prison. Nearly two years after the above incident, the same prisoner sent us the following message:

I got off into some real bad shit here in July. I seen an inmate beaten up by prison authorities and I reported it to two federal Judges and the Federal Bureau of Investigation in Houston, Texas and life has been pretty miserable ever since.

We damn ner' had the shit stopped but one day it started all over again like it never stopped at all. So in January and in August there were two nonjudicial murders on this Unit and I feel the way things are going I am going to be number three. But so goes life. But some of us will have to sacrifice in order to accomplish our goal. No change is comfortable on the outside or inside. The only difference that I can see is that prison officials get away with a lot more because of the "exception" in the 13th Amendment. Ever so slight but still there is a little movement forward instead of backward. . .

This prisoner's fears are well-founded, for those who run the Texas prison system have also been named for the following indictments, testified to in a 1978 federal court hearing:

[A] former prisoner told of losing both his arms below the elbow after he was ordered by supervisors at a state prison farm to feed silage into a threshing machine by hand, a violation of normal safety procedures. . . .

One prisoner, John W. Johnson, serving a three year sentence for possession of marijuana, testified that, after he awakened from a hernia operation in a prison hospital, the attending physician explained that he had accidentally lost a testicle, assuring the patient "You don't need it. You can go through life without it."[32]

From plantation to plantation in the antebellum South, from nation to nation throughout history, the "modus operandi" of human bondage has been distinguished by atrocity. Whenever a people are denied the practices of democratic rights, their sufferings defy description. Until the practices of citizenship, human and labor rights are restored to prisoners, prison reform will continue to apply band-aid solutions to this deep sickness. The cancer of our justice system will only heal when its source - slavery - is cut out root and branch. As California prisoner Ruchell MaGee has written:

To some degree, Slavery has always been outlawed and condemned by hypocritical mockery of chattering lips, but on the inside of people and prisons, where slavery is imbedded and proudly displayed as a Western Way of Life and a privilege of God Himself, Slavery is condoned on all of its numerous levels.

Notes

1. *Plessy v. Ferguson,* 163 U.S. 537, 542 (1896).

2. Henry Campbell Black, *Black's Law Dictionary,* 5th ed. (1979), s.v. "involuntary servitude," "slavery."

3. On June 30, 1981, there were 30,954 people imprisoned in Texas. This figure includes prisoners under Texas state jurisdiction but not those under "state custody." (U.S. Department of Justice, *Prisoners at Midyear 1981.)* In 1978, 47 percent of Texas prisoners were reported doing agricultural labor, with most prisoners working their first six to eight months in the fields (Kevin Krajick, "Profile Texas," *Corrections Magazine,* vol. 4, no. 1 (March 1978), pp. 11, 13). Controversy over the Texas system is also examined by the March, 1978, issue of *Corrections Magazine* (see Krajick, pp. 5-7, 9-21). On p. 5, Kevin Krajick reports:

> According to its admirers, who are numerous, the Texas prison system is the most successful and efficient anywhere. "They do well all the things that prisons are supposed to do," says C. Paul Phelps, director of the neighboring Louisiana Department of Corrections. "They keep you in, they keep you busy and they keep you from getting killed." According to critics, also numerous, the system is dehumanizing and repressive, *because* of its very orderliness and efficiency. "The Texas Department of Corrections is probably the best example of slavery remaining in the country," says Arnold Pontesso, former director of corrections in neighboring Oklahoma.

See also Danny Lyon, *Conversations with the Dead* (New York: Holt, Rinehart and Winston, 1971), an important photographic essay of prison life in Texas.

4. Katheryn Watterson Burkhart, *Women in Prison* (Garden City, N.Y.: Doubleday & Company, Inc., 1973), p. 286, interview with Arizona prison superintendent Frank Eyman.

5. Mitford, p. 190.

6. Ibid., p. 193.

7. Ibid., pp. 196-197.

8. U.S. Department of Justice, *Bureau of Justice Statistics Bulletin,* "Prisoners at Midyear 1981," opens with:

> The prison population of the United States swelled by more than 20,000 during the first half of 1981, adding more persons to the rolls of the nation's correctional institutions in 6 months than were added during the previous 12 months. On June 30, 1981, State and Federal correctional institutions held nearly 350,000 prisoners, compared with less than 330,000 yearend 1980 and 300,000 yearend 1977. The 6.2 percent increase during the first half of 1981 was equivalent to an annual growth rate of nearly 13 percent compared with increases of 4.5 percent in 1980 and just above 2 percent in 1979 and 1978.

9. National Moratorium on Prison Construction, "Average Maintenance Cost in Prisons and Jails per Prisoner per Year (Based on U.S. Department of Justice

Statistics, Prisoners in State and Federal Institutions on December 31, 1978 and U.S. Department of Justice [LEAA], Census of Jails and Survey of Jail Inmates, 1978, and on U.S. Department of Justice Expenditure Data for the Criminal Justice System, 1978.)" (Washington, D.C.: mimeo). $9,143 is the national average cost per state prisoner, as computed from direct costs ranging from $3,933 (Texas) to $36,944 (Wyoming) per prisoner year. These "direct costs" are limited to staff salaries, supplies, maintenance and other day-to-day institutional expenses. N.M.P.C. staff explain that this estimate of direct costs must be assumed to be lower than actual direct costs, since each state varies in budget items reported to the Justice Department.

The inadequacy of accurate cost analysis available to the public becomes clearer upon examining a 1978 report to the National Council on Crime and Delinquency by accounting and consultant firm Coopers and Lybrand. Entitled "The Cost of Incarceration in New York City," the study indicated that New York City spent $71.87 to imprison one person for one day, or approximately $26,000 per year per prisoner during the year ending June 30, 1976. Direct expenses were $58.12 per day [81% of total, and $21,213.80 per prisoner per year], and daily outside services such as legal, medical and education cost the city $13.75 per prisoner per day [19% of total, or $5,018.75 per prisoner per year]. In addition to these total "out-of-pocket" costs to New York City, the study states:

> We estimate societal costs [such as additional welfare benefits paid to prisoners' dependent families, lost earnings of imprisoned workers, and lost real estate taxes for property used by the city for "correctional" purposes] at $95.2 million per year, or $39.55 per prisoner per day. These costs are not included in the "out-of-pocket" costs outlined above.
>
> In addition to the costs described above, there are a number of other factors that should be considered.
>
> > A 6% inflationary impact on the present cost of incarceration would increase the annual "out-of-pocket costs" to 1.7 billion in 40 years. Expressed on a per prisoner basis, assuming no growth in the prisoner population, the cost per inmate day would be $697.47 and the annual cost per prisoner would be $255,000 in 40 years.
>
> The economic cost of alternative use of funds should also be considered. The impact can be quantified by measuring the cost of these "lost opportunities." For example, a dollar not spent on incarceration could be invested and interest earned; or City debt could be reduced. Using this concept and applying a 6% cost of money (a conservative rate by today's standards) to the out-of-pocket costs of incarceration, would result in a "lost opportunity" cost of $10.4 million for 1976 and an annual cost of $4.0 billion in 40 years. (Coopers & Lybrand, "The Cost of Incarceration in New York City" [Hackensack, N.J.: National Council on Crime and Delinquency, 1978], pp. 5-6.)

10. Mitford, pp. 202-203.

11. Ibid., p. 206.

12. Burkhardt, p. 289, and continues with:
    Hongisto said the commissary profit from San Francisco jails

alone totaled at least $18,000 a year. He planned to track down the money and start using it to improve direct services for inmates who live in what he called "outrageous and inhumane conditions." Hongisto said that he could only figure the money had been funneled off into private gain, because certainly it hadn't been used for inmate benefits.

13. See Michael Snedeker, "Con Law," *The Outlaw* (San Francisco: Prisoners' Union, 1974), 3: 6, 1-2; *Pell v. Procunier* 41 L. Ed 2nd 935, 504. *Wolff v. McDonnel* 41 L. Ed 2nd 935, 957; *Jones v. North Carolina Prisoners' Union, Inc.* 433 U.S. 119.

In *Pell v. Procunier*, the Supreme Court held that prison regulations banning prisoner interviews with the press did not violate the First Amendment:

> In this case, the restriction takes the form of limiting visitations. . . . In the judgment of the state correction officials, this visitation policy will permit inmates to have personal contact with those persons who will aid in their rehabilitation, while keeping visitations at a manageable level that will not compromise institutional security.
>
> Such considerations are particularly within the province and professional expertise of corrections officials, and . . . courts should ordinarily defer to their expert judgment in such matters.

In *Wolff v. McDonnel* regarding due process of law for prisoners in prison disciplinary hearings, the Court stated:

> The operation of a correctional institution is an extraordinarily difficult undertaking. Many prison officials, on the spot and with the responsibility for the safety of inmates and staff, are reluctant to extend the unqualified right to call witnesses; and in our view they must have the necessary discretion without being subject to unduly crippling constitutional impediments.

And in *Jones v. the North Carolina Prisoners Union, Inc.,* the Supreme Court ruled that prisoners' First Amendment rights "must give way to the reasonable regulations of penal management." (This case is examined in greater detail in Chapter 9.)

14. "Goon Squad" produced by Jim Jackson, *60 Minutes,* CBS News July 26, 1981 television broadcast transcript, (CBS, Inc., 1981; original broadcast January 11, 1981) vol. 13, no. 5, pp. 2-8.

15. Ibid.

16. Ibid.

17. John M. Crewsdon, "Inmates Tell of Texas Brutality," *New York Times,* November 11, 1978.

18. Ibid.

19. Mitford, pp. 139-140, as quoted from M.H. Pappanworth, *Human Guinea Pigs* (Boston: Beacon Press, 1968), p. 64.

20. Mitford, pp. 140-141.

21. Ibid., p. 149.

22. WCI Waupun Paralegal Program Sub-Committee on Prison Health, "Request for Assistance," March 25, 1980 (Waupun, Wisc.: memo to members of WCI Program Steering, Advisory and Procurement Committee), p. 1.

23. Prisoners' Commission, *Report from Prisoners Inside Indiana State Prison* (n.p.: *Prisoners' Commission,* 1980; mimeo), pp. 10-11, "April 20, 1980."

24. Ibid., p. 40, "Hospital/Medical Treatment."

25. Dr. Edgar Schein, at a meeting of U.S. wardens and social scientists in 1962, as quoted by Eddie Griffin, *Breaking Men's Minds: Behavior and Human Experimentation at the Federal Prison in Marion, Illinois* (St. Louis: National Committee to Support the Marion Brothers and the Task Force on Behavior Control and Human Experimentation of the National Alliance Against Racist and Political Repression, n.d.), p. 2.

26. Alberto Mares, released from the Control Unit as a result of a federal court order on December 6, 1973, quoted by Prison Research Education Action Project, 1976, p. 49, "Behavior Modification."

27. Ibid.

28. See Griffin, pp. 3-17.

29. Ibid., pp. 17-18.

30. *Webster's New World Dictionary of the American Language,* s.v. "civil rights."

31. Memorandum regarding "Malicious and Unjust Attacks on the World Community of Al-Islam in the West by the Attica Prison's Guards" to Governor of the State of New York, Commissioner of the Department of Correctional Services, Superintendent of the Attica Correctional Facility, et. al., from members of The World Community of Al-Islam in the West, in Attica Correctional Facility, May 5, 1980 (photo-copy).

32. Crewsdon, *New York Times,* Nov. 11, 1978.

Chapter 8:
Struggle Inside

Why, you welcomed the intelligence from France, that Louis Philippe had been barricaded in Paris · you threw up your caps in honor of the victory achieved by Republicanism over Royalty · you shouted a loud · "Long live the republic!" · and joined heartily in the watchword of "Liberty, Equality, Fraternity" · and should you not hail with equal pleasure the tidings from the South that the slaves had risen, achieved for themselves, against the iron-hearted slaveholder, what the republicans of France achieved against the royalists of France?

> **· Frederick Douglass**
> **Faneuil Hall, Boston**
> **June 8, 1849[1]**

Prisoners come from the most empoverished, most disempowered communities of this nation. Prison is the last stop on the line; here, behind cages of concrete and steel, through the sights of a gun and answering to a bill of no rights, government attempts to teach its captives to accept the "fate of the lower classes," to "rehabilitate" prisoners into accepting that fate.

The following letter from a California prisoner to a friend outside illustrates the futility constantly facing those locked inside without rights or resources to determine their own fate:

> A very sad prisoner came to me and explained that he had just received a letter from his wife in Detroit. Therein his wife told of a group of charity-oriented persons who brought some food and toys over for Christmas. His baby son refused the broken toys, started crying and shouted, "If you want to do something good then get my Daddy out of prison so *he* can buy me some toys!" Then he ran out of the project-apartment. The mother accepted the food and toys, and went on in her letter to beg her husband for assistance in relocating in California to be near enough to visit. I wanted to help · but I couldn't. February this prisoners got another letter in which his wife said she was going to get another old man "because the kids need a father and I need someone to help me make it through these rough times." The prisoner transferred to another joint and now doesn't give a damn whether he ever gets out or not. . . .

Prisoners are at the mercy of their keepers and, by virtue of their bondage, cannot determine the course of their own lives. They are forced into helplessness and their helplessness turns into despair. Prison slaves suffer atrophy of vital social abilities that prosper only with exercise of freedoms of speech, press, association, the rights to vote, petition, due process, and labor protections. These social "muscles" only become strong with practice of the rights to labor for just wages at a job of one's choice, safety from undue search and seizure and freedom from cruel and unusual punishment. Slavery and involuntary servitude are founded on denial of these vital protections.

Palsied by bondage, many leave prison with new disabilities, new bitterness, new futility. While society expects that they should have "learned their lesson," in reality their alternatives have been greatly diminished by the injustices they have suffered as slaves.

A person may develop numerous disabilities during and after release from prison. The ability to exercise citizenship rights becomes atrophied with denial of the opportunity to practice them, while new social muscles develop to contend with the primitive viciousness of contemporary punishment. Prisons train people to survive under cruel conditions; rehabilitation can only occur in the community. The task of crossing a street can overwhelm the new parolee who, having spent years behind high walls in a five-by-ten-foot cell, can no longer judge time, distance, and speed of oncoming traffic. In addition to losing such rights as "voting, holding offices of public and private trust, and serving as a juror," the prisoner and ex-prisoner may have lost "family by divorce or adoption proceedings resulting from conviction." The ex-prisoner may experience "difficulty managing . . . property, entering contracts and obtaining insurance, bonding, and pensions," and may also "be barred from a broad range government-regulated and private employment."[2]

Broken families, an already competitive labor market where jobs are even more difficult for an "ex-con" to find, and special restrictions the parolee must abide by in order to avoid being returned to prison - a traffic violation, for example, or leaving the state without obtaining authorization from a parole officer - are only a few of the additional handicaps the newly freed slave must endure. Just as the Black Codes were designed to return freed chattel slaves to their old masters, so parole regulations and social prejudices make it easy to recage newly freed prisoners. No wonder that 40 to 70 percent of those released from prison return. As one Louisiana prisoner put it:

> Prisons remind me of a machine that makes tin cans. When a can comes out of the machine with a dent in it, they put it back through the same machine to take out the dent. Instead of removing the dent, the machine dents the can worse! So, they repeat the process until the can becomes so dented that it can never be repaired. When will society consider the fact that it's the machine that needs repairing?[3]

Without practice of their citizenship and labor rights, prisoners' fates are no better than the tin cans this prisoner described. Another prisoner put it this way:

> We need to effect a program that will be for the benefit of those incarcerated, not a program that will beef-up security.

Walls, bars, and barbed wire fences do not help a human gain self-respect. What gives a person self-respect is the knowledge that he or she has accomplished something. This (something) is the building of a productive society that develops friendship and cooperation among its inhabitants. One day we will be returned to society and if we are conditioned into not being responsible decision-making humans, then surely we will make irrational decisions. A lot of prisoners have no one to turn to; so, they are in greater danger of returning because there is a lack of support.

Why not ask us (prisoners) what our needs are? Prison officials do not live with us, so how can they even begin to comprehend our problems? My experience with prisons would lead me to believe that we as prisoners could make our world better by having a voice....

Most prison administrators regard prisoner efforts to humanize their living conditions as a threat; any totalitarian regime is threatened by organized, peaceful attempts at self-empowerment by its subjects. Denied the right to vote and often punished for attempting to exercise free expression, American prisoners know the oppressions of bondage. While slavery breeds fear, complacency, frustration and powerlessness, it also breeds struggle for freedom. Thousands of stolen people jumped off slave ships and into the sea rather than face bondage, and slave insurrections left a trail through history of the blood spilled during the slavemasters' brutal backlash. The Underground Railroad was the American slave's only sucessful escape-route to freedom, but today there can be no underground railroad because no part to the country is free of "slavery...as a punishment for crime." The hidden nature of prison slavery's practice keeps many potential abolitionists immobilized by ignorance. Slaves have never been able to safely voice their needs or demands but the antebellum South's unashamed celebration of human bondage made it possible for citizens to witness and then to protest against slavery. Today, slavery is hidden in law and behind high bastilles which guard against physical escape and prevent public witness to daily brutalities.

Rebellion

Increased arrests for political crimes such as unlawful civil rights and anti-war marches; government infiltration and harrassment of organizations such as the Black Panther Party, the Student Nonviolent Coordinating Committee and the National Association for the Advancement of Colored People; and persecution and murder of leaders such as Martin Luther King, Jr., Fred Hampton, the Berrigan brothers, Angela Davis, Malcolm X, and many more, all led public attention to turn to prisons.

In 1969, black prisoners at the Indiana Reformatory petitioned the prison administration to forbid their keepers' use of derogatory racial epithets and arbitrary punishments. After written appeal brought no results, petitioners sat down in protest and guards opened fire, killing two and wounding 46 prisoners. Those who escaped injury were placed in segregation and denied visitors and writing privileges. "After deliberation the grand jury determined that the guards had committed no criminal act by firing into the group of seated prisoners."[4]

Struggle for Justice, a study of crime and punishment prepared for the American Friends Service Committee, reported:

> On August 11, 1970, three Philadelphia judges, reporting on the aftermath of a July 4 riot that left ninety-six persons injured at Holmesburg Prison, characterized the prison as a "cruel, degrading and disgusting place, likely to bring out the worst in man...Since the riot, the prison has, in addition, become a place ruled, as one of the prisoners certified, by 'cold-blooded terror'...."
>
> On the following day prisoners in the Tombs - New York's famous bastille, where accused suspects are held before trial - rioted, held several guards hostage, and presented a list of grievances that included inadequate food, filthy cells, brutality, lack of medical care, and insufficient representation by court-appointed lawyers. Less than two months later thousands of inmates in four New York City jails rebelled, taking control of the jails, holding hostages, and raising demands that challenged not only jail conditions but city court practices as well.[5]

That protest was also put down by force and, again, defenseless prisoners were brutally maimed. Significantly, "the New York City prison protests followed a decade in which that city had cooperated fully in implementing what has been widely regarded as the most significant program in the nation dealing with problems of pretrial detention."[6] Reform of slavery does not produce significant change. Victims of the slavery proviso in the Thirteenth Amendment, the prisoners at the Tombs were demanding relief for themselves from the incessant cruelties that had blighted the lives of slaves before them. In closing their petition, they stated:

> We are firm in our resolve and we demand, as human beings, the dignity and justice that is due to us by right of our birth. We do not know how the present system of brutality and dehumanization and injustice has been allowed to be perpetuated in this day of enlightenment, but we are the living proof of its existence and we cannot allow it to continue.
>
> The manner in which we chose to express our grievances is admittedly dramatic, but it is not as dramatic and shocking as the conditions under which society has forced us to live. We are indignant and so, too, should the people of society be indignant.
>
> The taxpayer, who, just happens to be our mothers, fathers, sisters, brothers, sons and daughters should be made aware

of how their tax dollars are being spent to deny their sons, brothers, fathers and uncles justice, equality and dignity.[7]

On January 13, 1970, in California's Soledad Prison, a spontaneous riot provoked by racist agitation occurred when previously segregated prisoners were put in the exercise yard together. Interracial tensions were high, no guards were sent into the yard with them, and, predictably, a fight erupted between two prisoners and led to havoc in the yard.[8]

> [Soledad guard] O.G. Miller had the reputation of being a hardline racist, and was known to be an expert marksman. He was stationed in the gun tower that day. He carefully aimed his carbine and fired several times. Three men fell: W.L. Nolen, Cleveland Edwards, Alvin Miller. They were all Black. A few days later the Monterey County Grand Jury was convened to hear the case of O.G. Miller. As could have been predicted, he was absolved of all responsibility for the deaths of the three brothers. The Grand Jury ruled that he had done nothing more serious than commit "justifiable homicide."[9]

Shortly after, three prisoners, George Jackson, Fleeta Drumgo and John Clutchette, were charged with the death of a Soledad guard. There was no evidence for the charge; these three black men had been singled out because of their continued protest of Miller's acquittal, because of their political beliefs and because of the respect they won from other inmates during discussions of the need for liberation of oppressed peoples: their conviction and execution would serve as an example to like-minded prisoners. In the year that followed, a committee to defend the Soledad Brothers was mobilized and, in May 1971, the State's star witness admitted in court to having given false testimony in exchange for an early parole and all charges against the Soledad Three were dropped.[10]

Barely three months later on August 3, 1971, George Jackson was murdered by San Quentin prison guards. Thinking slaves have always been selected for special punishment and George Jackson had become a symbol of freedom for too many people. In her autobiography, Angela Davis described the experience of hearing George Jackson's mother explain the conviction that had put him in prison:

> Georgia Jackson, Black, woman, mother; her infinite strength undergirded her plaintive words about her son.
> When she began to talk about George, a throbbing silence came over the hall. "They took George away from us when he was only eighteen. That was ten years ago." In a voice trembling with emotion, she went on to describe the incident which had robbed him of the little freedom he possessed as a young boy struggling to become a man. He was in a car when its owner - a casual acquaintance of his - had taken seventy dollars from a service station. Mrs. Jackson insisted that he

had been totally oblivious of his friend's designs. Nevertheless, thanks to an inept, insensitive public defender, thanks
to a system which had long ago stacked the cards against
young Black defendants like George, he was pronounced guilty of robbery. The matter of his sentencing was routinely
handed over to the Youth Authority.

With angry astonishment I listened to Mrs. Jackson
describe the sentence her son had received: one year to life in
prison. One to life. And George had already done ten times
the minimum.[11]

On August 3, 1971, 28 year old Jackson was sprayed with bullets by
guards who claimed he was trying to escape. Those familiar with the inner workings of prison knew that George Jackson had been executed.

On the other coast, in a prison named after an ancient Greek city-
state known for its keeping of slaves, Attica, prisoners were already
involved in peaceful attempts to convince their overseers to humanize
their living conditions. As the *Official Reports of the New York State
Special Commission on Attica* expressed it:

Into this atmosphere of frustration and futility came the news
of the shooting of George Jackson by prison guards at San
Quentin. If officials' explanations of the death of Fred Hampton in Chicago in 1969 were unacceptable to black people in
this country, the official account of the death of George
Jackson was regarded by Attica inmates as a flagrant insult.
California officials claimed that Jackson had attempted to
escape with a gun smuggled in to him by an attorney and con-
cealed by Jackson as he left the visiting area.

Every Attica inmate who had ever received a visit in prison
believed Jackson must certainly have been subjected to a
thorough search before entering and immediately upon leaving the visiting room. Even if a gun could have been conceal-
ed in his hair, inmates reasoned, it would certainly not escape
detection during such a search.[12]

George Jackson had been murdered and Attica convicts
demonstrated their outrage at that death in the quiet rebellion of black
arm bands and a hunger strike. A month earlier, in July, a petition had
been submitted listing Attica prisoner grievances:

Their demands centered largely on improvement of the conditions of their imprisonment, not the end of that imprisonment
itself. Among other things, they demanded legal representation before the Parole Board; improvement in medical care,
visiting facilities, food and sanitary conditions in the mess
hall, personal hygiene, clothing, recreational facilities, and
working conditions in the shops; a uniform set of rules in all
prisons; adjustment of commissary prices; and "an end to the
segregation of prisoners from the mainline population
because of their political beliefs."[13]

Come September, nearly nine months had passed without any response to prisoners' requests to negotiate with the Attica administration. Denied access to the media and appeal to public support, Attica prisoners, like all other prisoners, were stymied in their attempts to effect needed change. John Cohen, friend of Sam Melville, one of those killed in the September massacre, wrote:

> By subjecting prisoners to total degradation - one inmate described Mancusi as "not a warden, but a concentration camp commandant to whom inmates are not even dogs, just numbers" - and by refusing the inmates any hope for significant change in prison conditions, the pigs created enough anger, frustration and despair to generate any number of riots. And by refusing the prisoners access to the media the pigs actually *encouraged* riots. As Sam wrote, "We are left with nothing except riots to bring our plight before the public."[14]

On September 8th, the growing tension exploded when a guard accused a prisoner of a rule infraction and ordered him into lock-up. Other prisoners went to his defense, a hostage was taken and soon prisoners were holding the yard. The prisoners' attempt to force the administration into fruitful negotiations ended at the order of Governor Nelson Rockefeller on September 13th:

> *First,* a special gas was sprayed into the yard before the police opened fire. Rockefeller described the effects of this gas as "fantastic." Inmates said it was extremely powerful, sending men into convulsions.[15]

State snipers, perched on the high walls encircling the yard, fired into the prisoners as troopers charged into the yard from below, spraying bullets as they ran. Reports later showed that

> Before they charged into D yard troopers loaded their shotguns with .32 caliber "pellets" - the size of pistol slugs - especially chosen so that each pellet would have murderous effect. Snipers loaded their rifles with .270 Winchester .30 gr. expanding bullets. Ammunition boxes discarded outside prison walls advertise "the exclusive Silvertip bullet with controlled expansion (and) soft-jacketed tip." In plain language, dumdum bullets, which international law outlaws in warfare.[16]

Today, no one questions why the slaves in the South rebelled, no one publicly disclaims their human right to equality and dignity under the law, or their historic right to throw off their chains. Villains of the nineteenth century like Nat Turner and John Brown are now national heroes. They, and millions before and after them, were responding to tyranny. They died demanding justice. There is an ongoing crisis in American prisons which comes to public light only after prison violence too massive and tragic to hide. The public wakes, pressure is put on prisons to remove the causes of violence but, shortly after, all is forgotten and the conditions which provoke prison violence remain. Nearly a decade after the Attica rebellion, we received the following from an Attica prisoner:

> As you may have heard or read, Attica has been in somewhat of a turmoil for the last few months. There has been a rash of killings, stabbings and daily fights amongst the inmate population. It would take more than this mere piece of paper to adequately explain the causes and effects, etc., but I will sum it up by merely saying, things are really bad, and you will definitely be hearing more from the Attica correctional facility!

Another prisoner also wrote in 1979 to explain the roots of prisoner unrest:

> I am a prisoner in the state of Washington and a Slave of the state. You have probably read or heard about the lock-down here and as everything comes to light, you will see that Slavery is the cause of it all. The brutality that was submitted here to hundreds of men, by officers with guns, clubs, leaded gloves, belts and whatever they could use to harm and beat innocent men, is only an act that was performed on slaves years ago prior to the abolishment of Slavery and yet it is allowed today to prisoners. WHY?
>
> What would happen if you took an animal and beat it with the instruments named above, for no reason at all?? If you took animals and caged them up so close that they could not move about in a normal manner, what would the Humane Society do to you?? If you worked the animals without proper food, what would the Humane Society do?? YET, the Constitution of the United States allows the above to happen to human prisoners.
>
> Are we not a maturing society? Should we not as prisoners, progress with a maturing society? If so, how can we progress when the Constitution has not progressed and still condones Slavery?

The next year violence overtook the prison at Santa Fe, New Mexico. The rage unleashed in Santa Fe was that of people who had been poked at, terrorized and brutalized for years.

Santa Fe, 1980

New Mexico has drawn the tears from my soul. These things are the result of man's inhumanity to man. In the name of God, Justice and Right Conduct, we will not be on earth if this continues for another two hundred years.

- Oji
Jessup Prison, Maryland
February, 1980

In the early morning of February 2, 1980, prisoners in the state penitentiary at Sante Fe, New Mexico, began a 36-hour siege that left an unknown number of prisoners dead, more than 100 wounded and $10 million in property damages - a "rampage of murder and mutilation," wrote one reporter, "that is apparently without precedent in the history of American prisons."[17]

The root causes of the February 2, 1980, prison slave rebellion at Santa Fe lay in the conditions under which those prisoners were forced to live and survive. From the outset, the tragedy of Santa Fe, of prisoners killing other prisoners, was caused by the brutal slave practices of that state prison.

New Mexico's violation of prisoners' rights became clearer in the American Broadcasting Company's television documentary "Death in a Southwest Prison." Severe overcrowding: ". . . there's about six inches between you and the next bed, " reported a former inmate; "you can't even move your arm over without hitting somebody in the face, and you've got all these radios and things on different stations full hog, and all these people are packed in." Flagrant violation of prisoners' rights to privacy and personal property: "They would go in and have [cell] shakedowns and throw his pictures of his children and his wife on the floor and walk on 'em, for no reason at all other than the fact that they just, you know, regarded that person as an inmate or a convicted criminal." Beatings and the "hole": a nine-by-six-foot cell which one ex-prisoner described as having "seven men thrown in there with one hole in the ground, and you have to eat in this place; there's no ventilation. You have a jug of water, where everybody shares it. You have to use a rest room in front of seven people, and if they [the guards] don't want to flush the toilet outside, they won't flush it. . . . there's a lot of individuals that are unable to take it. . . and pretty soon you got guards coming in beating on these guys."[18]

In this institution where 90 percent of its prisoners had less than 60 square feet each to live in and men have sentences as long as 250 to 1200 years,[19] there was even less hope for those who succumbed to mental illness. In September 1980, the *Albuquerque Journal* reported on Santa Fe's crude treatment of its mentally disturbed prisoners: solitary confinement, deliberate withholding of medication, medical treatment without supervision by a licensed physician in violation of state health codes, and, in some cases, immobilization of "violently suicidal inmates...in plaster bodycasts, which were left with holes for them to urinate and defecate through."[20]

> "Self-mutilators are numerous in any prison setting," Dr. [Frank] Rundle [New York psychiatrist and American Civil Liberties Union forensics health care consultant] told the *Journal*. "But the way prison people deal with it allows them to ignore the fact that the way they're running the prison and treating people is what's leading prisoners to do it.
>
> "Prison officials, rather than dealing with the basic problems, lock people up in cells, or put them in restraints, or in some cases, knock them out with tranquilizers...
>
> "Everybody knew the problems were there - everybody, all the way up to the governor."[21]

While imprisoned, cousins Dwight and Lonnie Duran challenged unconstitutional prison conditions in court and won. In December 1979, Santa Fe prisoners told corrections officials that a rebellion would occur if partial court orders of *Duran v. King* were not complied with immediately. Two weeks before the riot, a memo from a prison psychologist informed the prison administration that an uprising would occur, predicting it to the very day. Nothing was done. Ten days before the February riot, Dwight Duran completed his sentence and was released from prison. Now working at the National Prison Project of the American Civil Liberties Union, Dwight explained that the prison rebellion was anticipated at the same time New Mexico's corrections department was waiting for the legislature to respond to its request for more funds. Dwight said that such "coincidences" had occurred many times before:

> A lot of investigative reporters have done work in this area. It's a fact, a very well known fact that they knew it was coming: memos were sent by staff and security days ahead.
>
> They knew it was coming. But up to that point in New Mexico the riots had been contained in one or two living units. They could easily quell them and they would go to the state legislature, request what they needed, and get funding. But this time they underestimated the rage.
>
> A couple of months before, they had a mass escape of eleven inmates...If you check the balances of records for escapes and disturbances, you find the corrections officials have also had an appointment to go to the state legislative finance committee or such. And it's too frequent to be coincidence.

Prison riots tend to occur at crucial times for state appropriations; New Mexico is not unique in experiencing prison disturbances which occur just in time to help convince politicians to appropriate more money for corrections. Prison rebellions frighten taxpayers into believing more dollars must be spent to better "protect" them from "dangerous criminals" already locked away.

Since January 1980, the State of New Mexico has appropriated $300 million to its corrections budget, largely in reaction to that February tragedy in Santa Fe. A considerable portion of the money, Dwight told us, has gone to pay consultants to study the system. But studies on the New Mexico prison system are not new - one quarter of a million dollars paid for a study in 1977 and, two years later, a half million funded another. In December 1979, only one clause of the findings of a study on Santa Fe's staffing was released: "It said that the State of New Mexico was playing Russian roulette with the lives of the inmates, the staff, and the public alike. And that was two months before the riot. They stuck it in the bottom drawer and never released the findings." A few days after the riot, $95 million was appropriated for the construction of two new prisons, shortly followed by another $14 million for renovation and building expenses. The 1980 budget shows a 65 percent increase for operational expenses, and when we asked Dwight where the money had gone, he said: "Higher salaries, uniforms and nice offices. Inmates are still wearing rags and eating slop."

Mice and vermin in prisoners' half-cooked meals, arbitrary disciplinary procedures, vengeful staff and inhumane treatment, cavity searches, routine harrassment of prisoner visitors and intolerably long sentences were among the conditions that created the intense rage unleashed on February 2, 1980. This in a state which spends $8,000 each year to keep one person in prison.[22]

Beyond vile living conditions, Santa Fe prison keepers showed traditional overseer vigilance in maintaining slavemaster control. Slaveholders have always planted informants among their chattel and no prison is without its snitches. As the ABC documentary reported, the snitch system at Santa Fe was deliberate, widespread and recruitment of prisoner informants was laced with brutality. If a prisoner refused to be an informer, as one ex-inmate reported,

> They'll take him and throw him in with a bunch of hard timers. . . . knowin' that they're going to beat him, they're gonna rape him and everything else. Then, when he gets out of the hospital the Captains and Lieutenants tell him, All right, you do what we want to, and. . . we'll keep 'em away from you.[23]

Public report suggested the prisoner violence that night was aimed at the snitches, but no reporters were allowed to interview the prisoners to find out what really happened. As Dwight Duran told us, of the 33 prisoners reported killed, only 13 were found in the protective custody unit where prisoner informants were housed. Nor did the riot result from drug-induced hysteria: as Dwight remarked, the drugs prisoners were alleged to have obtained from the medical dispensary were sedatives and could have only helped to quell the rage, not intensify it.

On September 3, 1981, the *Santa Fe Reporter* published findings of the Inter-Media Investigative Group, "a group of newspaper, television and radio reporters and several other individuals, all of whom had become frustrated in their independent efforts to get to the bottom of New Mexico's scandal-ridden corrections system."[24] One of the results of their intensive five-month investigation revealed that, while the prison administration's report lists 33 dead, 120 Santa Fe prisoners are unaccounted for, missing since the riot. The investigative group also interviewed prisoners who reported seeing piles of bodies after the riot, deaths not accounted for in official reports.[25]

Little has changed in New Mexico's Santa Fe prison since that horrible national media event. The court order resulting from *Duran v. King* has not been enforced; there have been isolated prisoner killings and suicides; and, as the Inter-Media Investigative Group reports, there exists no credible fiscal accounting system for the prison.[26] The man in charge of Santa Fe's prison, Felix Rodriguez, whom many blame for the tyranny and brutality which rules the prison, still reigns. Prisoners still have six months of visiting privileges taken away if they touch their visitors more than twice, upon greeting and farewell. As Dwight Duran explains, it is not uncommon for a guard to take a baby out of his imprisoned father's arms and charge the prisoner with violating visiting rules.

New Mexico continues to punish its citizens with intolerable long and harsh sentences while several of its towns are competing for the next new prison location and employment that prisons can bring. In the aftermath of Santa Fe, however, there is a growing movement among New Mexico citizens to force the state government to bring humane treatment to its prisoners. Like freedom fighters before them, prisoner rights activists have been threatened with violence. In an interview with ABC, activist Juan Lopez stated:

> They have made threats on my life. My line...rings all the time...and...at one time my daughter came to me and she was crying and screaming, she says: they're after you, Dad, they want to kill you, a threat has been made. They told me to tell you...stop the investigation...or else.[27]

And, like antebellum slave leaders, prisoners who have used their even limited access to the courts to effectively challenge unconstitutional brutality are further isolated in modern slaveholding attempts to render them powerless. Lonnie Duran, co-plaintiff *Duran v. King,* who is serving 300 years and who was instrumental in saving hostage lives during the February riot, was transferred to Lompoc prison in California. There he met friend David Ruiz who was transferred from a Texas prison. Like Duran, Ruiz was responsible for important litigation, *Ruiz v. Estelle,* which was decided in favor of Texas prisoners. Shortly after, Lompoc prison keepers charged both men with instigating an alleged work strike which never took place.[28] Ruiz was then transferred to the federal penitentiary at Marion, Illinois, and Duran was sent to Leavenworth, Kansas. Like slave leaders before them, they had been "sold South" as punishment.

What happened in Santa Fe prison provided brief, intense insight into the suffering hidden by prison walls. Prison slavery breeds rebellion, results in human destruction and incites riot. Like the systems of human bondage which permeated the antebellum South, the severity of contemporary punishment varies from state to state, from prison to prison, but, as one Texas prisoner put it:

> Slavery, man. Human slavery. You write that down. That's all you need to write, because that puts it all in one word.[29]

Notes

1. Foner, *Life and Writings of Frederick Douglass,* vol. 1, p. 399.

2. President's Commission on Law Enforcement and Administration of Justice Task Force Report: Corrections 88 (1967) *The Collateral Consequences of a Criminal Conviction, Vanderbilt Law Review,* 23 (1970): 939.

3. Letter from Louisiana prisoner Billy McLeod as printed in "Jake McCarthy, a personal opinion," St. Louis, Mo. *Post-Dispatch,* January 18, 1978.

4. *Struggle for Justice,* A Report on Crime and Punishment in America Prepared for the American Friends Service Committee (New York: Hill & Wang, a division of Farrar, Straus and Giroux, 1971), p. 6.

5. Ibid., p. 1.

6. Ibid., p. 7.

7. Ibid., pp. 5-6.

8. Angela Davis, *Angela Davis: An Autobiography* (New York: Random House, Inc., 1974), p. 252.

9. Ibid.

10. Ibid., p. 253; *If They Come in the Morning,* p. 73 n.

11. *Angela Davis: An Autobiography,* pp. 253-254.

12. New York State Special Commission on Attica, *Attica: The Official Report of the New York State Special Commission on Attica* (New York: Bantam Books, Inc., 1972), p. 139.

13. Ibid., p. 134.

14. Samuel Melville, *Letters from Attica,* introduction by John Cohen (New York: William Morrow & Company, Inc., 1972), p. 70.

15. Ibid., p. 73.

16. Ibid., pp. 75-76.

17. Cynthia Gorney, "New Mexico Prison Toll Reaches 35; At Least 20 Murdered," *Washington Post,* February 5, 1980.

18. "Death in a Southwest Prison," produced by Stephen Fleischman, *ABC News Closeup* September 23, 1980 television broadcast transcript (American Broadcasting Companies, Inc., 1980).

19. Craig Pyes, "Priority Given to Crisis in Mental Care at Pen," *Albuquerque Journal,* September 25, 1980; length of prison sentences told to us by former Santa Fe prisoner Dwight Duran.

20. Craig Pyes, "Plaster Casts Employed as Prisoner Restraints," *Albuquerque Journal,* September 23, 1980.

21. Craig Pyes, "Mentally Ill State Prison Inmates Receive Crude Treatment," *Albuquerque Journal,* September 21, 1980.

22. National Moratorium on Prison Construction, "Average Maintenance Cost in Prisons and Jails per Prisoner per Year."

23. *ABC News Closeup,* "Death in a Southwest Prison."

24. Inter-Media Investigative Group, "Frustration was the Common Bond," *Hell On Earth: A Special Report, Santa Fe Reporter,* September 3, 1981, p. 2. Members of the investigative team: Roger Morris (team leader), Toni Drew, Kingsley Hammett, David Hendry, Karen McDaniel, Kathy Morris, Peter Morris, Mary Lynn Roper, Diana Stauffer, Charles Zdravesky, and other members who were not identified "because their work within the penitentiary and the Corrections Department, and their contacts within the system, would be jeopardized by public exposure of their role." (p. 2).

25. Ibid, "The Unknown Toll: We'll Never Know," p. 3.

26. Ibid., "They Thought It Was Their Prison," pp. 7, 10.

27. *ABC News Closeup,* "Death in a Southwest Prison."

28. As reported to us by Dwight Duran.

29. Krajick, p. 17.

Chapter 9:
A New
Abolitionist Movement

That slavery has begun its fall is plain, but. . .its fall will be resisted by those who cling to it. . . . The end will be slow. Woe to abolitionists if they think their work is well nigh done.

- Theodore Weld, 1852[1]

Groups and organizations within the prisoners' rights and criminal justice arenas are joining the struggle to abolish prison slavery at an increasing rate, and their growing rank-and-file membership is also calling for prison slavery's abolition. Habilitation or rehabilitation demands affirmation of human dignity and exercise of the responsibilities inherent in the practice of democratic rights. We cannot expect to have safe streets when we dehumanize lawbreakers and return them to society full of new rage accumulated during years of bondage and with new helplessness caused by enforced powerlessness and denial of democratic protections. Abolition of prison slavery will humanize our systems of punishment and encourage use of humane alternatives to imprisonment.

Unlike nineteenth century bondage, modern slavery is hidden rather than proudly displayed. It selects victims from those most impoverished and its perpetuation depends on national misunderstanding. Slavery is a cancer in our justice system; any remnant of the dreaded illness allows it to flourish, maim and kill. Until prison slavery is abolished, we will continue putting band-aids on cancerous wounds only to have them fester and recur in various forms of suffering throughout our body politic.

The old abolitionist movement did not complete its work. As the struggle against one form of bondage gathered momentum, another was developing in its place. Prison slavery was sealed into the very constitutional amendment which achieved chattel slavery's prohibition. Like chattel slavery before it, modern prison slavery is the most blatant form of human bondage in its time, revealing and requiring elimination of its many contributing oppressions.

Overwhelmingly poor and minority prison populations testify to government's continued effort to train citizens to submit willingly to the "fate" of the lower classes. As American political leadership moves further away from sheltering the rights of people to advocating the rights of a few to accrue wealth, we come to a new era of struggle. Slavery protects the rights of profit rather than the rights of people; advocacy of civil rights has become a defensive political position rather than the vanguard of government policy changes, and we face expansion of slave punishments.

Like the developers of seventeenth century workhouses, the contract labor and convict lease systems, some "reformers" are lobbying to readmit private industry to American prisons and open the free market to prison-made products. Even the Chief Justice of the Supreme Court, Warren E. Burger, has gone on record for building "factories with fences around them."[2] Touting liberal-sounding labels such as the "free venture system," modern advocates in harnessing prison labor for profit present sophisticated arguments for the rehabilitative value of work and the additional benefit of reducing the cost of imprisonment. Among the unmentioned dangers is the threat to American workers: letting private industry into prison would open the way for corporations unwilling to meet the demands of organized labor. With the unorganized and exploitable labor force in prisons, industrialists who have moved their shops to third-world countries for cheap labor could come home again. Prisons would become profitable for government and big business and serve to depress wages by making free American workers compete with imprisoned workers. Until prisoners are guaranteed the practices and protections of citizenship, labor rights and human rights, all of us remain unprotected victims of their potential exploitation.

Recognizing the immediate dangers of American inequality, we must pick up the prematurely discarded banner of slavery abolition to build a new abolitionist movement. The nineteenth century dictum remains true: while slavery is reserved for one of us, none of us is free. Building on the tradition of abolitionists before us, we need to focus on slavery's last lawful stronghold: "slavery...as a punishment for crime."

Lessons from Old Abolitionists

John Woolman gave witness to the relationship between unequal wealth and oppression; Frederick Douglass contributed a former slave's leadership and clarity of perception to the often confused charity of his fellow abolitionists; Dred Scott persisted in fighting for his right to freedom in the courts; Harriet Tubman led her people up from slavery; John Brown died for abolition; workers and slaves fought the Civil War to bring freedom to this nation; Charles Sumner fought slavery in Congress and joined forces with abolitionists like Douglass to ensure the civil rights of emancipated freedmen; Wendell Phillips took his abolitionist training to the labor movement and Susan B. Anthony helped forge the women's movement; the Molly Maguires were hanged for their insistence on justice; W.E.B. DuBois urged his people on to freedom; Dr. Martin Luther King, Jr., George Jackson and unmentioned others have left a legacy and example for us to carry forward. From them, and by examining the development of their struggles, we learn much of what abolition of prison slavery demands. As we hold to the strengths of our abolitionist heritage, we must also avoid its past mistakes.

Sources of the old movement's weaknesses lay in the superficial understanding of inequality that guided some of its most influential members. Sheltered by relatively affluent lifestyles, several remained ignorant of slavery's roots in economic exploitation. Because of this, the movement generally failed to embrace workers' struggles against class-based oppression. The festering wound of prison slavery was a natural outgrowth of ignored inequities. The movement failed to encourage leadership from ex-slaves within it, even though those who suffer under slavery have always known it best. Frederick Douglass, appalled by victimization of the "free" poor, which he said reminded him "of the plantation, and my own cruelly abused people," was ignored when he argued against postwar disbanding of the movement. He criticized those abolitionists who would abandon the ballot box or let the South secede in order to be cleansed of partaking in a slaveholding government. From the earliest abolitionist struggles we learn that slavery oppresses all, even the slavemaster, but that it is the slave who loses nothing by breaking slavery's chains. It is from the ranks of those most oppressed that we learn what abolition demands. Today, those who know slavery best are behind prison walls; not only have they experienced denial of their rights as prisoners, but their direct victimization by social, political and economic inequities contributed to their imprisonment. The success of a renewed abolitionist movement depends on bridging the abyss which has kept slave and free from working together.

Slavery thrives on divisions among its victims. While it seeks to divide caged victims by fostering racial animosity and offering crumbs of privilege to those who contribute to fellow slave disempowerment, it also prospers from divisions among the "free" who fight it. Labor and civil rights movements have been natural allies but the well-fostered misunderstandings which separate economic and political struggles for equality in this country have served to divide them. The struggle against slavery is a fight against all inequality. If the old abolitionist movement had defended labor, workers would have swelled abolitionist ranks; if slave leadership had been fully recognized, tragic mistakes could have been avoided. With each of slavery's victims contributing to the other's understanding of oppression, the injustices which helped slavery expand and change forms might have been eliminated.

Mandate for a United Front

When the abolitionist movement prematurely disbanded, the modern prisoners' rights movement began. The unfinished work of abolition has also continued in other arenas: civil rights, labor rights, minority rights, women's rights, the peace movement, advocacy for the poor and the struggle to end oppression from unequal wealth. While important victories have been won, the struggles have continued along a divided front.

This disunity can be examined, in microcosm, in the prisoners' rights movement. Organizations are severely underfunded to carry out their programs and competion develops between like-purposed organizations for meager resources. Despite hard-won battles for justice, the oppressions which have faced prison slaves for centuries appear in new forms again and again. Prisoner needs continue to overwhelm the capacity of any one organization or coalition of organizations to serve. Most prisoners' rights activists have been victimized by the long-prevailing notion that slavery was abolished, that rights are to be protected rather than won. Unaware of this important contradiction, twentieth century prison reform can be likened to humanizing the system of bondage which victimized this nation before the Civil War: it cannot be done without abolishing the institutionalized structure of punishment - slavery.

Since the end of the Vietnam War, there has been a resurgence of the attitudes which upheld antebellum slavery. "Taking government off the backs of the people" has become the political slogan for granting new license for exploitation to the robber barons of burgeoning corporate cartels. The call to balance the national budget by slashing programs which helped protect consumers, workers and the unemployed, minorities, children, the elderly and the poor has given new impetus to "profits before people." Government's renewed war on crime promises that prison populations will increase, punishing those who rebel against growing repression and hiding those who fall victim in the intensifying struggle to survive. Recent burnings of books by "moral majority" censors and cross-burnings by the "new" Klan serve as signposts for the dismantling of our liberties.

The weakened posture of the people's progressive forces is a defensive one, one that assumes this country is free of slavery when it is not and that has failed to grasp the essential unity of interest of those too oppressed to act as one. The Thriteenth Amendment's authorization of prison slavery provides a tactic for a new offensive for people's rights, but abolition of prison slavery and of contributing inequalities requires unprecedented unity. Too much work exists for any single group, organization or coalition, and the struggle is too large to waste precious resources by failing to coordinate efforts.

A United Front to Abolish Prison Slavery would help answer America's need for a new abolitionist movement. Based on the understanding that each quest for equality finally depends upon the abolition of slavery, this federation of abolitionists and their respective organizations could reach out to support other struggles for people's rights while carefully coordinating prison slavery abolitionist activities. By sharing resources and responsibility and avoiding duplication of efforts through cooperative organizing, the United Front would be able to forge an offensive to stop the expansion of modern slavery.

WORK TO BE DONE

We face a social, economic and political problem which must be attacked at the sources of its proliferation: local, state, and federal criminal (in)justice systems. Progressive change in law is worthless without community vigilance and understanding in seeking its enforcement. Slavery abolition is a people's struggle which must work up from the deepest grassroots levels.

Grassroots and State Lobbying

Grassroots lobbying combines organizing, assistance and services, community education about the negative conditions of prison slavery and political action. An empowering grassroots educational and political tactic is petitioning, and the Petition to Abolish Prison Slavery is a basic organizing tool. By presenting the Thirteenth Amendment with its offensive proviso capitalized for emphasis, the document calls attention to the long-ignored exception for slavery in the Constitution:

> Neither slavery nor involuntary servitude, EXCEPT AS A PUN-ISHMENT FOR CRIME WHEREOF THE PARTY SHALL HAVE BEEN DULY CONVICTED, shall exist within the United States, or any place subject to their jurisdiction.

and asks that the Constitution be amended, deleting the exception for prison slavery so that the Thirteenth Amendment would read:

> Neither slavery nor involuntary servitude shall exist within the United States or any place subject to their jurisdiction.

The lesson of the old abolitionists' struggle is clear on petitioning: they so flooded American institutions with their petitions that policy makers were forced to deal with slavery. Today, slavery is hidden by government instruments which support it, assumed to have been abolished by most Americans, and remains unidentified by many prison slaves. The Petition to Abolish Prison Slavery serves as a stimulus to re-examine failing justice systems, create new understanding, empower habilitation of caged Americans through struggle for their own emancipation, and lobby for political change.

Petition signatures are obtained everywhere, in churches and in bars, on street corners and at home, at rallies and at concerts, at community gatherings and by going door to door, through the mail, in prisons and in branches of government. Although many who have signed

C.A.P.S.'s petition have done so immediately, exclaiming that "this ex ception to slavery explains everything," others have not been as ready. New truth is often resisted and modern abolitionists need to embrace people's questions with new knowledge, perspectives and solutions. Those circulating petitions will not always know all of the answers. In such circumstances, it is always best to state that you will research the matter to find the answer.

Political use of petitioning takes two forms, informal and formal. Informal political petitions are used to persuade lawmakers to introduce local and state legislation calling for abolition of prison slavery and involuntary servitude. Formal use employs the initiative/referendum process of citizens petitioning to qualify abolitionist legislation for voter consideration in state elections. Political organizing can be expanded to support abolitionist candidates and to oppose the election of those who demonstrate slaveholding positions on prisoners' rights. Continued lobbying is also needed to introduce selected prisoners' rights legislation such as voting rights, right to petition, freedoms of speech and press, equal pay for equal work, abolition of the death penalty and abolition of civil death statutes.* The key objective of state political organizing is winning support for national legislation and its ultimate ratification in the various state legislatures.

Prisoner-Support Chapters

The Petition to Abolish Prison Slavery is helping prisoners develop mutual identity. Recognizing the exception within the Thirteenth Amendment is the first step in tracing responsibility for suffering to its source in a philosophical and material system of injustice. It has helped transform prisoner alienation into constructive class conciousness, stimulating needed unity in the quest for abolition. In correcting the misunderstanding which has kept slavery's victims divided, the struggle to abolish prison slavery calls on the vital wisdom of this nation's most oppressed class.

Community-based education and action programs are needed to bridge the abyss of misunderstanding currently existing between outside and inside communities because the key to understanding prison slavery lies behind prison walls. Prisoners hold that key and abolition requires the effective participation of prison slaves. As chattel slaves were most vulnerable to slavemaster retribution when the institutionalized structure of their bondage was attacked, so are prisoners. The first step of any abolitionist program is to address the survival needs of those slavery most severely victimizes. From that protection and advocacy comes the needed participation of the imprisoned, their family members and the communities from which they come.

---

*Please see Appendix.

Today there is no underground railroad for slave protection and outside abolitionists must reach behind slavery's walls to insure prisoner participants against special punishments. Such a "lifeline" to emancipation depends on active communication and advocacy sustained by free abolitionists. Correspondence, visitation and organizing with prisoners creates this bridge. Together, slaves and abolitionists learn what must and can be done. Based on the common goal of abolishing prison slavery, today's slave-and-advocate relationship works against reprisals facing prisoners who petition for slavery abolition and aims to empower both participants working together for effective change. The bulwark of abolition is built on this lifeline.

Through this lifeline, the public can be informed of news of prisoner oppressions, crisis-provoking prison tensions can be addressed through legal and political action before riots result, legal and political protection can be obtained for imprisoned abolitionists, and survival needs of prisoner family members can be met through community-based projects which help restore vital family ties.

The most viable support base is prisoner families, most often poor people without adequate resources to organize for their collective self-determination. Abolitionist organizing empowers participants through projects which address survival needs while creating the means to organize further. Appropriate projects include emergency food closets, car pool transportation for prison visits, and collective child care. Establishing a community-based office provides an organizing center outside prison needed to recruit volunteers, provide services and assistance, build community education projects, raise funds, petition, lobby and coordinate other chapter activities.

Abolitionism stresses the need to guard against slaveholding principles which warp programs by claiming to represent the best interests of equality while failing to invoke the participation of the unfree. Without their contributions abolition becomes a pompous label for activity by the self-righteous and the misled.

Boycotts

Galley slavery and the convict lease system prospered when blatant slavery and its clearly visible profits were acceptable. Today, slavery exists within every prison and jail in every state. The profits from this exploited labor force are hidden because prisoners work at a variety of jobs so that no one particular product comes to national attention. The average citizen pays little attention to the source of slave-made products since they fall withing the realm of "government" services. As nineteenth century abolitionists refused to buy fabrics dyed with slave labor, the renewed abolition movement can draw public attention to the slave economy of many government services. Economic boycotts work.

Prisons are run by slave labor: laundry, clothing, food, repair and maintenance, all are done by prisoners. Services provided by prison slave labor may vary according to the budget needs of each state: plantation labor, road construction and repair, license plates, computer print-outs for government agencies, standard equipment for state and veterans' hospitals, furniture used in prisons, government offices and the homes and offices of correctional personnel, barbeque grills and picnic tables for state and rest areas, road signs, fire fighting services, prison construction and American flags make up an incomplete list of the products and services provided to the State by the slave labor of prisoners within "Corporate Penal Industries".[3] A list of products sold by the Texas Department of Corrections, for example, provides the beginning of a list of one state's prison-slave products which could be targeted for boycott. As reported by a Texas prison slave, these products include license plates, inspection stickers, canned goods, boxes, mops, brooms, microfilming, plastic signs, plastic name tags, furniture, shoes, soaps, street signs and poultry.[4] A Pennsylvania prisoner reports that all "Pencor" products are slave-made and easily recognizable by the label advertising their trade name.

One recent example of a boycott for prisoners' rights is provided by the internationally supported avoidance of British-made products to protest denial of political prisoner status for Irish Republican prisoners. Other contemporary examples of boycott effectiveness are found in the past decade's boycott of grapes and lettuce by the United Farmworkers' Union and in the more recent boycott of products by Nestlé, the international trafficker in infant formulas, especially harmful in third-world countries. Both campaigns won nationwide support and were instrumental in changing repressive corporate policies. Boycotting prison slavery's products* could create public education and political pressure. While calling attention to slavery's continuance, economic action throws a wrench into the slave economy, forcing institutional consideration of slavery-free solutions.

Slavery abolition remains a moral, political, legal and economic struggle belonging in international, national, state and local arenas. Today's worldwide condemnation of slavery and involuntary servitude places a new abolitionist movement on advantaged footing. Least known, but crucial to the strategy of a United Front, are the various state constitutional provisos for slavery and involuntary servitude to punish crime.

---

*Because the sale of their art work is often the most equitable source of income available to prisoners, boycotts should not include prisoner crafts.

THE STATES

The war between the North and South was fought to forcibly reunite a "house divided" over slavery. Since that great Civil War, a common geographical reference point for socioeconomic and political comparisons has been between states north and south of the old Mason-Dixon Line.

There is another frame of reference for measuring today's house-divided concept: a prison slavery abolitionist perspective.

A Prison Slavery Abolitionist Perspective

The significance of the various state constitutional provisos on prison slavery cannot be ignored in a workable strategy for abolition. Behind each state's modern prison oppressions are laws and traditions in denial of prisoners' rights deeply ingrained from centuries of practice.

The states fall into four primary catagories: prison slave, changed, involuntary servitude, and no proviso. Those states whose constitutions call for prison slavery and involuntary servitude are referred to as *prison slave* states. Originally there were 29 *prison slave* states; now there are 14.

29 ORIGINAL PRISON SLAVE STATES

Those 15 states which changed their prison slavery provisos are known as *changed states*. As a result of these constitutional changes, there are now only 14 *prison slave* states.

15 CHANGED & 14 PRISON SLAVE STATES

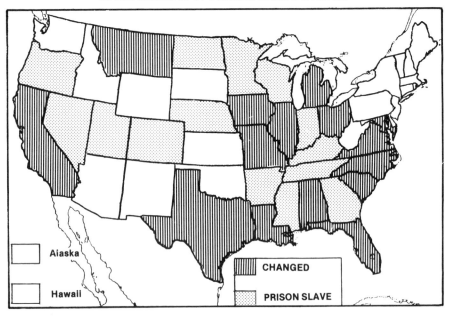

Those 10 states whose constitutions prohibit slavery but provide for involuntary servitude as a punishment for crime are referred to as *involuntary servitude* states.

10 INVOLUNTARY SERVITUDE STATES

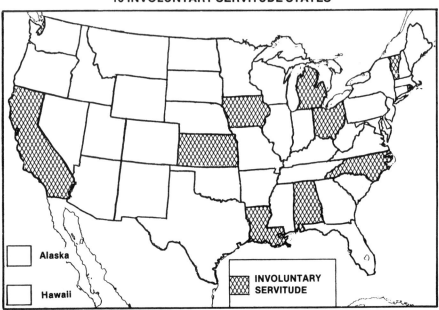

Those 26 states making no mention of either slavery or involuntary servitude are referred to as *no proviso* states.

26 NO PROVISO STATES

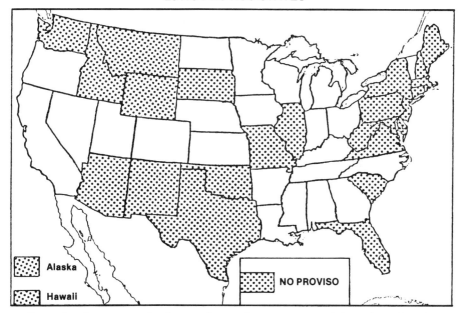

Georgia, for example, is a *prison slave* state and Article I, Section I of its constitution blatantly says so:

> There shall be within the State of Georgia neither slavery nor involuntary servitude, SAVE AS A PUNISHMENT FOR CRIME AFTER LEGAL CONVICTION THEREOF.

Michigan is one of those states whose constitution changed from prison slave to *involuntary servitude.* Article 18, Section 11 of its 1850 constitution stated:

> Neither slavery nor involuntary servitude, UNLESS FOR THE PUNISHMENT OF CRIME, shall ever be tolerated in this State.

In 1963, Michigan became an *involuntary servitude* state by its new constitution's Article I, Section 9:

> Neither slavery, NOR INVOLUNTARY SERVITUDE UNLESS FOR THE PUNISHMENT OF CRIME, shall ever be tolerated in this State.

Montana is a state which changed from prison slave to *no proviso.* Article III, Section 28 of its 1889 constitution stated:

> There shall never be in this state either slavery or involuntary servitude, EXCEPT AS A PUNISHMENT FOR CRIME,

>WHEREOF THE PARTY SHALL HAVE BEEN DULY CON-
>VICTED.

This section was omitted from Montana's 1972 constitution and no reference was made to either slavery or involuntary servitude.

The notion that prison slavery is an emotional term with no functional significance is refuted by the fact that 15 states have *changed* their state constitutional provisos to *involuntary servitude* or *no proviso.* There were two major periods of state constitutional changes on prison slavery, during the period of Radical Reconstruction and the era of controversy over private business use of prison labor when seven states changed their slavery provisos; and, again, during the sixties' and seventies' struggles for civil rights and against the war in Vietnam, when eight states changed their constitutional provisos. Including the pre-Civil War proviso change in Iowa during 1857, 15 states changed their constitutional rulings on prison slavery:

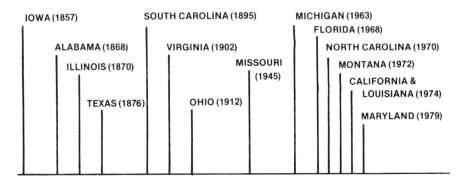

Excepting Texas, California and Montana, the change states are in the South and the Northwest Territory. Eight of these 15 are now *no proviso;* the remaining seven are *involuntary servitude* states.

These 15 state governments must be confronted with their constitutional changes, and more research is needed to reveal the political motivation for each change. Efficient organizing strategy can be designed following additional research to determine the statistical signatures of oppression within and among each of the states. Changed states provide important historical examples of legislative dealings with the embarrassing constitutional sore of modern slavery.

California - from Slavery to Involuntary Servitude

Until 1974, California authorized slavery and involuntary servitude to punish crime. The old Article I, Section 18 read:

>Neither slavery nor involuntary servitude, UNLESS FOR THE
>PUNISHMENT OF CRIMES, shall ever be tolerated in this State.

The prisoners' rights, civil rights and anti-war movements of the late sixties and early seventies helped influence the California legislature to amend its state constitution to prohibit "slavery...for the punishment of crime." Article I, Section 6 of the 1974 California constitution. reads:

> Slavery is prohibited. Involuntary servitude is prohibited EXCEPT TO PUNISH CRIME.

In 1975, California followed the tradition of other involuntary servitude states by removing its authorization of Civil Death for prisoners and parolees. Section 2600 of the Penal Code had stated:

> A sentence of imprisonment in a state prison for any term suspends all the civil rights of the person so sentenced, and forfeits all public offices and all private trusts, authority, or power during such imprisonment. But the Adult Authority may restore to said person during his imprisonment such civil rights as the authority may deem proper...[5]

The replacement for Section 2600, however, shows little effective change from the old:

> A person sentenced to imprisonment in a state may, during any such period of confinement, be deprived of such rights, and only such rights, as is necessary in order to provide for the reasonable security of the institution in which he is confined and for the reasonable protection of the public.[6]

The institutional structure of Califorina punishment has not changed, even though its labels have. Prisoners still cannot vote, they are caged and chained, due process and free expression are severely limited, they are forced to live in unsafe, crowded and unhealthy environments with inadequate nutrition and medical care: citizenship rights continue to give way to the "reasonable security" of prison slavery.

Abolition of any form of slavery requires radical change in the institutional structures which have disfranchised and victimized the oppressed. For example, one of the first acts of nineteenth century Radical Reconstruction was passage of the Fourteenth and Fifteenth Amendments, guaranteeing voting and citizenship rights to emancipated slaves. Rather than restore rights to prisoners, California's new penal code orders that rights "be deprived...in order to provide for the reasonable security of the institution...[and] public." If California legislators were intent on abolishing the perpetuation of slavery, Section 2600 would state:

> The 1974 prohibition of "slavery...for the punishment of crimes" in California guarantees that all citizenship, labor and human rights are restored to prisoners and to persons henceforth sentenced to state prisons. The inalienable rights

of citizenship, and the practice thereof, are necessary for the reasonable security of the institution, for the reasonable protection of society, and for the reasonable habilitation of the offender. During such period of confinement the practice of these rights shall not be denied but shall be guaranteed.

The hypocrisy of slavery prohibition in California is further illustrated by the 1976 addition of Section 2652.5 to its Penal Code:

Chain or mechanical restraint around neck of prisoner; prohibition; violations misdemeanor

No person employed by the Department of Corrections, the Department of the Youth Authority, or any city or county jail facility shall place any chain or other mechanical restraint around the neck of any prisoner for any purpose. Any violation of this section shall be a misdemeanor.[7]

Removing a chain from the neck of a slave does not emancipate the slave, it merely makes less blatant the visible atrocity of human bondage by eliminating one of its symbols. Furthermore, how can shackling a person be merely a misdemeanor in a "slave free" state?

As in other involuntary servitude states, no serious attempt at "radical reconstruction" occurred in California. The continued denial of prisoners' rights was merely reworded, camouflaged by replacing "slavery" with "involuntary servitude." The essential process facing "involuntary servitude" states is the same process that faced Congress after the passage of the Thirteenth Amendment. At the very least, prohibition of slavery must be enforced by guaranteed protection of prisoners' citizenship, voting, and labor rights.

A prison slavery abolition program in California could focus on that state's 1974 prohibition and unconstitutional continuance of "slavery...to punish crime." While California has had sufficient time to promote citizens' understanding of the responsibilities inherent in its state constitutional change and to establish serious guarantees for prisoners' rights, it has failed to do so. California prison slavery abolitionists can cite the relatively meaningless state penal code changes since 1974 as testimony of this failure. An effective program for slavery abolition in California could maintain that continued denial of prisoner citizenship and labor rights be declared unconstitutional, immediately restrained and all appropriate orders be issued against further such unconstitutional practices. It could call for establishment of a Caring Community Board with authority to guarantee protection of prisoners' rights as citizens, thereby ensuring radical reconstruction of that state's prison system, and it could maintain that monetary damages of no less than $100 per day be awarded to each prisoner who suffered under the unconstitutional yoke of slavery since 1974.

Each "involuntary servitude" state continues its unconstitutional practice of slavery as a punishment for crime; each provides its abolitionist citizens with a unique opportunity for struggle. While their constitutions proclaim abolitionist intent, the involuntary servitude states have merely called slavery by another name. In addition to seeking state legislative action, citizens of involuntary servitude states can bring their struggle to the courts where their states' prohibition of prison slavery could be used to challenge violation of prisoners' rights. The potential of such litigation is illustrated by a prison slavery abolitionist analysis of a 1977 U.S. Supreme Court case.

Jones v. the North Carolina Prisoners Union

An important opportunity to use modern slaveholding language against itself was missed in a 1977 Supreme Court case challenging denial of First Amendment rights to North Carolina prisoners. North Carolina had changed its constitution to prohibit slavery and permit only involuntary servitude to punish crimes. That state's prior prison slavery proviso was found in Article I, Section 33 of the 1868 Constitution:

> Slavery and involuntary servitude, OTHERWISE THAN FOR CRIME, WHEREOF THE PARTIES SHALL HAVE BEEN CONVICTED, shall be, and are hereby forever prohibited within this State.

Article I, Section 17 of the 1970 Constitution ended North Carolina's license to practice slavery by permitting only involuntary servitude to punish the convicted:

> Slavery is forever prohibited. Involuntary servitude, EXCEPT AS A PUNISHMENT FOR CRIME WHEREOF THE PARTIES HAVE BEEN ADJUDGED GUILTY, is forever prohibited.

As a consequence of the new North Carolina Constitution, labor rights but not citizenship rights could be denied to prisoners. As we have seen, however, slavery is enforced by means of denying citizenship rights to ensure involuntary servitude, slavery's mode of production. The North Carolina prison system violated prisoners' new constitutional protection from slavery when it prevented them from associating in the North Carolina Prisoners' Union. Prisoners, still under complete control of the state, were being denied their First Amendment rights and the prison administration violated its state prohibition of "slavery.... for crime." Even though the U.S. District Court granted the North Carolina Prisoners' Union "substantial injunctive relief, having concluded that prohibiting inmate-to-inmate solicitation 'border[ed] on the irrational,'" the U.S. Supreme Court ruled against the union, stating that "the challenged [prison] regulations do not violate the First Amendment as made applicable by the Fourteenth."[8] The June 23, 1977 U.S. Supreme Court decision on *Jones v. The North Carolina Prisoners' Labor Union, Inc.* held that state prison officials can prohibit prisoners from asking fellow inmates to join a union, can refuse to distribute inmates' bulk mailings from outside union organizers, and can prohibit the use of prison facilities for union meetings. Writing for the Court's majority, Justice William H. Rehnquist stated that such regulations do not violate a prisoner's rights to freedom of speech and association since prisoners' First Amendment rights "must give way to the reasonable regulations of penal management."[9] Nowhere were the "reasonable regulations of penal management" challenged as being based in North Carolina's unconstitutional practice of "slavery . . . . for crime."

In spite of this missed opportunity to challenge the unconstitutional practice of prison slavery in the Court, the dissenting opinions of Justices Brennan and Marshall provided some hope for future litigation efforts. Written by Justice Marshall, their dissent reminded the court of the affirmation of prison slavery in the 1871 ruling of *Ruffin v. The Commonwealth of Virginia:*

> There was a time, not so very long ago, when prisoners were regarded as "slave(s) of the State," having "not only forfeited (their) liberty, but all (their) personal rights . . ." *Ruffin v. The Commonwealth of Virginia,* 62. Va., 790, 792 (1871). In recent years, however, the courts increasingly have rejected this view, and with it the corollary which holds that courts should keep their "hands off" penal institutions. Today, however, the Court, in apparent fear of a prison reform organization that has the temerity to call itself a "union," takes a giant step back towards that discredited conception of prisoners' rights and the role of the courts. I decline to join in what I hope will prove to be a temporary defeat . . . .[10]

Like the nineteenth century court cases which tossed Dred Scott and his family from slavery to freedom to slavery again, the "hands on/hands off" doctrine towards prisoners' rights merely describes United States judicial policies on slavery: hands off, hands on, then hands off "slavery . . . as a punishment for crime." Since *Ruffin,* the courts have conveniently circumvented reference to the Thirteenth Amendment with terms such as the "reasonable regulations of penal management" used by Justice Rehnquist. The various state constitutional rulings on prison slavery, however, provide important opportunity for abolitionists to confront the institutional structure of punishment, even in the courts.

Had the North Carolina Prisoners' Union focused on the difference between the U.S. Constitution and the North Carolina Constitution rulings on prison slavery, it might have won its case by using the authority of the Tenth Amendment, which guarantees that all states can guarantee more but not fewer rights than the federal constitution. It could have confronted the Supreme Court's judicial responsibility to uphold the legal meanings of constitutional language through prison practices by presenting North Carolina's 1970 prohibition of "slavery. . . . for crime." The U.S. District Court had been correct in restoring First Amendment rights to North Carolina prisoners and the U.S. Supreme Court overstepped its constitutional authority by granting fewer rights to prisoners than authorized by Article I, Section 17 of the North Carolina Constitution.

Maryland - A Timely Example

Shortly after the American Civil War, the Thirteenth Amendment to the United States Constitution passed through the two houses of Congress, was submitted to the states for ratification and was certified as law on December 18, 1865. In 1867, Maryland added the then new Article 24 to its Declaration of Rights.

> THAT SLAVERY SHALL NOT BE RE-ESTABLISHED IN THIS STATE; but having been abolished under the policy and authority of the United States, compensation, in consideration thereof, is due from the United States.

112 years later, in 1979, Article 24 was completely removed from the Maryland Constitution. At first glance it would seem appropriate to eliminate the antiquated last portion. However, upon careful examination we note that this legislative action nullified the progressive first portion ("That slavery shall not be re-established in this State") by allowing sanction for prison slavery to be "re-established" in Maryland under the authority of the Thirteenth Amendment. Simply, rescinding of Article 24 deferred constitutional authority on slavery from Maryland to the U.S. Constitution's Thirteenth Amendment whereby slavery is sanctioned "as a punishment for crime."

The U.S. Constitution allows each state to grant more rights, but not fewer than exist on the federal level. Upon C.A.P.S.'s informing Maryland House of Delegates Representative Wendell Phillips of his state's error in nullifying its abolitionist ruling, Delegate Phillips decided to introduce legislation to amend the Maryland State Constitution to "abolish and prohibit slavery absolutely." On February 29, 1980, Delegate Phillips submitted his proposed amendment to the Maryland House of Delegates' Constitutional and Administrative Law Committee.* C.A.P.S. testified at this hearing, criticizing the rescinding of all of Article 24 in 1979, explaining the meaning of Maryland's legislative history, and urging solicitation of prisoner participation in designing legislation in their own behalf.

If the 1980 bill had passed, it would have abolished the permissible practice of slavery as a punishment for crime in Maryland by requiring Maryland to discontinue those aspects of punishment which can be fairly regarded as attributes of slavery. In their simplest context, those attributes are denial of the practice of citizenship, labor, and human

---

*Please see Appendix for the 1980 proposed legislation in Maryland.

rights to prisoners. The bill did not pass the Constitutional and Administrative Law Committee.

In 1981, Delegate Phillips introduced further legislation to abolish prison slavery and C.A.P.S. sent the following communication to its members and to Maryland legislators in support of that legislation:

> We respectfully urge your support of Maryland House Joint Resolution No. 70, "A House Joint Resolution concerning Slavery or Involuntary Servitude for the purpose of urging the amendment of the United States Constitution to remove any trace of the acceptability of slavery or involuntary servitude. . . ."
>
> Most legislators do not know that slavery is still legal or that the United States Constitution authorizes slave punishment within the Thirteenth Amendment. Nor do legislators know that prisoners are slaves through the institutionalized denial of the practices of their citizenship, labor and human rights. The abolition of prison slavery would mean the restoration of prisoners' rights to vote, free speech, due process, freedom from undue search and seizure, freedom from cruel and unusual punishment (slavery is just this), the right to a just and equitable wage for their labor, the right to join a labor union, and many more inalienable rights which are currently being denied to prisoners.
>
> In seeking your support of House Joint Resolution No. 70, we ask that you consider the following unheeded appeal by Senator Charles Sumner in 1864:
>
>> In placing a new and important text into our Constitution, it seems to me we cannot be too careful in the language we adopt. . . . Therefore, it seems to me, we have every motive, the strongest inducement in the world, to make that language as perfect as possible.
>
> In due respect to the spirit of the proposed bill, we further request that prisoners be included in the democratic process which will consider passage of House Joint Resolution No. 70. Their testimony and representation is an important part of the emancipative process and would demonstrate the State of Maryland's clarity in considering this most historic appeal to the U.S. Congress.

The failure of these two legislative appeals provides important lessons for twenty-first century abolitionists. Maryland citizens were not informed about the practices of prison slavery in their state, prisoners were not consulted or asked to testify in behalf of their best interests and no preparation was made to create a needed grassroots movement to participate in designing legislation or to lobby in its behalf. Simply put, those pushing for submission of the legislation failed to accept responsibility for bridging the abyss between the outside and inside communities so that their proposed change in law would be representative of the will of a large abolitionist community inside and outside prison walls. The lesson for abolition is clear: legislative efforts to abolish slavery must be accompanied by grassroots organizing and lobbying efforts from the bottom up. Without community participation in this process, we face probable failure of well-meaning legislation, possible misrepresentation of the needs of prisoners and community members, and a misrepresentation of the very democratic process which abolition seeks to correct and expand.

Since abolition cannot be achieved until slavery is prohibited and that prohibition enforced, the 1980 proposed bill to amend the Maryland Constitution - "That slavery is abolished and shall be prohibited absolutely" - was technically incorrect and misleading. If passed, the 1980 bill could have served to make Maryland citizens assume there was no need for radical reconstruction of state penal practices. However, the 1981 proposed legislation, which would have called on Congress to amend the Thirteenth Amendment, was far more representative of abolitionist needs, citing the U.S. Constitution's authorization for prison slavery and consequent violation of the United Nations Declaration of Human Rights.

State by State Abolition

When a people's status is reduced by denying them practice of their citizenship rights, they become slaves and their bondage cannot be legitimized or camouflaged by not mentioning it or calling it something other than it is. To a lesser or greater degree, all states deny or negate prisoners' citizenship, labor and human rights; all states practice slavery as a punishment for crime. Regardless of constitutional category, each state practices prison slavey and each community bears its own responsibility for slaveholding. Abolition must expose local and state traditions, laws and practices in slave punishment and eradicate them, one by one. As Germantown Quakers gave up slaveholding in 1648 and were followed by all Quakers in 1806, so the power of abolition can spread from one community through an entire state and the nation.

UNITED NATIONS APPEAL

The international authority in support for the proposed abolitionist legislation in the United States is found in Article 4 of the United Nations Universal Declaration of Human Rights.

> Article 4. No one shall be held in slavery or servitude; slavery and the slave trade shall be prohibited *in all their forms.* [Emphasis added.]

In 1967, the United States Senate ratified the "Supplementary Convention on the Abolition of Slavery, the Slave Trade, and Institutions and Practices Similar to Slavery." Simply put, the Senate ratified Article 4 of the U.N. Declaration of Human Rights.

The obvious contradiction is that, unlike the Thirteenth Amendment to the U.S. Constitution, Article 4 contains *no exception* for either slavery or involuntary servitude - both are "prohibited in all their forms." Hence, the United States seems to be in violation of an international treaty on human rights.

The 1981 proposed Maryland House Resolution No. 70 addressed this violation of international treaty by maintaining:

> WHEREAS, With the states' ratification of Amendment XIII of the United States Constitution in 1865, the legality of slavery and involuntary servitude was restricted to "punishment for crime whereof the party shall have been duly convicted"; and
>
> WHEREAS, With the United States Senate's ratification of the Supplementary Convention on the Abolition of Slavery, the Slave Trade, and Institutions and Practices Similar to Slavery in 1967, we recognized the illegality of the "status or condition of a person over whom any or all of the powers attaching to the right of ownership are exercised"; and
>
> WHEREAS, We have become increasingly aware that by accepting as just any form of slavery or involuntary servitude we reduce a human being's personhood and are responsible for the abominable consequences that flow therefrom; and
>
> WHEREAS, In spite of this growing awareness, United States Courts have been bound by Amendment XIII of the Constitution to accept the proposition that "the labor of a convict belongs to the state"; now, therefore, be it
>
> RESOLVED BY THE GENERAL ASSEMBLY OF MARYLAND, That the United States Constitution should be amended to remove any trace of the acceptability of slavery or involuntary servitude; . . . .

While the above resolution never received full consideration by either house of the Maryland state legislature, it serves to show the importance of international appeal. Abolitionist appeal to the United Nations could bring world-wide pressure to bear on the United States to abolish its prison slave practices, thereby providing important assistance to a campaign for national abolitionist legislation.

NATIONAL LEGISLATION

The national legislative focus of a United Front to Abolish Prison Slavery would be amendment of the Thirteenth Amendment to prohibit all slavery and involuntary servitude and passage of supporting laws to enforce that prohibition.

Thirteenth Amendment:

> Neither slavery nor involuntary servitude, EXCEPT AS A PUN-
> ISHMENT FOR CRIME WHEREOF THE PARTY SHALL HAVE
> BEEN DULY CONVICTED, shall exist within the United
> States, or any place subject to their jurisdiction.

Proposed Amendment Change:

> Neither slavery nor involuntary servitude shall exist within the
> United States or any place subject to their jurisdiction.

Prohibition would be accomplished by amending the Thirteenth
Amendment; abolition would begin when the newly worded amendment is enforced by supporting law.

Prohibition

There are three basic stages to amending the Constitution to prohibit all slavery and involuntary servitude: writing and submitting a bill
to Congress to prohibit all slavery and involuntary servitude; passage
of the proposed Amendment by two-thirds majority in each house of
Congress; and ratification of the new Amendment by 38 states, three-
quarters of the United States. Each stage requires sustained grassroots and legislative lobbying from a well-coordinated national base.

As exemplified by the nineteenth century abolition struggle, arriv-
ing at the first stage of national prohibition involves a protracted campaign. While the old movement laid the groundwork by prohibiting
chattel slavery, misrepresentation of the continued practice of prison
slavery must be understood and eliminated to ensure that a new
amendment leaves no provision for slavery under any other name.
Complete and explicit prohibition of involuntary servitude is absolutely essential.

Once enough Congressional allies agree to sponsor a bill prohibiting prison slavery and involuntary servitude, intensive lobbying and
abolitionist education will be needed throughout Congress. As before,
slaveholding lawmakers will adopt different forms of resistance, the
danger in their efforts being explicit enforcement of slave punishments or compromise of an abolitionist victory.

The success of the correct rewording of the Thirteenth Amendment
and its subsequent passage depends on the amount of pressure coming from the grassroots and international levels. The old movement
kept pressure on Congress from their communities, from millions of
petitioners, through the separate abolitionist victories in each state
and with the help of vocal support abroad. Successful organizing
would combine state-by-state victories with effective petitioning of
the United Nations to achieve national prohibition.

Perhaps the best example of what is needed to win ratification is found in examining the long struggle for the Equal Rights Amendment, a movement also rooted in nineteenth century abolitionism. Most significant in this recent lesson of parliamentary struggle is the growing power of relatively small groups of opponents of equality. With well-funded campaigns they have sent their powerful allies to influence the political process and have infiltrated the media and flooded the mails with convincing deceit aimed at creating opposition to the E.R.A. While their numbers are small, their financial backing is strong. Prison slavery abolitionists have the same opponents. Changing the Constitution to prohibit all slavery will depend on preparing ground for abolition: grassroots organizing and state by state constitutional changes can build national victory.

Abolition

Prohibition is only the beginning; abolition requires radical reconstruction of our systems of justice. It is the building of a community of care, a safe society which replaces vindictive punishment with habilitation, restitution and social justice. Abolition enforces equality instead of exploitation, cutting out all remnants of slavery root and branch.

In the second section of the Thirteenth Amendment, the Constitution states:

> Sec. 2. Congress shall have the power to enforce this article
> by appropriate legislation.

Congressional response to this mandate for enforcement came during the short but official post-bellum period of Radical Reconstruction when the Fourteenth and Fifteenth Amendments were passed granting citizenship and voting rights to former slaves. Both of these amendments also had sections calling for Congressional enforcement. The most recent application of reconstructionist law came when the Voting Rights Act was passed at the height of the civil rights movement, banning the use of literacy tests, poll taxes and other devices used to keep black and other minority citizens from voting and requiring those states with a history of voting rights discrimination to obtain clearance ahead of time from the Justice Department for any changes in state or local election laws.

After the first section of the Thirteenth Amendment is amended to abolish all slavery and involuntary servitude, the second section will be needed to enforce prison slavery prohibition. Abolition of prison slavery requires "radical reconstruction" at many levels: restoring the right to vote to the convicted as well as other protections and practices of citizenship, returning their labor rights as citizens, and the enforcement of their human rights in all aspects of their treatment, including the right to healthful living conditions. The death penalty, the ultimate expression of slavemaster power, must be eliminated; the building of human cages must also stop. Each negative condition now suffered must end: prisoners can tell you what they are - ask them.

By removing the yoke of slavery from our systems of justice, we will also open the way to alternatives to imprisonment: victim-offender mediation, victim restitution, community service, counseling and teaching for those that need them. Eventually, prison will take its place in a history which will refer to a time long past when humankind had not yet learned how to heal.

CONCLUSION

Much remains to be done before Americans grasp the reality of the exception to slavery within our Constitution and how it epitomizes the many sufferings of prisoners. Meanwhile, continued denial of the practices of citizenship, labor and human rights in our nation's systems of punishment makes a mockery of any attempt to create a truly safe society. There can be no Safe Society without a Caring Community, and there can be no Caring Community which permits "slavery... as a punishment for crime."

Abolition is a struggle for universal emancipation. As one prisoner put it, "You won't find members of the ruling clique in places like this, but you will find their victims." The exception to slavery in the Constitution represents many inequalities Americans have yet to eliminate. There will be - as there presently are and as history has shown there to be - many twists and turns, ebbs and flows in the road to abolition. We have proposed organizing projects which can accomplish the work needed to produce an abolitionist movement for the 1980's and beyond and we have sought to clarify the unity of struggle which abolition requires.

The problem of prison slavery, like its historical counterparts, cannot be separated from the need for fundamental progressive change in the social, political and economic structure of the United States. The abolition of prison slavery is an integral part of that change.

The task is ours - together, we must begin.

Notes

1. Lerner, p. 305.

2. "Remarks of Warren E. Burger, Chief Justice of the United States, at the University of Nebraska," December 16, 1981, Lincoln, Ne. (Washington, D.C.: Supreme Court Public Information Office), p. 2.

3. Burkhardt, pp. 284-286.

4. "A Few of the Products Available from T.D.C.," as listed in a Texas prisoner's letter and published in the Spring 1980 issue of C.A.P.S.' newsletter *The Abolitionist:*

License Plates	Diesel Mechanics
Inspection Stickers	Dental Prosthetics
Cattle	Plastic Signs
Canned Goods	Plastic Name Tags
Boxes	Swine
Mops	Clothes
Brooms	Uniforms
Scouring Powders	Laundry
Soaps	Dry Cleaning
Furniture	Mattresses
Building Materials	Wielding and Stock Trailers
Shoes	Street Signs
Complete Microfilming	Building Trades
Automobile Repairs	Bus Renovations
Engine Repairs	Poultry

5. *West's Annotated California Codes, Penal Code* (St. Paul, Minn.: West Publishing Company, 1970), vol. 51A, p. 48.

6. *West's Annotated California Codes, Penal Code, Volume 51A Supplementary Pamphlet 1970 to 1981,* p. 14.

7. Ibid., p. 21.

8. *Jones v. North Carolina Prisoners' Union, Inc.,* 433 U.S. 119 (1976).

9. Ibid., p. 132.

10. Ibid., p. 139.

Appendix

The States

Proposed Maryland Legislation

PRISON SLAVE STATE CONSTITUTIONS

ARKANSAS	NEBRASKA
COLORADO	NEVADA
GEORGIA	NORTH DAKOTA
INDIANA	OREGON
KENTUCKY	TENNESSEE
MINNESOTA	UTAH
MISSISSIPPI	WISCONSIN

CONSTITUTION OF ARKANSAS

Article 5, Section 37   (1868)
No citizen of this State shall be disfranchised, or deprived of any rights or privileges secured to any citizen thereof, unless the same is done by the law of the land, or the judgement of his peers, except as hereinafter provided. There shall be neither slavery nor involuntary servitude, either by indentures, apprenticeships, or otherwise, in the State, EXCEPT FOR THE PUNISHMENT OF CRIME, WHEREOF THE PARTY SHALL HAVE BEEN DULY CONVICTED.

NOTE:

Arkansas "was re-admitted to representation in Congress, upon the fundamental condition that its Constitution should never be amended or changed so as to deprive any citizen or class of citizens of the United States of the right to vote, who were entitled to vote by the Constitution then recognized, except as a punishment for such crimes as are now felonies at common law, whereof they shall have been duly convicted, under laws equally applicable to all the inhabitants of the State..."[1]

Article 2, Section 27   (1874)
There shall be no slavery in this State, nor involuntary servitude, EXCEPT AS A PUNISHMENT FOR CRIME....

CONSTITUTION OF COLORADO

Article 2, Section 26   (1876)
Slavery Prohibited. There shall never be in this state either slavery or involuntary servitude, EXCEPT AS A PUNISHMENT FOR CRIME, WHEREOF THE PARTY SHALL HAVE BEEN DULY CONVICTED.

CONSTITUTION OF GEORGIA

Article I, Section 4   (1868)
Sec. 4. There shall be within the State of Georgia neither slavery nor

involuntary servitude, SAVE AS A PUNISHMENT FOR CRIME AFTER LEGAL CONVICTION THEREOF.

Art. I, Sec. 1 Paragraph XIX. Slavery and Involuntary Servitude.   (Current)

Same wording as Article I, Section 4 of the Constitution of 1868. This section was S-2117 of the 1945 Constitution.

CONSTITUTION OF INDIANA

Article I, Section 37   (1851)
There shall be neither slavery nor involuntary servitude within the State, OTHERWISE THAN FOR THE PUNISHMENT OF CRIMES, WHEREOF THE PARTY SHALL HAVE BEEN DULY CONVICTED. No indenture of any Negro or Mulatto, made and executed out of the bounds of the State, shall be valid within the State.

Article I, Section 37   (Current)
Slavery Prohibited. There shall be neither slavery, nor involuntary servitude, within the State, OTHERWISE THAN FOR THE PUNISHMENT OF CRIMES, WHEREOF THE PARTY SHALL HAVE BEEN DULY CONVICTED. No indenture of any Negro or Mulatto, made and executed out of the bounds of the State, shall be valid within the State.

CONSTITUTION OF KENTUCKY

Article I, Section 25   (1891)
Slavery, except as a punishment, forbidden. Slavery and involuntary servitude in this state are forbidden, EXCEPT AS A PUNISHMENT FOR CRIME, WHEREOF THE PARTY SHALL HAVE BEEN DULY CONVICTED.

CONSTITUTION OF MINNESOTA

Article I, Section 2   (1857)
Sec. 2. No member of this State shall be disfranchised, or deprived of any of the rights or privileges secured to any citizen thereof, unless by the law of the land, or the judgement of his peers. There shall be neither slavery nor involuntary servitude in the State OTHERWISE THAN IN THE PUNISHMENT OF CRIME, WHEREOF OF THE PARTY SHALL HAVE BEEN DULY CONVICTED.

Article I, Section 2   (Current)
Sec. 2. No member of this state shall be disfranchised or deprived of any of the rights or privileges secured to any citizen thereof, unless by the law of the land or the judgement of his peers. There shall be

neither slavery nor involuntary servitude in the state OTHERWISE THAN AS PUNISHMENT FOR A CRIME OF WHICH THE PARTY HAS BEEN CONVICTED.

CONSTITUTION OF MISSISSIPPI

Article I, Section 19 (1868)
Sec. 19. There shall be neither slavery nor involuntary servitude in this State, OTHERWISE THAN IN THE PUNISHMENT OF CRIME, WHERE-OF THE PARTY SHALL HAVE BEEN DULY CONVICTED.

Article 3, Section 15 (Current)
Same wording as Article I, Section 19 of the 1868 Constitution.

CONSTITUTION OF NEBRASKA

Article I, Section 2 (1875)
Sec. 2. There shall be neither slavery nor involuntary servitude in this state, OTHERWISE THAN FOR PUNISHMENT OF CRIME, WHEREOF THE PARTY SHALL HAVE BEEN DULY CONVICTED.

CONSTITUTION OF NEVADA

Article I, Section 17 (1864)
Sec. 17. Neither slavery nor involuntary servitude, UNLESS FOR THE PUNISHMENT OF CRIMES, shall ever be tolerated in this State.

CONSTITUTION OF NORTH DAKOTA

Article I, Section 17 (1889)
Sec. 17. Neither slavery nor involuntary servitude, UNLESS FOR THE PUNISHMENT OF CRIME, shall ever be tolerated in this state.

CONSTITUTION OF OREGON

Article I, Section 35 (1857)
Sec. 35. There shall be neither slavery nor involuntary servitude in the State, OTHERWISE THAN AS A PUNISHMENT FOR CRIME, WHERE-OF THE PARTY SHALL HAVE BEEN DULY CONVICTED.

Article I, Section 34. Slavery or involuntary servitude. (Current)
Same as Article I, Section 35 of Constitution of 1857.

CONSTITUTION OF TENNESSEE

Article I   (1870)
Sec. 33. That slavery and involuntary servitude, EXCEPT AS A PUN-ISHMENT FOR CRIME, WHEREOF THE PARTY SHALL HAVE BEEN DULY CONVICTED, are forever prohibited in this State.

Sec. 34. The General Assembly shall make no law recognizing the right of property in man.

Sec. 33. **Slavery prohibited   (Current)**
    Same as in 1870 Constitution.

> *Compiler's Notes.* Section 33 did not appear in the Constitu-tion of 1796 and 1834.
>   The amendments to the Constitution made February 22, 1865, abolishing slavery in this state were substantially the same as S 33, 34 of this article. . . .
>   Slavery was recognized and protected by the Constitution of the United States, until abolished by the 13th amendment, becoming effective the 18th day of February, 1865. By the fourth condition in North Carolina's cession act ceding to the United States the territory subsequently becoming the State of Tennessee, it was provided "That no regulations made or to be made by congress shall tend to emancipate slaves."[2]

Sec. 34. **Right of property in man.   (Current)**
    Same as Article I, Section 34 of 1870 Constitution.

CONSTITUTION OF UTAH

Article I, Section 21   (1896)
Sec. 21. **Slavery forbidden**
Neither slavery nor involuntary servitude, EXCEPT AS A PUNISHMENT FOR CRIME, WHEREOF THE PARTY SHALL HAVE BEEN DULY CON-VICTED, shall exist within this State.

CONSTITUTION OF WISCONSIN

Article I, Declaration of Rights   (1848)
Sec. 2. There shall be neither slavery, nor involuntary servitude in this state, OTHERWISE THAN FOR THE PUNISHMENT OF CRIME, WHEREOF THE PARTY SHALL HAVE BEEN DULY CONVICTED.

> This state was the fifth and last one formed out of the Ter-ritory North-West of the Ohio River, established in 1787.[3]

INVOLUNTARY SERVITUDE
STATE CONSTITUTIONS

ALABAMA	MICHIGAN
CALIFORNIA	NORTH CAROLINA
IOWA	OHIO
KANSAS	RHODE ISLAND
LOUISIANA	VERMONT

CONSTITUTION OF ALABAMA
(Changed State)

Article I, Section 34   (1865)
Sec. 34. That hereafter there shall be in this State neither slavery nor involuntary servitude, OTHERWISE THAN FOR THE PUNISHMENT OF CRIME, WHEREOF THE PARTY SHALL HAVE BEEN DULY CONVICTED.

Article I, Section 35   (1868)
Sec. 35. That no form of slavery shall exist in this State; and there shall be no involuntary servitude, OTHERWISE THAN FOR THE PUNISHMENT OF CRIME, OF WHICH THE PARTY SHALL HAVE BEEN DULY CONVICTED.

Article I, Section 33   (1875)
Same as in 1868, Article I, Section 35.

Article I, Section 32   (1901)
Sec. 32. That no form of slavery shall exist in this state; and there shall not be any involuntary servitude, OTHERWISE THAN FOR THE PUNISHMENT OF CRIME, OF WHICH THE PARTY SHALL HAVE BEEN DULY CONVICTED.

CONSTITUTION OF CALIFORNIA
(Changed State)

Article I, Section 18   (1849)
Sec. 18. Neither slavery nor involuntary servitude, UNLESS FOR THE PUNISHMENT OF CRIMES, shall ever be tolerated in this State.

Article I, Section 6   (1974)
Sec. 6. Slavery is prohibited. Involuntary servitude is prohibited EXCEPT TO PUNISH CRIME.

CONSTITUTION OF IOWA
(Changed State)

Article I, Section 23 (1846)
Sec. 23. Neither slavery nor involuntary servitude, UNLESS FOR THE PUNISHMENT OF CRIMES, shall ever be tolerated in this State.

Article I, Section 23 (1857)
Sec. 23. There shall be no slavery in this State; nor shall there be involuntary servitude, UNLESS FOR THE PUNISHMENT OF CRIME.

CONSTITUTION OF KANSAS

Bill of Rights, Section 6 (1859)
Sec. 6. **Slavery prohibited.** There shall be no slavery in this state; and no involuntary servitude, EXCEPT FOR THE PUNISHMENT OF CRIME, WHEREOF THE PARTY SHALL HAVE DULY CONVICTED.

CONSTITUTION OF LOUISIANA
(Changed State)

Title I, Article 3 (1868)
Art. 3. There shall be neither slavery nor involuntary servitude in this State, OTHERWISE THAN FOR THE PUNISHMENT OF CRIME, WHEREOF THE PARTY SHALL HAVE BEEN DULY CONVICTED.

Article I, Section 3. Right to Individual Dignity (1974)
Sec. 3. No person shall be denied the equal protection of the laws. No law shall discriminate against a person because of race or religious ideas, beliefs, or affiliations. No law shall arbitrarily, capriciously, or unreasonably discriminate against a person because of birth, age, sex, culture, physical condition, or political ideas or affiliations. Slavery and involuntary servitude are prohibited, EXCEPT IN THE LATTER CASE AS PUNISHMENT FOR CRIME.

CONSTITUTION OF MICHIGAN
(Changed State)

Article 18, Section 11 (1850)
Sec. 11. Neither slavery nor involuntary servitude, UNLESS FOR THE PUNISHMENT OF CRIME, shall ever be tolerated in this State.

Article 2, Section 8 (1908)
Same as Article 18, Section 11 of 1850 Constitution.

Article 1, Section 9   (1963)
Sec. 9. **Slavery and involuntary servitude.** Neither slavery, nor involuntary servitude UNLESS FOR THE PUNISHMENT OF CRIME, shall ever be tolerated in this state.

> Convention Comment
> No change from Sec. 8, Article II, of the present [1908] constitution except for the insertion of a comma after the word "slavery" and elimination of a comma after the word "servitude". The old punctuation conceivably made slavery permissible as a punishment for crime.[4]

CONSTITUTION OF NORTH CAROLINA
(Changed State)

Article I, Section 33   (1868)
Sec. 33. Slavery and involuntary servitude, OTHERWISE THAN FOR CRIME, WHEREOF THE PARTIES SHALL HAVE BEEN CONVICTED, shall be, and are hereby forever prohibited within this State.

Article I, Section 17   (1970)
Sec. 17. **Slavery and involuntary servitude.** Slavery is forever prohibited. Involuntary servitude, EXCEPT AS A PUNISHMENT FOR CRIME WHEREOF THE PARTIES HAVE BEEN ADJUDGED GUILTY, is forever prohibited.

CONSTITUTION OF OHIO
(Changed State)

Northwest Territory Ordinance, Article 6   (1787)
Art. 6. There shall be neither slavery nor involuntary servitude in the said territory, OTHERWISE THAN IN THE PUNISHMENT OF CRIMES, WHEREOF THE PARTY SHALL HAVE BEEN DULY CONVICTED; *Provided, always,* that any person escaping into the same, from whom labor or service is lawfully claimed in any one of the original States, said fugitive may be lawfully reclaimed and conveyed to the person claiming his or her labor or service as aforesaid.

Article 8, Section 2   (1802 Constitution of Ohio)
Sec. 2. There shall be neither slavery nor involuntary servitude in this state, OTHERWISE THAN FOR THE PUNISHMENT OF CRIMES, WHEREOF THE PARTY SHALL HAVE BEEN DULY CONVICTED; nor shall any male person, arrived at the age of twenty-one years, or female person arrived at the age of eighteen years, be held to serve any person as a servant, under the pretense of indenture or otherwise, unless such person shall enter into such indenture while in a state of perfect freedom, and on condition of a bona fide consideration receiv-

ed, or to be received, for their service, EXCEPT AS BEFORE EXCEPTED. Nor shall any indenture of any negro or mulatto, hereafter made and executed out of the state, or if made in the state, where the term of service exceeds one year, be of the least validity, except those given in the case of apprenticeships.

Article I, Section 6 (1851)
Sec. 6. There shall be no slavery in this state, nor involuntary servitude, UNLESS FOR THE PUNISHMENT OF CRIME.

Article I, Section 6 (1912)
Sec. 6. **Slavery and involuntary servitude.** There shall be no slavery in this state; nor involuntary servitude, UNLESS FOR THE PUNISHMENT OF CRIME.

Note the difference between the two versions of Art. I, Sec. 6 contained in punctuation: the 1851 version has a comma (,) after the word "slavery" while the 1912 version has a semicolon (;). This singular alteration created great change in meaning of Ohio's constitutional law: from slavery and involuntary servitude "FOR THE PUNISHMENT OF CRIME" in 1851 to involuntary servitude without slavery "FOR THE PUNISHMENT OF CRIME" in 1912.

CONSTITUTION OF RHODE ISLAND

Article I, Section 4 (1842)
Sec. 4. Slavery shall not be permitted in this State.

CONSTITUTION OF VERMONT

Chapter I, Article 1st (1793)
Art. 1st. That all men are born equally free and independent, and have certain natural, inherent, and unalienable rights, amongst which are the enjoying and defending life and liberty, acquiring, possessing and protecting property, and pursuing and obtaining happiness and safety; therefore no person born in this country, or brought from over sea, ought to be holden by law, to serve any person as a servant, slave or apprentice, after he arrives to the age of twenty-one years, unless he is bound by his own consent, after he arrives to such age, or bound by law for the payment of debts, damages, fines, costs, or the like.

Annotations
4. Slavery. No inhabitant of this state can hold a slave. Selectmen of *Windsor v. Jacob* (1802) 2 Tyl. 192.[5]

NO PROVISO STATE CONSTITUTIONS

ALASKA	NEW HAMPSHIRE
ARIZONA	NEW JERSEY
CONNECTICUT	NEW MEXICO
DELAWARE	NEW YORK
FLORIDA	OKLAHOMA
HAWAII	PENNSYLVANIA
IDAHO	SOUTH CAROLINA
ILLINOIS	SOUTH DAKOTA
MAINE	TEXAS
MARYLAND	VIRGINIA
MASSACHUSETTS	WASHINGTON
MISSOURI	WEST VIRGINIA
MONTANA	WYOMING

CONSTITUTION OF ALASKA

NO PROVISO

Article I, Sec. 12   (1956)
Sec. 12. **Excessive Punishment.** Excessive bail shall not be required nor excessive fines imposed, nor cruel and unusual punishments inflicted. Penal administration shall be based on the principle of reformation and upon the need for protection of the public.

CONSTITUTION OF ARIZONA

NO PROVISO

CONSTITUTION OF CONNECTICUT

NO PROVISO

CONSTITUTION OF DELAWARE

NO PROVISO

CONSTITUTION OF FLORIDA
(Changed State)

Declaration of Rights   (1868)
Sec. 18. Neither slavery nor involuntary servitude, UNLESS FOR THE PUNISHMENT OF CRIME, shall ever be tolerated in this State.

Declaration of Rights (1885)

Sec. 19. **Slavery prohibited; penal servitude.** Neither slavery nor involuntary servitude, EXCEPT AS A PUNISHMENT FOR CRIME, WHEREOF THE PARTY HAS BEEN DULY CONVICTED, shall ever be allowed in this State.

Historical Note
The Constitution of 1868, in which this section first appeared, did not specify that one must be duly convicted before the imposition of involuntary servitude as a punishment for crime.[6]

NO PROVISO (1968 Revision)

References to slavery and involuntary servitude omitted from the 1968 Declaration of Rights.

The 1968 revision of the Florida Constitution omitted Section 19 of the 1885 Declaration of Rights; and in 1969, Florida "transferred all powers, duties and functions of the division of corrections of the board of commissioners of state institutions to the division of adult corrections . . . of the department of health and rehabilitative services."[7]

CONSTITUTION OF HAWAII

NO PROVISO

CONSTITUTION OF IDAHO

NO PROVISO

CONSTITUTION OF ILLINOIS
(Changed State)

Article 4, Section 1 (1818)

Sec. 1. Neither slavery nor involuntary servitude shall hereafter be introduced into this State, OTHERWISE THAN FOR THE PUNISHMENT OF CRIMES, WHEREOF THE PARTY SHALL HAVE BEEN DULY CONVICTED. . . .

Article 13, Section 16 (1848)

Sec. 16. There shall be neither slavery nor involuntary servitude in this state, EXCEPT AS A PUNISHMENT FOR CRIME WHEREOF THE PARTY SHALL HAVE BEEN DULY CONVICTED.

NO PROVISO (1870)

CONSTITUTION OF MAINE

NO PROVISO

CONSTITUTION OF MARYLAND
(Changed State)

Declaration of Rights, Article 24   (1867)
Art. 24. THAT SLAVERY SHALL NOT BE RE-ESTABLISHED IN THIS STATE; but having been abolished under the policy and authority of the United States, compensation, in consideration thereof, is due from the United States.

NO PROVISO   (1979)

CONSTITUTION OF MASSACHUSETTS

NO PROVISO
  (See PENNSYLVANIA)

CONSTITUTION OF MISSOURI
(Changed State)

From *American Constitutions* by Franklin B. Hough:

> A petition from the Territorial Legislature, asking for a State government, was received in Congress December 18, 1818, which was referred to the Committee on Territories. On the 13th of February, 1819, the House went into Committee of the Whole and took up the bill upon this subject, and several amendments were adopted on the 15th, the most important of which, moved General James Tallmadge, of New York, was as follows:
>
> *"And provided, also,* that the further introduction of slavery or involuntary servitude be prohibited, EXCEPT FOR THE PUNISHMENT OF CRIMES, WHEREOF THE PARTY SHALL HAVE BEEN DULY CONVICTED; and that all children of slaves, born within the said State, after the admission thereof into the Union, shall be free, but may be held to service until the age of twenty-five years."
>
> This amendment was adopted by a vote of 87 to 76, upon that part ending with the word "convicted," and upon the residue, by a vote of 82 to 78. In this form it was referred back to the House, and on a third reading it passed, as amended, by a vote of 98 to 56.
>
> In the Senate, the latter part of the amendment was stricken out, by a vote of 27 to 7, and on the remainder, the

vote for striking out was 22 to 16. Upon being referred back to the House, they refused to concur, by vote of 69 to 74, and so the bill was lost. . . .

When the war of the rebellion began, the Governor of Missouir (C.F. Jackson) proved to be in sympathy with secession, and a strong effort was made to carry this State with the South. The Legislature voted, on the 16th of January, 1861, to call a Convention, which was elected, and met on the 28th of February, 1861; but that body proved to be in favor of remaining in the Federal Union, and refused to secede therefrom. It remained in existence by adjourments until the 1st of July, 1863. In October, a remnant of the Legislature who adhered to the fortunes of the rebellion, were assembled by Governor Jackson at Neosho, and went through the farce of secession. The Constitutional quorum of the Legislature was 67 in the House and 17 in the Senate; but at the session at Neosho, there were present but 35 of the former, and 10 of the latter. A few days after they were joined by five other members and one Senator, which was the nearest approach made to a quorum in either House.

Nevertheless, persons claiming to have been elected, appeared to represent Missouri in the Confederate Congress in December, 1861, and the shadow of a State government in sympathy with the rebellion, continued for some time after.[8]

Article I, Section 2   (1865)
Sec. 2. That there cannot be in this state either slavery or involuntary servitude, EXCEPT IN PUNISHMENT OF CRIME, WHEREOF THE PARTY SHALL HAVE BEEN DULY CONVICTED.

Article 2, Section 31.   (1875)
Sec. 31. **Slavery prohibited.** That there cannot be in this State either slavery or involuntary servitude, EXCEPT AS A PUNISHMENT FOR CRIME, WHEREOF THE PARTY SHALL HAVE BEEN DULY CONVICTED.

NO PROVISO   (1945)
Constitution of 1945 makes no reference to slavery or involuntary servitude - 1875 Article 2, Section 31 is omitted.

CONSTITUTION OF MONTANA
(Changed State)

Article 3, Section 28   (1889)
Sec. 28. There shall never be in this state either slavery or involuntary servitude, EXCEPT AS A PUNISHMENT FOR CRIME, WHEREOF THE PARTY SHALL HAVE BEEN DULY CONVICTED.

NO PROVISO   (1972)

CONSTITUTION OF NEW HAMPSHIRE

NO PROVISO

Bill of Rights, Article 18   (1792)
[Art.] 18th. [Penalties to be Proportioned to Offenses; True Design of Punishment.] All penalties ought to be proportioned to the nature of the offense. No wise legislature will affix the same punishment to the crimes of theft, forgery, and the like, which they do to those of murder and treason. Where the same undistinguishing severity is exerted against all offenses, the people are led to forget the real distinction in the crimes themselves, and to commit the most flagrant with as little compunction as they do the lightest offenses. For the same reason a multitude of sanguinary laws is both impolitic and unjust. *The true design of all punishments being to reform, not to exterminate mankind.* [Emphasis added.]

CONSTITUTION OF NEW JERSEY

NO PROVISO

> Slavery existed prior to the adoption of the constitution of 1844, and was not abolished by that constitution, but was abolished by Act April 18, 1846, Rev. St. 1847, p. 382. State v. Post, 21 N.J.L. 699 (1848); State v. Post, 20 N.J.L. 368 (1844.)[9]

CONSTITUTION OF NEW MEXICO

NO PROVISO

CONSTITUTION OF NEW YORK

NO PROVISO
 (See PENNSYLVANIA)

CONSTITUTION OF OKLAHOMA

NO PROVISO

CONSTITUTION OF PENNSYLVANIA

NO PROVISO

Historical Note

The book *Free Men All,* by Thomas D. Morris, "follows the developments in five free states (Massachusetts, New York, Pennsylvania, Ohio, and Wisconsin) in which 'Personal Liberty Laws' were passed. These laws variously guaranteed a jury trial to a person who claimed to be free; extended habeas corpus to cover the claims to freedom of fugitives; required state procedures in addition to, or as an alternative to, the federal fugitive rendition procedures; punished state officials for performing duties under the federal fugitive slave acts, or withdrew jurisdiction from state officials in such cases; denied the use of jails to house alleged runaways; provided counsel for blacks or persons claimed as slaves; and provided punishment for persons convicted of kidnapping. Not all were in effect in any one state, and some were later repealed by prosouthern state legislatures. The most bold and threatening (the first three listed above) were ruled unconstitutional or void in *Prigg [Prigg v. Pennsylvania,* 41 U.S. (16 Pet.) 539 (1842)] and *Ableman v. Booth* [62 U.S. (21 How.) 506 (1859)] as conflicting with valid federal law."[10]

CONSTITUTION OF SOUTH CAROLINA
(Changed State)

Article I, Section 2   (1868)
Sec. 2. Slavery shall never exist in this State; neither shall involuntary servitude, EXCEPT AS A PUNISHMENT FOR CRIME, WHEREOF THE PARTY SHALL HAVE BEEN DULY CONVICTED.

NO PROVISO   (1895)

CONSTITUTION OF SOUTH DAKOTA

NO PROVISO

CONSTITUTION OF TEXAS
(Changed State)

Article I, Section 19   (1869)
Sec. 22. Importations of persons under the name of "coolies," or any other name or designation, or the adoption of any system of peonage, whereby the helpless and unfortunate may be reduced to practical bondage, shall never be authorized or tolerated by the laws of this State; and neither slavery nor involuntary servitude, EXCEPT AS A PUNISHMENT FOR CRIME, WHEREOF THE PARTY SHALL HAVE BEEN DULY CONVICTED, shall ever exist in this State.

NO PROVISO   (1876)

CONSTITUTION OF VIRGINIA
(Changed State)

Article I, Section 19   (1870)
Sec. 19. That neither slavery nor involuntary servitude, EXCEPT AS LAWFUL IMPRISONMENT MAY CONSTITUTE SUCH, shall exist in this State.

NO PROVISO   (1902)

CONSTITUTION OF WASHINGTON

NO PROVISO

Article 6. Elections and Elective Rights
Sec. 3. **Who Disqualified.** All idiots, insane persons, and persons convicted of infamous crime unless restored to their civil rights are excluded from the elective franchise.

CONSTITUTION OF WEST VIRGINIA

NO PROVISO

CONSTITUTION OF WYOMING

NO PROVISO

Notes

1. Hough, vol. 1, p. 82.

2. *Tennessee Code Annotated,* vol. 1, 1980 replacement ed. (Charlottesville: Michie Company, 1980), pp. 399-400.

3. Hough, vol. 2, p. 493.

4. *Michigan Compiled Laws Annotated,* vol. 1 (St. Paul: West Publishing Comany, 1967), p. 560.

5. *Vermont Statutes Annotated, Title I through Title 3,* 1972 replacement ed. (Orford, N.H.: Equity Publishing Corporation, 1972), p. 98.

6. *Florida Statutes Annotated,* (St. Paul: West Publishing Co., 1970), vol. 25, p. 98.

7. Ibid., vol. 24, p. 234.

8. Hough, vol. 1, pp. 96-98.

9. *New Jersey Statutes Annotated, Constitution of New Jersey, Articles I-III* (St. Paul: West Publishing Co., 1970), p. 127.

10. Wyeth Holt, pp. 1066-1067; see also Thomas Morris, *Free Men All, The Personal Liberty Laws of the North, 1780-1861* (Baltimore: Johns Hopkins University Press, 1974), pp. 195-199, which Holt cites as "a good summary of the types of Personal Liberty Laws, and what became of them."

Civil Death Statutes

Prison slavery state constitutional changes would be meaningless without subsequent changes in state statutes. This technical conformity focuses on the changes in state civil death statutes.

Three *prison slave* and 6 *no proviso* states have civil death. Three *changed* states had civil death statutes - now they have one. *Involuntary servitude* states had 3 - now they have none.

CIVIL DEATH STATES

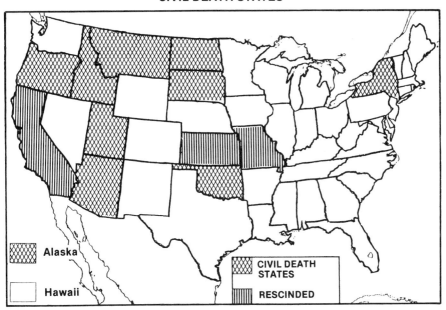

Further research in state statute and policy changes will empower critical analysis of the practices of prison slavery and involuntary servitude. Correlation and cross-correlation of several factors will establish state signatures and both positive and negative effects of state constitutional changes. Factors needing research and correlation include: civil death, death penalty, prison sentences, time served before release, prison construction, unconstitutional prison conditions, the existence of labor union-busting "right to work laws," passage or failure of the Equal Rights Amendment, abortion rights legislation, affirmative action, the distribution of nuclear power plants, and unemployment, poverty, and incarceration rates.

CONSTITUTIONAL AMENDMENT
HOUSE OF DELEGATES
No. 1087

By: Delegate Phillips
Introduced and read first time: February 4, 1980
Assigned to: Constitutional and Administrative Law

A BILL ENTITLED

AN ACT concerning

Declaration of Rights - Abolition of Slavery

FOR the purpose of amending the Declaration of Rights of the Constitution of Maryland to prohibit the practice of slavery; and submitting this amendment to the qualified voters of the State of Maryland for their adoption or rejection.

BY proposing an addition to the Constitution of Maryland

Declaration of Rights
Article 47

SECTION 1. BE IT ENACTED BY THE GENERAL ASSEMBLY OF MARYLAND, (Three-fifths of all the members elected to each of the two Houses concurring), That it be proposed that section(s) of the Constitution of Maryland be repealed, amended, or added to read as follows:

Declaration of Rights

Article 47.

THE PRACTICE OF SLAVERY IS ABOLISHED AND SHALL BE PROHIBITED ABSOLUTELY.

SECTION 2. AND BE IT FURTHER ENACTED, That the General Assembly determines that the amendment to the Constitution of Maryland proposed by this Act affects multiple jurisdictions and that the provisions of Article XIV, Section 1 of the Constitution concerning local approval of constitutional amendments do not apply.

SECTION 3. AND BE IT FURTHER ENACTED, That the aforegoing section proposed as an amendment to the Constitution of Maryland shall be submitted to the legal and qualified voters of this State at the next general election to be held in November, 1980 for their adoption or rejection in pursuance of directions contained in Article XIV of the Constitution of this State. At that general election, the vote on this proposed amendment to the Constitution shall be by ballot, and upon each ballot there shall be printed the words "For the Constitutional Amendments" and "Against the Constitutional Amendments," as now provided by law. Immediately after the election, all returns shall be made to the Governor of the vote for and against the proposed amendment, as directed by Article XIV of the Constitution, and further proceedings had in accordance with Article XIV.

EXPLANATION: CAPITALS INDICATE MATTER ADDED TO EXISTING LAW.
[Brackets] indicate matter deleted from existing law.

HOUSE JOINT RESOLUTION No. 70

By: Delegates Phillips, Murphy, Dean, Rawlings, and Conaway
Introduced and read first time: February 13, 1981
Assigned to: Constitutional and Administrative Law

HOUSE JOINT RESOLUTION

A House Joint Resolution concerning

Slavery or Involuntary Servitude

FOR the purpose of urging the amendment of the United States Constitution to remove any trace of the acceptability of slavery or involuntary servitude.

WHEREAS, With the states' ratification of Amendment XIII of the United States Constitution in 1865, the legality of slavery and involuntary servitude was restricted to "punishment for crime whereof the party shall have been duly convicted"; and

WHEREAS, With the United States Senate's ratification of the Supplementary Convention on the Abolition of Slavery, the Slave Trade, and Institutions and Practices Similar to Slavery in 1967, we recognized the illegality of the "status or condition of a person over whom any or all of the powers attaching to the right of ownership are exercised"; and

WHEREAS, We have become increasingly aware that by accepting as just any form of slavery or involuntary servitude we reduce a human being's personhood and are responsible for the abominable consequences that flow therefrom; and

WHEREAS, In spite of this growing awareness, United States Courts have been bound by Amendment XIII of the Constitution to accept the proposition that "the labor of a convict belongs to the state"; now, therefore, be it

RESOLVED BY THE GENERAL ASSEMBLY OF MARYLAND, That the United States Constitution should be amended to remove any trace of the acceptability of slavery or involuntary servitude; and be it further

RESOLVED, That a copy of this Resolution be sent to the Maryland Congressional Delegation: Senators Charles Mc C. Mathias, Jr. and Paul S. Sabanes, Senate Office Building, Washington, D.C. 20510; and Representatives Royden P. Dyson, Clarence D. Long, Barbara A. Mikulski, Marjorie S. Holt, Gladys N. Spellman, Beverly B. Byron, Parren J. Mitchell, and Michael D. Barnes, House Office Building, Washington, D.C. 20515.

Petition to Abolish Prison Slavery

Committee to Abolish Prison Slavery
P.O. Box 3207, Washington, D.C. 20010   (202) 797-7721

I sign this petition in support of changing the status of prisoners from that of slaves to that of full citizens and in recognition that the Thirteenth Amendment to the United States Constitution presently reads:

> *Neither slavery nor involuntary servitude, EXCEPT AS A PUNISHMENT FOR CRIME WHEREOF THE PARTY SHALL HAVE BEEN DULY CONVICTED, shall exist within the United States, or any place subject to their jurisdiction.*

and should be changed to read:

> *Neither slavery nor involuntary servitude shall exist within the United States or any place subject to their jurisdiction.*

1. Print Name _____ Street Address_____ ID No. or Phone _____

Signature _____ City _____ State _____ Zip _____

2. Print Name _____ Street Address_____ ID No. or Phone _____

Signature _____ City _____ State _____ Zip _____

3. Print Name _____ Street Address_____ ID No. or Phone _____

Signature _____ City _____ State _____ Zip _____

4. Print Name _____ Street Address_____ ID No. or Phone _____

Signature _____ City _____ State _____ Zip _____

5. Print Name _____ Street Address_____ ID No. or Phone _____

Signature _____ City _____ State _____ Zip _____

DATE DUE

SEP - 5 1989			